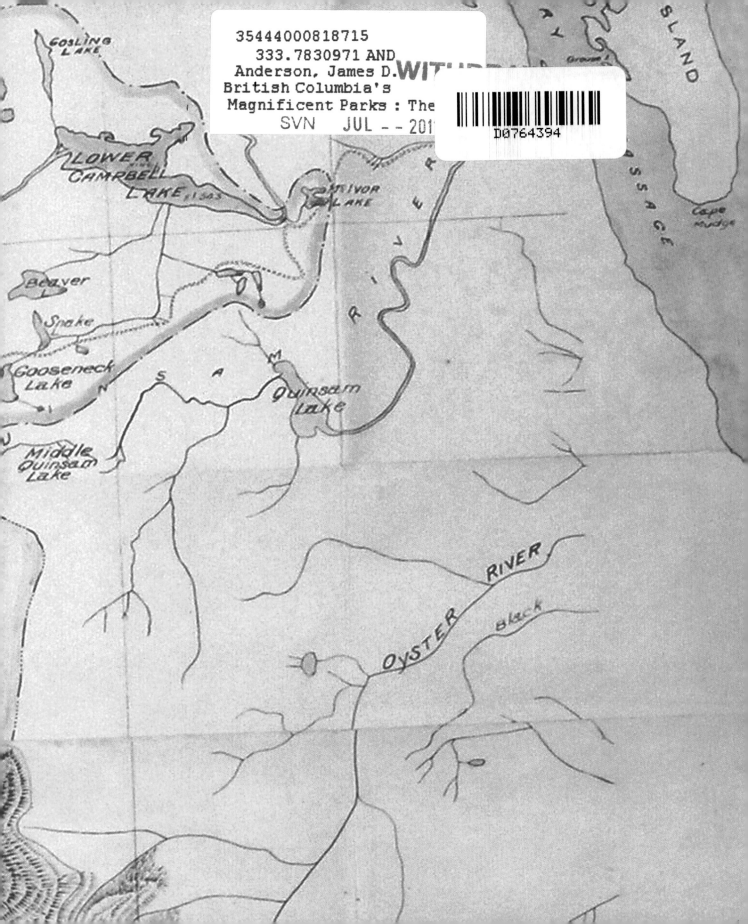

British Columbia's
MAGNIFICENT PARKS

British Columbia's
MAGNIFICENT PARKS
The First 100 Years

JAMES D. ANDERSON

Harbour Publishing

Harbour Publishing Co. Ltd.
P.O. Box 219, Madeira Park, BC, V0N 2H0
www.harbourpublishing.com

Dustjacket: Front, Hunlen Falls, Tweedsmuir Park (Vance Hanna Photo).
   Front flap: Khutzeymateen Grizzly Sanctuary. Back: Alice Lake Provincial Park.
Endsheets and back dust jacket: Detail, map of the Campbell River watershed by the BC
   Department of Lands Water Right Branch, 1920s. Courtesy Museum at Campbell River.
Edited by Betty Keller
Text design and map, page 23, by Roger Handling
Cover design by Anna Comfort
Index prepared by Ellen Hawman
Printed on FSC-certified stock containing 10% recycled content
Printed and bound in Canada

Harbour Publishing acknowledges financial support from the Government of Canada through the Canada Book Fund and the Canada Council for the Arts, and from the Province of British Columbia through the BC Arts Council and the Book Publishing Tax Credit.

Library and Archives Canada Cataloguing in Publication

Anderson, James D., 1941-
        British Columbia's magnificent parks : the first 100 years / James
D. Anderson.

Includes bibliographical references and index.
ISBN 978-1-55017-507-3

        1. Provincial parks and reserves—British Columbia. I. Title.

FC3813.A64 2011   333.78'309711   C2011-900780-0

Dedication

This history is dedicated to the "Elders and the Builders," those committed employees of the BC Parks Branch who were fortunate to have the opportunity and responsibility to provide for the growth and development of the provincial park system. This was a special personal journey for all involved and one that leaves a legacy of immense value to the citizens of this province. It is only in retrospect that these employees realize they were engaged in an endeavour of considerable merit. By their efforts, park elders ensured the preservation of special places in our province, and provided opportunities for residents and visitors to treasure and enjoy them. In particular, the author and his colleagues recognize the contribution of R.H. Ahrens, C.J. Velay, J. Masselink and D. Thompson and trust that others will appreciate the leadership they provided to the cause of parks in British Columbia and Canada. The contributions of the next generation of park planners and managers who continue this proud tradition is also recognized.

This legacy represents and protects special places and the province by providing the finest provincial system in the world—the equivalent of many national parks systems. As we approach the 100th anniversary, it is appropriate to celebrate the diversity and riches of our park system and to learn and remember how it came to be.

Paintbrush and lupins bloom in Manning Park.
Bill Merrilees

Contents

Page 1: The spectacular wilderness of Dune Za Keyih Provincial Park, centred in the Rocky Mountain Trench, includes part of the Kechika River valley, BC's largest unlogged watershed.

Page 3: Camping in a muskeg area in Naikoon Provincial Park on Haida Gwaii. This park includes Rose Spit Ecological Reserve, critical habitat for local and migratory birds. *All Canada Photos, David Nunuk*

This page: A sailboat anchors at the entrance to Kynoch Inlet in Fiordland Provincial Recreational Area on the Central Coast. *All Canada Photos, Chris Cheadle*

Foreword

Stephen Hume

$\mathbf{A}$ big red sun rolled down the dark rim of the Sooke Hills and a breeze ruffled Victoria's Inner Harbour on the fine July evening in 1910 when Speaker David McEwen Eberts bustled down from the British Columbia legislature to the CPR steamship terminal.

Eberts was bidding bon voyage to a party led by Conservative cabinet minister Price Ellison. The travellers awaited the night sailing of the S.S. *Queen City* to Vancouver, where they would pick up supplies before venturing into some of BC's wildest country to assess its suitability for a new provincial park.

Viewed from a century in their future, the explorers who were to begin the process recounted in *British Columbia's Magnificent Parks*, Jim Anderson's meticulous history of how Canada's largest provincial parks system came into being, resembled not bureaucrats and planners but the exotic cast from a high Victorian adventure like H. Rider Haggard's 1885 novel, *King Solomon's Mines*.

....

Above: Guide "Lord" Hugh Bacon's dog, Man, supervises as the crew of an Ellison expedition canoe paddle and pole their way up the Campbell River in mid-July 1910. *Museum at Campbell River, 010106*

There was Ellison, "The Chief," a beefy, imperturbable, walrus-moustached newspaper owner from Vernon. Born in Britain and apprenticed as a blacksmith, he'd been a prospector in the California and Cariboo goldfields before assembling one of the biggest ranches in the Okanagan Valley.

William Washington Bolton was an adventurous Cambridge-educated school master, both sky pilot and poet. There were devil-may-care students and cool-headed military men. The dashing Colonel William Josiah Hartley Holmes, former commanding officer of the Rocky Mountain Rangers was officially the team's science officer, although his closely guarded "instrument box" was later found to be full of "bottled goods." Walter Fletcher Loveland had been wounded in action five times and twice mentioned in dispatches while a corporal with the Imperial Light Horse in the South African War.

A. Lionel Hudson was an affable, urbane Englishman. "One of the finer types of English gentleman, resourceful, adaptable, ready for anything, very fond of shooting, unlimited perseverance, even temper, always polite, even in the strangest situations," remarked Harry McLure Johnson, "former law student," Ellison's nephew and the expedition's unofficial chronicler.

Johnson was an American from Peoria, Illinois. His witty, keenly observant journal survives—I once spent two days engrossed in a copy at the Campbell River Museum—and so does the work of Frank Ward, the expedition's official photographer, an accomplished artist who had studied in Boston. Johnson admired Ward's dry humour in trying circumstances.

Peter Jamieson, the camp cook, former chef to British aristocrats including

The Price Ellison expedition gathered on the balcony of the Willows Inn in Campbell River before setting off to explore Strathcona Park in July 1910. *Museum at Campbell River, 0101389*

Governor-General Earl Grey, had been seconded from the legislature's dining room despite "his great avoirdupois, about 250 lbs."

Dan, Dave and Bob Gaboriau, three tough and tireless Cowichan Indian packers would paddle freight in a carved dugout canoe. Charlie Haslam, a quiet, Vancouver-born timber cruiser and son of the province's chief log scaler would prove indispensible in the bush. James Dickson Twaddle was a trapper. Jim Manning, the head packer, was a Gulf Islands homesteader. The rest of his crew included university students earning tuition and immigrants fresh off the boat.

Hugh Francis Bacon, the party's wilderness guide, had dubbed himself the "Lord" of Vancouver Island. He moved through the woods like a ghost and was incomparable in a canoe on white water.

Bacon might have stepped from the pages of *Trader Horn* or *Last of the Mohicans*. He lived alone in the mountains, accompanied only by his little fox terrier "Man," except when moved to visit the saloon in Campbell River, where he'd drink the best Scotch and recite Kipling to drunken loggers.

"He never seems to hurry, yet always gives the impression of speed," Johnson wrote after watching him. "He slides along just like a cat—more properly 'like a cat of the woods,' a cougar, so like a thing of the woods is he, always alert, every muscle under perfect control, always masterful, seeing every exigency before it happens and always ready to meet it."

And what adventure yarn would be complete without a feisty young heroine? The Chief's daughter, Myra King Ellison, just turned twenty, was a beautiful, brilliant blue-stocking who had been accepted at McGill at sixteen in a time when few women were encouraged by their fathers to pursue a higher education. The honour student in economics would astound everyone with her high spirits, endurance and skill.

Ellison's mission was to explore the "*hyas mesachie illahie*," the very bad country in the interior of Vancouver Island, isolated behind rapids and terrain so difficult that even First Nations were loathe to venture there, although stories of its unpardonable beauty filtered out with trappers and long-range timber cruisers.

The expedition would trek up the Campbell River, ascend Crown Mountain, explore the surrounding lakes, rivers and valleys, cross the divide, descend to the western sea and report to the legislature on whether it was suitable for the province's first park.

But when Eberts arrived at the dock, he found the adventurers already in disarray—Ellison had forgotten his boots. And now he couldn't find a pair sturdy enough for six weeks in the bush. The Speaker sent a fast runner home to bring back a pair of Eberts' own boots. Fortunately, the borrowed footwear fit "The Chief."

Opposite: After two weeks of gruelling travel, nine of the Ellison party were selected for the assault on Crown Mountain. Myra King Ellison stands third from the left, her father, Price Ellison, fourth from the left. *Museum at Campbell River, 010138*

Above: Myra King Ellison led the way on the final morning of the climb to the top of Crown Mountain on July 29, 1910. She holds the Union Jack she will plant on the summit. *Museum at Campbell River, 010149*

That crisis overcome, the party next looked in dismay at the ship that would take them to Campbell River, then just a beachfront hotel and a bare-knuckle logging camp. S.S. *Queen City* was "a dirty little tug" retired from service on the outer coast of Vancouver Island and McLure Johnson complained that "a howling dog among the freight tortured our ears during the goodbyes," although he did find the cabins satisfactory.

If the bumbling start seemed inauspicious, Ellison's report would prove the genesis of the provincial parks system that celebrated its 100th anniversary in the spring of 2011.

Today, that parks system is one of Canada's incomparable—if often beleaguered—treasures. It ranges from tiny but special places like Shawnigan Lake's Memory Island, less than a hectare in area, to entire ecosystems that extend from tidewater to mountaintop, like the grizzly bear sanctuary of the Khutzeymateen or the desolate seabird sanctuary of Triangle Island.

Protected landscapes range from the sodden coastal rainforests to dry antelope brush deserts, from lush, teeming estuaries to barren rock, ice and alpine tundra.

Tweedsmuir Park, larger than some European countries, is a trackless, inaccessible wilderness. Manning Park in the Cascades, provides access to the outback within a few hours' drive of vast urban populations. Golden Ears Park in the

British Columbia's massive parks system contains treasures like Canada's only grizzly bear sanctuary, Khutzeymateen Park, located 45 kilometres northeast of Prince Rupert.

Fraser Valley and Goldstream Park near Victoria are close enough for day trips from downtown.

The total number of visits to BC's almost 1,000 parks and protected areas for camping, boating, hiking, picnics and sight-seeing is more than 200 million over the last decade. That represents customer traffic that is 50 times the provincial population—the parks system is a powerful engine in the economy.

Yet, in 1910, the entire population of the province numbered only 370,000 people, 80 percent of whom lived in the Fraser Valley and around Victoria. Most of the province was uninhabited wilderness. It took a special kind of visionary to foresee the need for parks a century in the future, as it will take another kind of visionary to foresee the parkland demands of a hundred years from now.

When Ellison's exploring party arrived in Campbell River, the largely transient non-native population consisted of bunkhouse loggers and well-heeled sportsmen who came to fish and hunt.

The Willows Hotel, where the explorers awaited the arrival of their guide and packers, catered to both.

It featured brass beds, hot and cold running water and a spectacular bar with tiled floor, mirrors and ornamental iron ceiling.

"The Captain had told us there was a good hotel but we had no reason to believe it would be as good as this (Miss E. did not see the bar)," Johnson wrote.

"Loggers are restricted to one end of the hotel and the corridors leading to their rooms are separated from the rest of the hotel by partitions and closed doors so that the loggers, if inclined to be boisterous, will not interfere with the patrons of the hotel of quieter instincts."

Golden Ears Park, on the north side of the Fraser River, has an extensive system of trails for hiking and horseback riding, but the mountainous backcountry is extremely rugged.

Sometime that evening, as the party relaxed on verandas overlooking the beach, "Lord" Hugh Bacon, who was to be their guide, slipped in from the woods with a pack on his back and his dog at heel.

"Lord is not an ordinary person," Johnson wrote. "He spends his time in the fastnesses of his forest home back in the Buttle Lake region, and comes down to the settlements only when the silence of the forest palls on him and he feels it his duty to come down and straighten out the rabble."

With a bit of lubrication, the astonishing recitations of Kipling would follow.

"Loggers ask who Kipling is, does he live with him in the mountains, does he ever come down to the settlements? Lord B. tells us with a straight face that he is the author of five books: *Travels, Advice to Young Ladies* and *Immorality of the Modern Age*. . .those who know him say they are different each time he tells about them."

Two days later, the expedition was underway, first by freight wagon to McIvor

A red fox warily observes a photographer in Ts'il-os Provincial Park. In addition to providing recreational opportunities, wilderness areas protect vegetation, wildlife and fish habitats.

Lake, then a portage to the Campbell River, provisions following with Charlie Haslam and the Cowichan packers "in a big Siwash war canoe gaily ornamented with carvings and blue and black paint at the bow and stern. The prow is a long-beaked bird of some description similar to the figures of the Totem poles."

On the first day, the landscape asserted itself. Johnson paused in his canoe, the cold, deep water perfectly clear but reflecting three gleaming ranges of snow peaks, a painfully blue sky and puffy white clouds that changed as he watched dusk fall on the first camp.

"The peaks are blue, then pink, and the forests all about and up the mountain sides are every delicate shade. The water about us takes on all sorts of shades of light and dark blue, green, yellow and pink…Even after the sun and its brilliance is gone, and afterglow of twilight remains."

Bacon, too, had paused, ostensibly to bail his leaky canoe "but rather, I discover, to slip a bottle out of his pack and take a swig while The Chief is out of sight."

As the others set up camp, the guide had a bath.

"Lord Hughey goes in with his underclothes on. He has bought new ones at Campbell River and thinks this a good opportunity to wash himself and his old ones before putting on the new. He dons also a pair of socks when he comes out, a bright blue with a silk finish."

Soon, however, the romance gave way to reality: ferocious rapids, cruel portages packing more than a ton of supplies through deadfalls that restricted travel to a few kilometres a day and clouds of torment from mosquitoes, midges and, "the worst of our insect foes," blackflies.

For all his peculiarities, the guide would soon prove invaluable. He knew how to build a smudge to keep off the biting insects, where to pitch camp to catch breezes that blew them away, how to read and negotiate fast water—"a solid, wild, foaming, roaring torrent interspersed with rocks, others just submerged and causing wondrous turmoil"—which became more frequent as the expedition moved deeper into the mountains.

"The ascent is very exciting," Johnson wrote. "Lord B. is standing in the stern, quick as a cat, poling, now on one side of the canoe, now on the other, always keeping the bow straight on the current and fighting to push her ahead, inch by inch."

"Lord B. takes Miss E. into Charlie's small canoe," he noted. "I follow them along and watch. Lord B. is a wonder—never makes a mis-stroke or loses control for a second—every stroke of his paddle tells—seems to do it much more easily than the Indians."

The danger of what was easy to Bacon was emphasized when the canoe carrying Ellison capsized in a rapid. Caught in the thwarts, Ellison was trapped head down in the water.

The marine life in the intertidal zone off Bamberton Provincial Park, just 45 kilometres north of Victoria, invite inspection, especially by school children.

"Miracle that his head was not dashed against the stones on the bottom and life sent fleeting," Johnson wrote. "Providence ordered it otherwise." The expedition's leader came through with only a bad knock on the knee, although the injury would plague him.

Then after portaging around six violent rapids, a whirlpool Bacon called "the Devil's Dream" and traversing a huge blowdown, the explorers reached "this jewel of a lake" among rugged mountains.

"Who will say anything in the Alps or Selkirks is finer," Johnson wrote. "We have to look in silence. The brilliant blue sky, with a few puffs of white clouds, perfectly reflected in the water of the lake completes the magical scene."

Once again the reverie would evaporate. Two days later they were struggling through a green hell, "walking a narrow log when the least swinging of your pack to one side or the other will throw you off to the ground below, maybe into a stream, maybe into the yawning chasm of a gulch," Johnson wrote. "You land on your face in Devil's Club or salmon berries if you are not impaled upon a sharp, dead branch or a pointed rock."

Jamieson, with his enormous girth, was particularly plagued by the terrain and frequently fell behind, lumbering into camp late and then fretting over supplies. Yet none of his companions regretted having him along.

"Our 'fat cook' is one of the features of the trip that we would not dispense with for anything," Johnson wrote. "He is always complaining of lack of ingredients and tools to work with, but produces wonderful dishes nevertheless. When will we forget his lobster pates, clam chowder, canned mutton a la Spanish, plum puddings and hot cakes? Good old Pete!"

On July 19, after two weeks of exhausting travel, the expedition camped to rest up for the assault on Crown Mountain. Johnson took a canoe and went fishing by moonlight and was astounded by the sight of "snow-capped crowns—conical masses of molten silver."

But strains were beginning to show. Ellison's injured knee was so painful he sometimes cried out, Haslam had dysentery, "all the packers hate the colonel for some reason and would rather be kicked than do anything for him" and even the colonel was "nervous" about the coming climb.

Ellison called a council of war. He produced "a bottle of champagne, Moet & Chandon, 1900, to drink good luck to ourselves." Charlie and the boys preferred rum toddies, "the woodsman's friend."

Three days later, carrying 30-kilogram packs, a climbing party of nine including the injured Ellison, his remarkable daughter—"Miss E. looks perfectly fresh"—Holmes and Johnson set out for the distant peak.

It would take them a week of difficult travel, sometimes a few kilometres in a day, traversing one criss-cross tangle of fallen trees two metres in diameter and climbing another mountain en route.

On July 29, they broke camp at daybreak and, with Myra Ellison leading the way up a precipitous ridge, reached the summit at 7:50 a.m.

"Miss E. had a British Union Jack in her hand as she reached the summit and

A squirrel finds a cosy home within a spruce tree in Charlie Lake Provincial Park at the junction of the Alaska Highway and Highway 29. Moose, black bears and both white-tailed and mule deer are common in this area.

waved it joyously," Johnson wrote. "I had a surprise in store for them, for I pulled out of my pocket 'Old Glory,' an American Star Spangled Banner larger than her Union Jack.

"While nobody was looking, I tied it to the barrel of the rifle and with a hurrah waved it over their heads. I came near to being mobbed. Charlie jumped on me and bore me to the earth. Scotty (Twaddle) assisted him. Jim Haworth (a student at the University of Washington packing for the summer) came to my rescue being an American also, but they were too many for us, and got the flag away from me and threatened to throw it overboard off the peak.

"I grabbed the Union Jack and said I would do the same to it. That brought them to reason and I regained possession of my flag. As the Colonel came aboard, followed closely by The Chief, I waved it over them. The Colonel is highly incensed. 'Throw out the American,' he repeats over and over."

Ellison defused the tiny international incident above the clouds. Both flags were tied to the rifle barrel, the Union Jack above the Stars and Stripes according to proper protocol, after which Miss E. fired the rifle, a note was signed by all members and placed in the brass cartridge and a cairn was built.

Sealed in an empty butter tin were the cartridge, a *Vancouver Province* from July 12, 1910, a baseball pass made out to photographer Frank Ward and his wife, an 1892 Queen Victoria quarter, a 1910 King Edward VII quarter, a Queen Victoria dime and an 1894 American nickel.

The shoreline of Dionisio Point Provincial Park on Galiano Island features unique sculpted sandstone shelves and pebble beaches. It is only accessible by boat.

Then Myra produced her own surprise, a bottle of champagne, and the climbers began their descent to rejoin the trek at Buttle Lake, then press on to the high divide, Great Central Lake and Alberni on the Island's west coast.

On the way, they met a scout sent from Alberni five days earlier to find them. "He doesn't see how 'the lady' is going to make it," Johnson wrote. "We are not alarmed because we know Miss E."

By August 10 the explorers were camped beside a lake so high that it froze by night. They fortified themselves with a bottle of port, this time produced by Vancouver's Charlie Haslam. On the ascent, they passed a spectacular waterfall and named it after the redoubtable Miss E. —Myra Falls and Myra River are still on the map. The next night, Myra slept in a dugout canoe on Great Central Lake and by August 12, six weeks after setting out, they were in Alberni.

"Our vicissitudes and our great trip are over," Johnson wrote. "We adjourn to a candy shop there is in town and satiate ourselves with sweets, ice cream and drinks from the soda fountain."

Then a rare motor car drove them back to the Island's east coast.

"Lunch at the hotel, a walk about the streets of Nanaimo," he wrote, "then we board the Esquimalt and Northern Railway and are in Victoria at the Empress in time for dinner."

In 1911, on the basis of the explorers' report, the BC legislature set aside the

Nuth Khaw Yum Heritage Park, also known as Indian Arm Provincial Park, protects the shores of Indian Arm, which extends north from Burrard Inlet. It is jointly managed by the Tsleil-Waututh First Nation and the provincial government.

province's first park, named after Lord Strathcona, the railway tycoon who drove the last spike for the Canadian Pacific Railway at Craigellachie.

Over the last century, the system that began with the Ellison expedition has grown to 996 provincial parks, ecological reserves, conservancies, environmentally sensitive designations and recreation areas. They cover more than 13 million hectares—14.26 percent of BC's land base. The parks system makes available 340 campgrounds, 263 day-use areas, 118 boat launches and 6,000 kilometres of hiking trails, a distance greater than that stretching from Vancouver Island's west coast to the most easterly point of Newfoundland.

And British Columbians of the twenty-first century love and use their parks. More than 90 percent report having used a provincial park at least once. Six out of ten visit at least one park every year in search of everything from extreme outdoor sports to spiritual renewal.

It is to this amazing, triumphant and uplifting story that Jim Anderson, himself an intimate part of the process, brings his own deep knowledge and understanding of how it came about, what it means and what it yet may mean. Still, his carefully researched history of how the province's parks came to be a national treasure is as much a caution as a celebration.

Sprawling across the middle of Vancouver Island, Strathcona Park remains the

Indian Arm Provincial Park provides rustic camping, boating, kayaking, canoeing and scuba diving opportunities within an hour's boat travel north of Vancouver.

mountain wilderness encountered by the Ellison expedition in 1911. It is deeply carved by rivers tumbling seaward from glittering snowfields, glacier-fed lakes and dark mountain tarns. Dense old-growth forests flank alpine meadows renowned for their annual eruption of wildflowers in one of the world's richest ecosystems.

From Paradise Meadows on the Forbidden Plateau to Della Falls, at 440 metres the highest cascade in North America, Strathcona Park makes an ideal foundation—and metaphor—for the parks system so painstakingly assembled over a century.

As *British Columbia's Magnificent Parks* makes clear, that system is still a work in progress.

Yet if Strathcona Park represents the remarkable vision of some political leaders, it also represents the venality of others. While the Strathcona Park Act of 1911 clearly intended to protect the region from development, it took less than a decade for subsequent governments to begin despoiling it.

During its own troubled century, Strathcona Park has endured open pit mining, flooding from hydro dams and is still subject to almost constant pressure for logging, mineral and resort development.

British Columbians tend to take the glories of their provincial parks for granted. But citizen organizations still struggle to defend parks from economic and political interests that see them as a convenient resource bank from which to withdraw capital.

The conflicting interests symbolized by Strathcona Park are evidence that if people want their provincial wilderness legacy to survive for the British Columbians of 2111, they will have to be prepared to fight for them. Jim Anderson's history reminds us that people are prepared to fight and that these magnificent parks are well worth fighting for.

Stephen Hume, 2011
Author of *A Walk with the Rainy Sisters: In Praise of British Columbia's Places* and *Vancouver Sun* columnist and senior writer

Introduction

In early 2009 my wife and I went to Tanzania where we visited the famed Serengeti, home of the world's greatest populace of wildlife. This national park of 14,763 square kilometres was designated in 1951 but had been established first as a game reserve in 1929. Seeing this park, with its enormous variety and numbers of wildlife, is awe-inspiring and overwhelming.

Being there reminded me of why we need parks and the rationale for the United Nations objective of protecting 12 percent of the world's land base. It reinforced my own pride and commitment in what BC has been able to accomplish and the mission set forth by the elders of our Parks Branch[1]—an honourable and necessary contribution to society and indeed to all mankind.

Today, as we celebrate the centennial of the designation of Strathcona as the first BC provincial park, it is fitting that we look back over our history to understand

Above: Strathcona Provincial Park awaits the spring. Set aside in 1911 as British Columbia's first provincial park, it was promoted as the "Vancouver Island Alps," but the government of the day allowed mineral exploitation and logging.

how we arrived at our present state-of-parks (see map, opposite). This document offers and supports the premise that, from the late 1950s through the 1980s, the shape of British Columbia's parks system and the nature of park developments and park management practices were primarily a function of collective internal staff initiatives and leadership rather than that provided by outside groups, individuals or, for that matter, their political masters. Of course, the Parks Branch, like any other public agency, is not the master of its own destiny or that of its leadership. Instead, it reflects the impacts of political, economic and social changes and, particularly, legislative budget allocations. The political support the government has given to the Parks Branch is generally reflected in two ways: by its commitment to protect existing parks and to create new ones and by the size of budget allocations. Over time Parks has received a mixture of one or the other, occasionally both and sometimes neither.

The history of BC Parks system provides a lens through which to view most of the major headline stories and political issues of the times—unionization of the public service, hydro/highway development, regional government, biodiversity, aboriginal rights, fiscal restraint, privatization, urban versus rural values, hunting, endangered species, user fees, timber exchanges, land trust and more. This work covers the themes and issues that give land-use planning, resource management and politics such an interesting dynamic in British Columbia.

Politicians have provided a macro framework by deciding whether the park system will expand and by how much, and they have sole authority to determine the annual allocation of funding for park development. Interestingly, during the 1960s when adverse political decisions were made that threatened the integrity of parks, they were generally targeted at specific parks—Strathcona, Tweedsmuir and Hamber—and the destiny of hundreds of other parks remained untouched. These political interventions did not particularly affect internal Branch structure, staffing or operational activities. The prime political dynamic was a wildly fluctuating budgetary cycle of feast or famine while at the same time there was strong support for the development of numerous roadside and waterfront parks. Parks Branch staff, meanwhile, by careful and continuing on-the-ground planning reconnaissance, were able to choose where and which would be new parks and how they would be developed.

By the mid-1970s the public debate in support of parks versus resource development had become polarized and entered the public political arena. As conservation groups mounted vigorous public park advocacy campaigns, the leadership in park planning was no longer the sole purview of park planners and the Branch executive. Several public interest groups, including the Western Canada Wilderness Committee and the Valhalla Wilderness Society, had emerged as strong voices in support of conservation and parks. This debate (often referred to as the "war in the woods") is best typified by the saga of the Clayoquot Sound protests.

After 1982 Branch staff were absorbed in the monumental administrative task of implementing a dramatic shift to contracted visitor services delivery by the private sector. Contractual negotiations had to be completed and mechanisms put in place

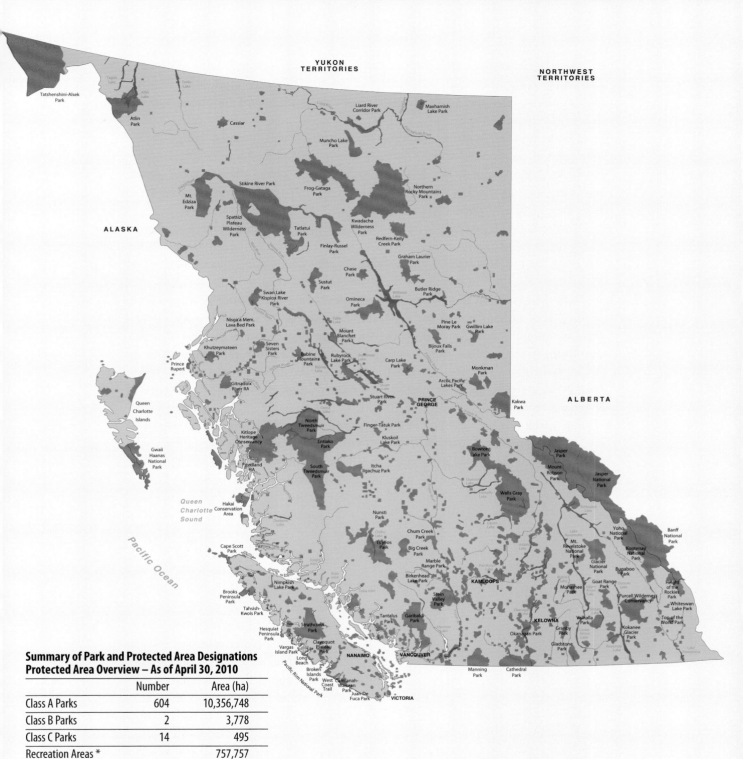

YUKON TERRITORIES

NORTHWEST TERRITORIES

ALASKA

ALBERTA

Pacific Ocean

Queen Charlotte Sound

Tatshenshini-Alsek Park

Atlin Park

Cassiar

Mt. Edziza Park

Stikine River Park

Spatsizi Plateau Wilderness Park

Tatlatui Park

Swan Lake Kispiox River Park

Nisga'a Mem. Lava Bed Park

Khutzeymateen Park

Prince Rupert

Seven Sisters Park

Gitnadoix River RA

Queen Charlotte Islands

Kitlope Heritage Conservancy

Gwaii Haanas National Park

Fiordland RA

Hakai Conservation Area

Cape Scott Park

Brooks Peninsula Park

Tahsish-Kwois Park

Hesquiat Peninsula Park

Strathcona Park

Nimpkish Lake Park

Clayoquot Plateau Park

Vargas Island Park

Long Beach

Pacific Rim National Park

Broken Islands Park

West Coast Trail

Carmanah-Walbran Park

Juan De Fuca Park

NANAIMO

VICTORIA

Frog-Gataga Park

Liard River Corridor Park

Maxhamish Lake Park

Muncho Lake Park

Northern Rocky Mountains Park

Kwadacha Wilderness Park

Redfern-Keily Creek Park

Finlay-Russel Park

Chase Park

Graham Laurier Park

Sustut Park

Omineca Park

Mount Blanchet Park

Babine Mountains Park

Rubyrock Lake Park

Carp Lake Park

Pine Le Moray Park

Gwillim Lake Park

Bijoux Falls Park

Butler Ridge Park

Monkman Park

Arctic Pacific Lakes Park

Stuart River Park

PRINCE GEORGE

Kakwa Park

North Tweedsmuir Park

Entiako Park

South Tweedsmuir Park

Finger-Tatuk Park

Kluskoil Lake Park

Itcha Ilgachuz Park

Bowron Lake Park

Jasper Park

Mount Robson Park

Jasper National Park

Wells Gray Park

Nunsti Park

Tsʼyl-os Park

Chum Creek Park

Big Creek Park

Marble Range Park

Birkenhead Lake Park

Mt. Revelstoke National Park

Yoho National Park

Banff National Park

Kootenay National Park

Glacier National Park

Bugaboo Park

Goat Range Park

Monashee Park

Purcell Wilderness Conservancy

Height of the Rockies Park

Whiteswan Lake Park

Top of the World Park

KAMLOOPS

Stein Valley Park

Tantalus Park

Garibaldi Park

Okanagan Park

KELOWNA

Granby Park

Valhalla Park

Kokanee Glacier Park

Gladstone Park

VANCOUVER

Manning Park

Cathedral Park

Summary of Park and Protected Area Designations
Protected Area Overview — As of April 30, 2010

	Number	Area (ha)
Class A Parks	604	10,356,748
Class B Parks	2	3,778
Class C Parks	14	495
Recreation Areas *		757,757
Conservancies	143	2,115,555
Designations under the Environmental and Land Use Act		71,450,113
Ecological Reserves**	148	162,632
Total	**989**	**13,142,741**

* The number and area figures for recreation areas reflect the outcome of land-use plans implemented to date. In some cases, orders in council may not have been passed yet to cancel a recreation area (e.g. Kwadacha; Mount Edziza; Stikine River). Accordingly, the actual number of recreation areas designated under the Park Act may be greater than the numbers reflected in this table. There is also some overlap between Recreation Areas and Class A parks (e.g. Kakwa) as land-use plan decisions have not yet been fully implemented. This overlap has been subtracted from the area figures for Recreation Areas.

**Three ecological reserves are also included in Class A parks. The area of overlap is approximately 67 hectares. Two ecological reserves are also included in Lac du Bois Grasslands Park established under the Environment and Land Use Act. The area of overlap is 270 hectares. This area of overlap has been subtracted from the total area figure above.

Note: One s. 6(1) trail under the Park Act (Babine Mountains Trail - 10 ha) is not included in the above numbers.

to ensure monitoring and accountability of both fiscal arrangements and quality standards for visitor services and facility maintenance. To their credit, this shift was fully in place within five years. It was a significant achievement and was reinforced by visitor satisfaction surveys.

The history of land-use planning and resource management policy in BC through the last three decades was also dominated by debate over forest policy. However, preservation of "wilderness areas" was only part of a much larger agenda to reform logging practices and to shift forest policy beyond integrated use objectives to recognize biodiversity.

Another tide had turned by the early 1990s and government policy again recognized the value of a more systematic regional land-use planning framework and the need for more protected areas. Four decades of planning reconnaissance by Parks staff now paid dividends in the strategic creation of new parks. The 1990s also saw the evolution of a dynamic system of public participatory processes, with local citizens tasked to lead and complete a comprehensive province-wide set of regional land and resource use plans. It was a process that also incorporated two significant policy shifts—highly centralized policy direction and recognition of Aboriginal rights. A key feature was the Protected Areas Strategy, which served as both a means to begin and a way to define the output of the Land and Resource Management Plans.

The result was the doubling of the parks systems within two short decades. Few provinces, if any, can match this achievement.

1:
Origins and Early Days

Origins

When Premier Richard McBride designated British Columbia's first provincial park in 1911, he was not inventing a new concept. There were precedents, especially in the United States and in eastern Canada, and he and his government incorporated some of the good ideas, and some of the bad ones, that made up the statutes that created those parks.

But the parks system that was eventually developed in British Columbia would prove to be unique, in part because of the political, economic and social structures in this far western province, but mostly because of its remoteness and remarkably varied geography. A hundred years after the designation of that first park 14 percent of this province's landmass would be protected within 996 national and provincial parks, ecological reserves, conservancies and recreation and wilderness areas.

Above: Roaring surf, spectacular coastal scenery and great wildlife viewing are all available to hikers travelling the trails of Juan de Fuca Provincial Park on southern Vancouver Island.

Above: The five large islands and numerous small ones designated in 2008 as the Lax Lwax/Dundas and Melville Islands Conservancy are traditional seafood harvesting areas for the Coast Tsimshian First Nation.

Right: A mature grizzly bear dines on grasses on the estuary of the Khutzeymateen River. Approximately 50 grizzlies are protected in this sanctuary, and viewing is only allowed under strict permit.

Left: Della Falls, which at 440 metres ranks as one of Canada's highest waterfalls, descends in three spectacular cascades. It is located near the southern end of Strathcona Provincial Park.

Below: Remote Atlin Park, in the northwest corner of the province is only accessible by boat or plane. Winter days are very short here, but there is no actual darkness on summer nights.

Glaciation in Northern Rocky Mountains Park has resulted in broad U-shaped river valley bottoms, mountain cirques and morainal ridges.

When contiguous protected areas are seen as a single unit, twenty-one of BC's protected areas are larger than 100,000 hectares; two of those areas are larger than one million hectares.

National Parks

Back in 1810 when the poet William Wordsworth described England's Lake District as a "sort of national property in which every man has a right and interest," he was expressing a radical concept: in a country where property ownership was traditionally restricted to the wealthy and titled, he was suggesting that ordinary working people should share in the ownership of this beautiful and romantic part of the Cumbrian countryside with its lakes and bogs and mountain crags. In effect, he was advocating a national park. Wordsworth's "national property" was not the untouched wilderness landscape that Canadians think of as a national park. The Lake District had been heavily populated since Neolithic times, denuded of forest cover by the reign of Elizabeth I and most of the land alienated for human dwellings, agriculture, commerce or industry. However, there were still mountains and tarns and heath that had not been claimed for man's purposes, and Wordsworth was advocating that every citizen of his country should have the right to access these unalienated parts of that landscape and enjoy their beauty. And that is the fundamental principle behind the national park concept.

Above: Kwadacha Wilderness Park, off the Alaska Highway, offers habitat for wildlife ranging from wolves to Siberian lemmings. For birders there are over 70 species to watch, including hawks, kestrels, falcons and eagles.

Left: Anderson Flats Provincial Park, established in 2007, is located on the southeast bank at the junction of the Skeena and Bulkley rivers. It preserves access to recreational salmon fishing sites.

In Europe national parks remained nothing more than the dreams of poets and idealists for another hundred years, but in 1909 Sweden became the first European country to create a national park. Switzerland followed in 1911. England's Lake District had to wait until 1951 for national park status. However, it was a different story in North America. Until well into the last half of the nineteenth century most of the western half of the continent was still untrammelled wilderness, and there were those who recognized the importance of protecting some of that wilderness in its natural state. The American painter, author and traveller George Catlin, touring the West in 1841, was one of the first to express the hope that the government would set aside a section of land for a national park that would contain "both man and beasts in all the wild and freshness of their nature's beauty." Fortunately there were also a few far-sighted politicians who saw the value of protecting some of it from private exploitation, and as a result, it was in the western United States that the first attempts were made to protect large blocks of land in their natural state. The first move came on April 20, 1832, when President Andrew Jackson signed legislation to create the Hot Springs Reservation in Hot Springs, Arkansas, to prevent

Above: A herd of resident mountain goats spend their summers amid the peaks of Seven Sisters Provincial Park, off Highway 16 between Hazelton and Terrace, and winter below in the valleys of Oliver and Hells Bells creeks.

Right: In most wilderness areas of British Columbia, including Babine Mountains Provincial Park, precautions should be observed to avoid close encounters with bears.

private development of the natural thermal springs there, although federal control of the area was not clearly established for another forty-five years.

The next attempt to set aside parkland came in 1864 when President Abraham Lincoln signed the Act of Congress that ceded the Yosemite Valley and the Mariposa Grove of Giant Sequoias to the state of California as a park. To make sure the intentions of Congress were not subverted, the act specified that "the said state shall accept this grant upon the express conditions that the premises shall be held for public use, resort and recreation." The naturalist John Muir arrived in the new park in 1868 and later wrote, "No temple made with hands can compare with Yosemite…[It is] the grandest of all special temples of Nature." Muir began a campaign to have Yosemite returned to the federal government as a national park; instead the federal government gave park status only to the high country. Muir then joined with other "preservationists" in 1892 to establish the Sierra Club to press for Yosemite's full protection. They were opposed by Gifford Pinchot, who became chief forester when the US Forest Service was established in 1905. He called himself a "conservationist" and saw parks as unused resources, a means of managing

Protecting Helmcken Falls, which at 141 metres high is the fourth-highest waterfall in Canada, was one of the main reasons for the creation of Wells Gray Provincial Park in 1939.

A porcupine takes a boardwalk stroll in Babine Mountains Provincial Park.

Junction Sheep Range Provincial Park is a unique landscape of rolling grasslands, cliffs and hoodoos at the confluence of the Chilcotin and Fraser rivers.

the nation's natural resources for long-term sustainable commercial use. His model for forest management—a system that was based on public ownership with logging carried out by private interests in exchange for a fee—was adopted throughout the United States (and eventually in Alberta). Pinchot also supported several hydro dam projects that would flood existing or proposed national parks. His debates with Muir set the scene for the vigorous policy differences between conservationists and preservationists that continue to this day.

In 1899 a new National Park Act elevated Yosemite to national park status but left it in the hands of the state of California; it was not transferred to federal control until 1906. However, this change did not entirely protect it. With the growth of population in San Francisco, pressure began to mount to dam the Tuolumne River in the Hetch Hetchy Valley to provide water and electrical power for the city. As this valley is within Yosemite National Park, an act of Congress was needed to start the project, and Muir pleaded with President Theodore Roosevelt, with whom he had camped in Yosemite, to scuttle the project. Roosevelt declined. His successor, William Howard Taft, did suspend approval for the Hetch Hetchy dam, but on December 19, 1913, after years of national debate, Taft's successor, Woodrow Wilson, signed the bill authorizing it. Construction of a sixty-nine-metre-high dam was completed in 1923; it was raised another twenty-six metres in 1938.

The progress of Yellowstone to national park status was smoother, but unlike Yosemite, the government's intention there was not to protect wilderness. The park was established to prevent private acquisition of geysers, hot springs and waterfalls and the wholesale slaughter of the wildlife that congregated there. On March 1, 1872, President Ulysses S. Grant signed an act of dedication to:

set apart a certain tract of land lying near the headwaters of the Yellowstone River as

Above: Access via mechanized or motorized vehicles to the wilderness areas of Height of the Rockies Provincial Park, southwest of Banff National Park, is prohibited.

Left: The glacier-carved granite spires of Bugaboo Provincial Park in the Purcell Mountains are among the world's greatest alpine rock climbing challenges. Only skilled mountaineers need apply.

a public park. Be it enacted by the Senate and House of Representatives of the United States of America in Congress assembled, that the tract of land in the Territories of Montana and Wyoming…is hereby reserved and withdrawn from settlement, occupancy, or sale under the laws of the United States, and dedicated and set apart as a public park or pleasuring ground for the benefit and enjoyment of the people; and all persons who shall locate, or settle upon, or occupy the same or any part thereof, except as hereinafter provided, shall be considered trespassers and removed therefrom.

The massive craggy peak of Mount Assiniboine, rising high above the tree line on the spine of the Rocky Mountains, attracts climbers from all over the world.

Initially, Yellowstone National Park was 404,686 hectares although it was increased in later years to 898,000 hectares. In 1886 the welfare of the park became the responsibility of the army, which oversaw public access while protecting its wildlife and natural resources, and the army remained its caretaker until after the US National Park Service was created in 1916.

Although isolated from the main population centres of the United States, Yellowstone became more accessible in the early 1880s when the Northern Pacific Railway built a train station at Livingston, Montana, allowing access via the park's northern entrance. After 1908 a Union Pacific branch line deposited visitors at the West Yellowstone entrance as well, but the real surge in visits came with automobile tourists, and by 1915 there were already a thousand cars entering the park every year.

In 1916 Congress passed the law that created the National Parks Service (NPS) to manage the country's sixteen national parks and twenty-two national monuments. The new service's official role was to "conserve the scenery and the natural and historic objects and wildlife therein, and to provide for the enjoyment of the same in such manner and by such means as will leave them unimpaired for future

Cathedral Park, which is located in the transition zone between the forested Cascade Mountains and the arid Okanagan Valley just north of the BC–Washington border, is a wilderness camper's heaven.

Left: Originally part of the Kettle Valley Railway line, the five Othello Tunnels and several bridges of Coquihalla Canyon Provincial Park provide a walking /cycling trail through the river's 90-meter-deep gorge.

generations." Thus, the job of the NPS was to manage both preservation and tourism. Stephen Mather, the first director of the NPS, was convinced that in order to gain support for national parks, his task was to increase park use, and he recruited the railways and newspapers for a "See America First" campaign and authorized road building within the national parks to accommodate more auto traffic. He also employed park rangers to protect resources and visitors, and by 1920 US national parks were receiving a million visitors a year. Five years later this number had doubled.

Canada's First National Park

In the early 1880s the Canadian Pacific Railway's general manager William Cornelius Van Horne, inspired by the Northern Pacific Railway's successful relationship with Yellowstone National Park, began urging Prime Minister John A. Macdonald to create park reserves along the CPR right-of-way. The prime minister was favourable to the idea, and in 1885 he designated the country's first national park reserve at Cave and Basin Hot Springs, which had been discovered two years earlier by some railway construction workers. This parcel of land on the eastern slope of the Rockies adjacent to the rail line was a mere 2,592 hectares, but on June 23, 1887, Parliament passed the Rocky Mountains Park Act, which transformed the reserve into a national park and enlarged its area to 67,400 hectares. That act specified that the land was "hereby reserved and set apart as public park and pleasure ground for the benefit, advantage and enjoyment of the people of Canada…and it shall be known as Rocky Mountains Park of Canada." In 1930 the name was changed to Banff National Park.

Manning Provincial Park is unique in providing both winter and summer recreational opportunities as well as protecting a dramatic natural heritage, half coastal rainforest, half dry Interior plateau.

Seventy-metre-high
Brandywine Falls, 47
kilometres north of
Squamish, is best seen from
a new viewing platform
perched on the edge of a
volcanic escarpment.

By night, the summit of Cypress Provincial Park provides a spectacular view of the Lions Gate Bridge, Stanley Park and the city of Vancouver.

The Great Glacier, now known as the Illecillewaet Glacier, towers over the Canadian Pacific Railway's Glacier House, which provided a dining facility for railway passengers. *BC Archives, B-02944*

The legislation, modelled on that for Yellowstone, allowed private enterprise to construct and operate hotels and lodges within the new park, and in 1888 the CPR, which already cut through the park's centre, built the Banff Springs Hotel and followed this five years later with Chateau Lake Louise. An international advertising campaign soon made both hotels profitable. The park was expanded to 1,140,000 hectares in 1902 so that it included Lake Louise and the headwaters of the Bow, Red Deer, Kananaskis and Spray rivers, although subsequent governments would shrink the park's size again to accommodate resource companies. In 1906 the Alpine Club of Canada was established to organize climbing and camping in the park's backcountry, and in 1911 the federal government organized the Dominion Parks Branch, mandated to protect and present nationally significant examples of Canada's natural and cultural heritage.

In 1886 the federal government had also reserved land for its second and third national parks, Glacier and Yoho, both in British Columbia. Glacier National Reserve protects 134,900 hectares in the Selkirk Mountains in the Interior wet belt of the province. Much of the higher terrain in the park, which is dominated by ten peaks ranging from 2,600 metres to 3,390 metres in height, is covered by glaciers. There are also unique stands of old-growth cedar and hemlock as well as critical habitat for wildlife species such as the mountain caribou, mountain goat and grizzly bear.

Like Banff, Glacier National Park is bisected by the Canadian Pacific Railway. As the CPR quickly discovered that dining cars added unnecessary extra weight to trains straining to climb the mountain passes, the company built Glacier House in Rogers Pass as a dining stop for its passengers. It proved to be very popular, but in 1916 the railway was forced to build the Connaught Tunnel to avoid the avalanches on the main line, and Glacier House no longer enjoyed direct rail service. It was closed in 1925 and subsequently dismantled.

The history of Yoho National Park is also bound up with the story of the CPR. Yoho lies on the western slope of the Rockies bordered by Banff National Park to the east, and includes Kicking Horse Pass through which the rail line runs. Within its boundaries are twenty-eight mountain peaks more than 3,000 metres in height. It also includes the Burgess Shale, one of the world's most important fossil beds.

In 1911 the Canadian Parliament passed the Dominion Forest and Reserve Act, which established the National Parks Commission to manage and develop national parks.

Provincial Parks

The first provincial park in Canada was established in Ontario on May 23, 1893. The initial boundaries of Algonquin Provincial Park included 379,700 hectares of forest, 2,400 lakes and 1,200 kilometres of streams and rivers. But this new park, situated in central Ontario between Georgian Bay and the Ottawa River, was intended not only to provide a "public park, health resort and pleasure ground for the benefit, advantage and enjoyment of all the people of the province" but also to control the rampant logging in the area. This latter concern takes precedence in the report by the five commissioners tasked with drawing up the park's mandate, a report that said in part that:

At high tide the first kilometre of the Indian River in Indian Arm Park is navigable by canoe or kayak, but beyond that boats must be abandoned in favour of hiking boots.

> *The experience of older countries had everywhere shown that the wholesale and indiscriminate slaughter of forests brings a host of evils in its train. Wide tracts are converted from fertile plains into arid desert, springs and streams are dried up, and the rainfall, instead of percolating gently through the forest floor and finding its way by easy stages by brook and river to the lower levels, now descends the valley in hurrying torrents, carrying before it tempestuous floods.*

However, the commissioners did not recommend an end to logging in the park; instead they proposed the protection of a tract of timberland where good forestry practices would be exemplified alongside a public recreation area. To ensure compliance with new logging practices, a park ranger service was established. The

A giant old-growth Douglas fir reaches into the skies above Cathedral Grove in MacMillan Provincial Park near Cameron Lake on Vancouver Island.

rangers also patrolled to enforce the no hunting or trapping rule, and within a few years wildlife numbers had increased.

Although no settlers were permitted to live within the park's boundaries, lumbermen did take up residence there, and after the Ottawa, Arnprior and Parry Sound Railway (which became part of the Grand Trunk Railway in 1905) was laid through the park in 1896, railway workers came to live there, too. The Hotel Algonquin was built on Joe Lake in 1908 followed closely by the Grand Trunk's Highland Inn, which was constructed overlooking the company's Algonquin Park train station. More hotels, lodges and camps were established in the following years, and in time the logging camps and the workers' cottages also became summer rental accommodation for vacationers. A second railway, the Canadian Northern, which was built in 1915, gave access to the park from the north side.

Ontario's second provincial park was designated just a year after Algonquin. Rondeau Provincial Park protects a unique eight-kilometre-long cuspate sandspit that extends almost three kilometres out into Lake Erie. It is also renowned as the largest area of Carolinian (deciduous) forest in Canada, and it is an important stopover for migrating birds. While it would be nice to believe that the government of Ontario was motivated to create this park in order to protect these ecological values, Rondeau was, in fact, created specifically to provide summer cottage land for the residents of the nearby city of Chatham. Forty cottage lots were surveyed at the outset and several hundred more in succeeding years, although the province retained title to the land and merely leased it to those who wished to build on it.

The province of Manitoba followed neither of these patterns for protecting wilderness areas. Instead, in the early 1900s the government established five forest reserves; in the 1950s these became the core of the province's parks system, although no parks department was established until 1960. Other provinces delayed establishing parks until nearly mid-century—New Brunswick's first provincial park was only designated in 1935—because regional parks satisfied local needs. Eventually it would be the lure of tourist dollars that would push all of the provinces to set aside parkland.

British Columbia's First Provincial Park

By 1908 when the British Columbia legislature passed its first Provincial Parks Act, giving the Lieutenant-Governor in Council the power to reserve public lands for provincial parks, the city of Victoria already had Beacon Hill Park (established in 1882) and the city of Vancouver had converted the First Narrows Military Reserve into Stanley Park (1888). Thus, most of the provisions of the act were an effort to regulate the kind of parks that already existed, so they referred to the management of parks for local use and dealt with boulevards, grass plots, licensing hacks, the sale of refreshments and the leasing of parkland to agricultural and athletic clubs as well as the creation of local park boards. Then in the spring of 1910 Premier Richard McBride became aware that the federal government was interested in establishing a national park on Vancouver Island, and to forestall that eventuality, he placed a reserve on a 203,314-hectare triangle of land in the centre of the island for future provincial government purposes, although primarily as a park. This single move by the premier embarked the province on a century of parks creation that would culminate in 14 percent of the land mass being protected as parks.

But designating a park in British Columbia would prove to have a whole range of problems that had not arisen in other regions of Canada, mostly because the geography and history of this coast had established a unique pattern of settlement. For the first century, human settlement had been dependent on water access and marine transport along the coast, inland to Yale via the Fraser or along Okanagan, Arrow and Kootenay lakes. Wherever free land had been offered, people had taken up homesteads, though more often parcels of land had been allocated for logging and mining, and townsites had grown up nearby. By need and design, flat valley bottoms and sites along rivers, lakes or ocean were the first to be taken up, and because of the terrain, elevated sites offering scenic views of the landscape were also taken up. Settlers discovered the Fraser Valley's long narrow pocket of farmland and the ribbon of fertile land in the Okanagan and later the Peace River country. Ranches were created in the East Kootenay and Cariboo–Chilcotin. Unfortunately the government had also encouraged settlers to try farming in circumstances where climate and soils were not favourable, and subsequently over the decades rural holdings were abandoned in such obscure places as the Queen Charlotte Islands, Cape Scott and the Bella Coola valley. On Vancouver Island, in order to attract a railway company, the government provided a land grant that covered 40 percent of the eastern portion of the island, which was valuable not only for its forest and mineral values (gold and coal) but, with its gentler terrain and moderate climate, was some of the most valuable real estate in the country. Consequently, when the BC government decided to create a parks system, the 5 percent of the province that was composed of easily accessible, low elevation, fertile land had all been alienated for private use. The 95 percent that was inaccessible and mountainous belonged to the Crown.

It is not surprising then that McBride and his government knew very little about the mountainous, heavily timbered central portion of the island where they proposed to create a park. It was the traditional territory of the Mowachaht and Muchalaht people of the Nuu-chah-nulth First Nation. In 1865 John James Taylor Buttle, who had come west with the Royal Engineers to serve as a botanical collector with the Oregon Boundary Commission, had led an expedition that explored the southwestern portion of the reserved triangle. The next officially noted expedition came in 1892 when the provincial government contracted with William Ralph to survey the western boundary of Robert Dunsmuir's Esquimalt and Nanaimo (E&N) Railway eight-thousand-square-kilometre land grant. Ralph surveyed a straight line extending northwest from Muir Creek near Sooke to the foot of Crown Mountain, which is twenty-five kilometres east of Campbell River. It was this survey line that McBride chose as the eastern boundary of his new reserve. For its southern boundary he drew a straight line on a map from east to west just north of Great Central Lake and for its western boundary another straight line due north and south. These arbitrary lines, which defy the dictum that parks should have natural boundaries

Left: Many of the old Kettle Valley Railway trestles on the main trail through Myra–Bellevue Park were destroyed in a 2003 forest fire, but they were rebuilt and the trail reopened in May 2005.

Below: Ever since Newcastle Island, just off the city of Nanaimo, opened as a Canadian Pacific Steamships resort in 1931, it has been attracting boatloads of day-trippers to swim and hike and picnic.

At the end of a hard day of canoeing upriver, members of the Ellison party gather beside a campfire at the lower end of Buttle Lake. *Museum at Campbell River, 10129*

such as water courses and heights of land, cut through watersheds, lakes, mountain-tops and other topographical features and were destined to provide many problems in the years to come.

McBride's next move was to instruct his chief commissioner of lands, Price Ellison, to lead an expedition into the triangle to assess its suitability as a park. Ellison, the beefy, fifty-eight-year-old, walrus-mustached owner of the *Vernon News*, had been born in England and apprenticed as a blacksmith but had left for the United States in 1873 to make his fortune in the California goldfields. When wealth had eluded him there, he tried the Cariboo then settled in the north Okanagan where he amassed one of the largest collections of orchards and ranchlands in the valley. When McBride sent him to investigate the reserve, he had been representing the Okanagan in the legislature for twelve years but had only recently been elevated to the cabinet.

The party of twenty-four adventurers that Ellison organized included several military men, a timber cruiser, a schoolteacher, a photographer, trappers, home-steaders and three Cowichan packers. Also in the party were Ellison's nephew, Harry McLure Johnson, who kept a journal of the trip; Ellison's twenty-year-old daughter,

Myra, who was a student of economics at McGill University; and Peter Jamieson, the 250-pound chef who usually presided over the legislature's dining room.

In Campbell River on July 2 the expedition's members met up with their guide, Hugh Francis Bacon, who called himself the "Lord of Vancouver Island." Bacon lived with his fox terrier, "Man," somewhere in the mountains, but he enjoyed visiting the logging town's bars where after a few glasses of Scotch he would recite Kipling to any who would listen. He was, however, an excellent woodsman.

The group set off two days later, using a freight wagon to take their supplies to McIvor Lake, canoeing across the lake then portaging to the Campbell River. From this point on, the trip was fraught with difficulties: poling upriver, they encountered whirlpools and whitewater rapids and were forced to portage through old-growth blowdowns and undergrowth laced with devil's club, all the while beset by mosquitoes, midges and blackflies. At one point, Ellison's canoe capsized and he was trapped head-down underwater, but he survived the incident with only a painful knee injury. Throughout all of their adventures, Myra Ellison was one of the stars of the show. A seasoned hiker and member of the Alpine Club of Canada, she had no difficulty keeping up with the men and always remained in good spirits. The other

Bowron Lake Provincial Park in the Cariboo Mountains provides a 116-kilometre canoe and kayak circuit that includes six lakes, two rivers and a number of small streams plus several portages. Wildlife abounds here.

star was chef Jamieson, who frequently fell behind and complained bitterly about the lack of culinary equipment but still managed to whip up four-course gourmet meals for the little band of explorers.

On July 22, after three weeks of extremely rough going, a climbing party of nine, which included Ellison, his daughter and his nephew, left the expedition to turn west into the Elk River Mountains. Their goal was 1,846-metre Crown Mountain, but it took them a week of horrendously difficult travel to reach the summit, each carrying a thirty-kilogram pack. Myra Ellison led the final assault to the summit where the party sealed coins and a page from the *Vancouver Province* into a butter tin that they left under a cairn of rocks.

When the climbers rejoined the expedition, the entire party canoed south on Buttle Lake, passing a spectacular waterfall en route. Sixty-four metres high, it plunged in half a dozen drops straight down a fault in the rock structure before the stream emptied into the aqua-blue water of Buttle Lake. Ellison named the falls and the stream in honour of his daughter. They completed the ascent to the divide the next day and reached Port Alberni via Great Central Lake on August 12, six weeks after setting out. A motor car took them to Nanaimo where they boarded the E&N and arrived in Victoria in time for dinner.

Ellison's enthusiastic report to the legislature (and the fact that McBride's thirty-six Conservative members easily out-voted the two Liberals in the House) ensured the easy passage of the Strathcona Park Act on March 1, 1911. The name was chosen to honour Donald Alexander Smith, first Baron of Strathcona and Mount Royal, one-time governor of the Hudson's Bay Company and president of the Bank of Montreal. He also had significance to BC's history as he was the railway promoter who in November 1885 drove the last spike at Craigellachie, completing the

Myra Creek in Strathcona Park descends in a series of eight waterfalls, with the final drop plunging straight into the aqua-blue waters of Buttle Lake.

main line of the Canadian Pacific Railway and finally uniting this province with the rest of Canada.

The Strathcona Park Act withdrew McBride's triangle of land from "sale, settlement or occupancy under the provisions of the Land Act or any other Act with respect to mining or any other matter," leaving it subject only to regulations that might be made by the Lieutenant-Governor in Council. But while this language appeared to protect the park from mining, logging and similar industrial exploitation, a further clause stated that "nothing in this Act contained shall be deemed to deprive any person of any vested rights or interests which he may have acquired within the limits of the park prior to the passing of this act." This clause neatly exempted the many mining claims and timber holdings that had already been granted there. The act also vested responsibility for the new park in the provincial Lands Service, but that department did not have the administrative capability, the supervisory manpower or the funding to oversee it. In addition, since neither rail nor road came close to the park's boundaries, the only people entering it over the next thirty years were prospectors, loggers and a few climbers intent on mastering its peaks and icefields. Almost all of them came at it from the more accessible eastern side, so few knew what was happening within the park as a whole. In 1913 the Management of Public Parks Act was repealed, allowing direct administration of parks by provincial officials rather than local boards, a move that avoided future public input into park use. Five years later the statute that created Strathcona was amended to open the park to the "location, acquisition and occupation of mineral claims under the Mineral Act," and in 1927 it was amended again to permit the raising of water levels in any of the park's watercourses. All of these changes would assure that Strathcona would not only be the first provincial park but the one with the worst history of exploitation.

2 :
Developing the
BC Parks System,
1913 to 1944

Mount Robson Provincial Park

After the designation of Strathcona Provincial Park in 1911, the provincial government created two more parks by special statutes. The first of these statutes was the Mount Robson Park Act, passed in 1913, shortly after the first ascent of the 3,954-metre mountain for which the park is named. This mountain, the highest in the Canadian Rockies, was conquered on July 31, 1913, by the famous Austrian-

Above: The glaciated face of Mount Robson rises to a towering 3,954 meters, the highest peak in the Canadian Rockies.

Opposite: Of all the falls in Mount Robson Park, the 45-metre-high Emperor Falls are the most well-known as they launch away from the cliff in a massive roostertail and create a cloud of spray when the water hits the rock below.

Right: Early twentieth century riders on the Berg Lake Trail in Mount Robson Provincial Park stop to admire Emperor Falls. *Vancouver Public Library Special Collections, 12302*

Below: The massive Berg Glacier in Mount Robson Provincial Park is one of the few living (or advancing) glaciers in the Canadian Rockies.

born climbing guide Conrad Kain, who led two members of the Alpine Club of Canada, W.W. Foster and Albert H. McCarthy, to the top.

Most of the 224,866-hectare Mount Robson Park lies east and south of the peak along the BC–Alberta border adjacent to Jasper National Park, and initially it was only accessible via the Yellowhead Pass, which is half in Mount Robson and half in Jasper. The Yellowhead had been the original route chosen for the Canadian Pacific Railway but had been abandoned in favour of the more southerly Kicking Horse Pass. It then became the choice of both the Grand Trunk Pacific and Canadian Northern railways. Trains began operating through it in August 1914 and as a result, Mount Robson Park became known as the province's first "railway park." (By 1923 both these rail lines had been absorbed into the Canadian National Railway.)

Mount Robson Park is also the site of the massive Berg Glacier, notable for being one of the few living or advancing glaciers in the Canadian Rockies. The park also protects the headwaters and first hundred kilometres of the Fraser River. From its beginnings here as an icy trickle, the Fraser, BC's most important river and the largest salmon-producing river in the world, flows 1,378 kilometres to the Pacific Ocean. Large portions of this rugged park have remained remote wilderness to this day despite being bisected by the rail line and later by the Yellowhead Highway.

Unfortunately, as in the statute that created Strathcona Park, nothing in the Mount Robson Park Act disturbed pre-existing rights and interests, which included mining claims and trapping and guiding rights. In fact, the owners of an adjacent guest ranch had constructed a seven-kilometre trail via Kinney Lake up to Berg Lake where they had built a chalet in the alpine area behind the mountain.

Garibaldi Provincial Park

Garibaldi Provincial Park, located in the heart of the Coast Mountains, just seventy kilometres north of Vancouver, was the last of the parks created by special statute. In 1907 a party of six Vancouver-based climbers had reached the summit of 2,678-metre Mount Garibaldi in the southwest corner of the designated park area, and this feat was followed by the establishment of summer hiking camps around nearby Garibaldi Lake. As a result of pressure from the climbing community, in 1920 the government gave park reserve status to a 194,000-hectare area to the north and east of the peak; this was followed by the Garibaldi Park Act of 1927, which made it a Class A provincial park and added the Golden Ears area, which lies to the south, to the original reserved area. (In 1967 the Golden Ears would become a separate park.) The park's boundaries were extended northward in 1928 to include Wedge Mountain and the Singing Pass area. A government brochure proudly announced that Garibaldi offered "all the glories and benefits of the Alps at Vancouver's very door."

The dominant peak, which was named in honour of the nineteenth-century Italian patriot and soldier Giuseppe Garibaldi, is a potentially active stratovolcano that began erupting about 250,000 years ago and has grown steadily since then. It is the only major Pleistocene epoch volcano known to have been formed on top of a

Opposite top: Members of the Vancouver Natural History Society stand amid rocky outcrops on an outing to Garibaldi Provincial Park in the mid-1930s. *Vancouver Public Library Special Collections, 67233*

Opposite bottom: Garibaldi Park, named after the towering, 2,678-metre peak that provides its centrepiece, offers over 90 kilometres of hiking trails for outdoor enthusiasts. When it was created in 1920, it was only the second park designated by the BC government.

Below: Lake Garibaldi, formed when a lava flow from nearby Price Mountain created a 300-metre-dam, reflects 2,678-metre Mount Garibadi in its still waters.

glacier, which caused the flanks of the volcano to collapse as the ice melted. The resulting slopes are fairly steep and composed of very loose, rotten lava and volcanic ash. A large icefield, known as the Garibaldi Neve, lies on the eastern and northern sides of the mountain.

Lava from other nearby Pleistocene epoch volcanoes flowed into an adjacent valley, creating a dam known as the Barrier, behind which the 250-metre-deep Lake Garibaldi formed, fed by melting glaciers. This dam is, however, unstable, and from time to time debris flows have been unleashed into the valley below it; the last of these flows occurred in 1855–56. Concern about the possibility of the Barrier's complete collapse during heavy rainfall, earthquakes or renewed volcanic activity caused the government to close the area below the lake in 1981 and relocate the residents of Garibaldi village, which lay in direct line of destruction if the Barrier failed.

After 1915 the corridor that runs north from the town of Squamish along the western and northwestern sides of the park was serviced by the Pacific Great Eastern Railway, but road access into the park itself was non-existent. Most early hikers and skiers, therefore, came by boat from Vancouver to Squamish in order to make their way into the area around Lake Garibaldi. It was not until the 1940s that a road was built from Squamish along Paul Ridge, allowing vehicles to access the highlands and glaciers close to Mount Garibaldi. The Sea to Sky Highway, completed in the mid-1960s from Horseshoe Bay to Squamish, made access easier.

The First Order-in-Council Parks

The original Provincial Parks Act of 1908 had given the government the power to create local boards to manage provincial parks that were designated under either the Lands Act or the Forests Act. Then in 1911 the legislature amended the act in order to allow the government to establish new parks by orders-in-council rather than legislative acts, thus avoiding the distractions of both political debate and input from the general public.

In February 1922 the government created its first two parks by order-in-council. Both were in the Nelson Forest District. The boundaries of Kokanee Glacier Park originally encompassed 25,900 hectares straddling the crest of the mountain ridges between Slocan and Kootenay lakes; another 6,000 hectares were added in 1995 to add more separation between the park's grizzly bear population and its human visitors. Most of this park is above 1,500 metres in elevation, and it includes three glaciers—Kokanee, Caribou and Woodbury—that feed over thirty good trout fishing lakes. The finger-like veins of gold and silver ores found in the granite bedrock of these mountains had caused a mining boom here at the end of the nineteenth century, and the network of trails left by the miners has been developed and extended for the recreational users of the park.

In 1922 the Kokanee Mountaineering Club paused for a photo while en route to the opening ceremonies for the newly created Kokanee Glacier Provincial Park in the Selkirk Moutains. *BC Archives, D-06521*

Left: The Kokanee Glacier can be viewed from the rugged summit of Sunrise Mountain, which is also within the park.

Below: Cabins in Kokanee Glacier Provincial Park, in the Selkirk Mountains between Slocan and Kootenay lakes, are managed by the Alpine Club of Canada.

Bottom: The three glaciers of Kokanee Glacier Park—Kokanee, Caribou and Woodbury—feed over 30 lakes and streams.

Above: On a clear summer day moutaineers embark over the broken rock of the lower slopes of Mount Assiniboine.

Below: The first ascent of 3,618-metre Mount Assiniboine was made by James Outram in 1901. The park surrounding it was not designated until 1922.

Mount Assiniboine Park is situated along the spine of the Rocky Mountains on BC's border with Alberta. When it was created in 1922, it was only 5,180 hectares, but it was increased in size in 1947 and again in 1973 so that it is now 38,600 hectares. Like Kokanee Glacier Park, this entire park sits above 1,500 metres in elevation and includes several peaks that exceed 2,700 metres in height; they include Mount Assiniboine, Mount Magog, Mount Sturdee and the Marshall and Lunette Peaks. However, Mount Assiniboine, named to honour the Native people of this area, towers above the others at 3,618 metres. There are no roads into this park so that it remains a rugged wilderness, ideal for hiking and camping.

The only other important park to be designated before 1930 was the result of a gift of land. On December 9, 1921, Victoria pioneer John Dean donated 32.37 hectares of his farm on the Saanich Peninsula to the Crown to be used as a park. He kept only the eight hectares surrounding his cabin, Illahie, for his personal use, although this too would be left to the Crown on his death. A board was created to manage John Dean Provincial Park in 1934, but it lay undeveloped for another two years. At that time, the BC Forest Service began work on an access road and a trail system. The park was later enlarged by a series of land donations so that it now

Swan Lake / Kispiox River Provincial Park on the Kiskatinaw Plateau in the Peace River Country south of Dawson Creek is a popular recreation destination for swimmers, canoers, campers, fishermen and birdwatchers.

stands at 173 hectares and encompasses the high land lying between North and Central Saanich.

Between 1918 and 1930 a half-dozen small, local-use parks, all of them designated under the Forests Act, were created with little fanfare, generally in response to requests for protected recreation areas. They ranged in size from the 2-hectare Inonoaklin Park in the Nelson Forest District to the 138-hectare Princeton Park in Kamloops Forest District. Some of them, such as the 4.8-hectare White Rock Park created in 1930 and the 35-hectare Salt Lake Park created as a local swimming area for Prince Rupert in 1925, disappeared as magically as they had appeared. However, 67-hectare Swan Lake Park in the Peace River area south of Dawson Creek became—and continues to be—a valuable community resource as is the 57-hectare park at Nakusp Hot Springs, designated in 1925.

In 1922 BC's first tourist brochures, *Park Guide Books*, were published for Garibaldi, Kokanee, Mount Robson and Strathcona parks under the authority of Minister of Lands Duff Pattullo. This was not an original initiative as similar promotional material was being published by both US and Canadian National Parks departments. However, there was one big difference: while the national parks of both countries were being developed with access roads, trails, hotels and campgrounds, BC's parks lacked facilities of any kind and most had no access roads. In fact, no budget had been set aside for the administration of parks or for building roads, trails or camping amenities. This reality led the volunteers who made up the Garibaldi Park Association to propose an extreme solution. According to the late University of BC agricultural scientist Vernon (Bert) Brink, in the late 1930s the association decided to raise funds for improvements by allowing some logging within the park. Their announcement met with public outrage. Led by Brink, Donald Buchan and a Mrs. Cracknell, the anti-logging forces organized petitions, which were signed by

Peregrine falcon nest—the lake chain in the southwest portion of Swan Lake / Kispiox River Provincial Park provides spawning and rearing habitat for salmon, which provide food for a large population of swans, buffleheads, goldeneyes and common mergansers.

thousands of people. As a result, the park escaped logging, but a budget to manage it was still not granted until after World War II.

Changing the Rules

In 1924 an amendment to the Parks Act gave the Lieutenant-Governor the power to "acquire lands, make timber or land exchanges" and even reduce the size of parks where no boards had been appointed. In fact, very few boards had been appointed by this time, so the government was in a position to make and unmake parks at will. The statute was amended again in 1927 to permit the level of any watercourse within a provincial park to be raised. And in 1933 both the Garibaldi and Mount Robson Park acts were rewritten to allow reductions in size via a simple order-in-council. All of these changes made the creation, reduction and abolition, the flooding, mining and logging of parks a simple matter of the stroke of a pen.

By 1930 British Columbia had twelve provincial parks totalling approximately 279,638 hectares, although 90 percent of this total was made up of the land included in Strathcona, Mount Robson, Garibaldi, Kokanee Glacier and Assiniboine parks. The first three were administered by special acts, the other two by the Lands ministry; a few of the remaining ones were administered by local, unpaid park boards.

Mount Seymour Provincial Park, located just 30 minutes from downtown Vancouver, has provided a convenient playground in both winter and summer for almost a century.

Park Development in the Depression Years

When the Great Depression hit North America in 1930, the federal governments of both Canada and the United States were challenged to create economic opportunities for men who had been thrown out of work. In 1933 US President Franklin D. Roosevelt introduced a program called the Civilian Conservation Corps (CCC), which put unemployed men to work on projects related to the conservation and development of natural resources, especially within national parks. Over the next nine years more than three million young men were employed by the CCC to build thousands of miles of public roadways, plant nearly three billion trees and construct more than eight hundred parks.

In Canada the federal government enacted the Unemployment and Farm Relief Act to provide for public works projects on roads and in national parks. As a result, jobless men were put to work on the Big Bend Highway between Revelstoke and Golden and the Banff–Jasper highway during the Depression years, and within Banff National Park workers constructed a new bathhouse and pool at the Upper Hot Springs. Then in 1934 the Public Works Construction Act was passed, providing continued funding for public works projects such as construction of an administrative building in Banff.

Above: The original campsite among the maples and birches at Bear Creek on the west side of Okanagan Lake was operated by the Forest Branch. *Kamloops Museum & Archives*

Left: BC Forest Service workers hired on the Young Men's Forestry Training Plan build the Verdun fire lookout tower between Francois and Ootsa lakes in 1936. *BC Archives, H-02965*

It was not until May 1935 that BC's Liberal government under Premier Duff Pattullo followed the example of the federal government and instituted the Young Men's Forestry Training Plan (YMFTP). This program employed some of the thousands of jobless men who had "ridden the rails" west in the hope of finding employment or to avoid freezing to death in eastern Canada's harsher winters. Those enrolled in this new program were between the ages of eighteen and twenty-five, with priority given to those coming from "disadvantaged families or applicants in necessitous circumstances." They were sent off to work on special projects for the Forest Branch—among them the Cowichan Lake Research Station—where they were paid a dollar a day plus room and board to construct a camp complex and build roads and trails. As BC's provincial parks were the responsibility of the Forest Branch at this time, they also profited from this program—the parks were still essentially wilderness areas with no trails, roads or campgrounds. The success of this program prompted the federal government to institute the Youth Forestry Training Plan (YFTP), which hired young men to work in forestry camps, many of them in BC. In 1936 the provincial government funded a Forest Development Program, but this time 50 percent of the men enrolled were directed into provincial and regional park development. Work camps were set up in the smaller provincial parks where the men built picnic shelters, bridges and rock walls.

Among the parks to benefit from the YMFTP and the Forest Development Program was Mount Seymour Park, created on January 31, 1936, and named for Frederick Seymour, governor of British Columbia from 1864 to 1869. This park, though only 274 hectares (another 3,200 hectares were added in the 1960s), was created primarily for its recreational values. The first recorded climb to the top of Mount Seymour was made in 1908 by members of the BC Mountaineering Club, but it was not until 1929 that the Alpine Club of Canada explored it as a potential

Skiers pose at the top of the Seymour Mountain ski run in the mid-1930s. The first ski jump was built here in 1941. BC Archives, I-61525

ski area. The following year the club was granted a twenty-one-year lease of the primary ski slopes, but they allowed the lease to lapse during the Depression years. It was then that the provincial government was persuaded to designate it as a park. That same year entrepreneur Harold Enquist bought the adjoining 200 hectares from the provincial government in order to develop a private ski area. Two years later the BC Forest Service surveyed and built a road that would take skiers halfway up the mountain to a parking lot and the beginning of the trail to Enquist's rustic ski and accommodation facilities. The first ski jump was built in 1941.

The partnership between Enquist and the Forest Service broke down in 1949, and the government bought out his interests then provided him with a Parks Use Permit (PUP) to operate the facilities. At this time the first rope tow was installed and the access road was extended. Unfortunately, the administration of the PUP in such matters as rental, revenue sharing, renewal, expansion and upgrading of facilities engendered legal disputes and political interference in favour of the operator. When Enquist's permit expired in 1951, new concessionaires took over portions of the operation until 1984 when the facilities were purchased by Mount Seymour Resorts Limited.

Another small park to benefit from the work programs of the Depression years was Peace Arch Park at the Douglas border crossing, which was officially dedicated on November 7, 1939. Although the Peace Arch itself was built in 1921 as a symbol of the good relations between the US and Canada, the lands surrounding it on both sides of the border—nine hectares on the Canadian side—were purchased in the years that followed through donations and fundraising efforts by school children. The gardens at the Peace Arch Provincial Park were begun by workers in the YMFTP program.

A moss-draped fir tree provides the foreground for spectacular Helmcken Falls in Tweedsmuir Provincial Park.

The Era of the Large Parks

Between 1938 and 1944, five immense parks were created in British Columbia. Tweedsmuir was the first. Although it was not designated as a park until 1938, it had been on the government's list of possible park sites since 1925 when Harlan Smith, an archeologist with the Geological Survey of Canada, had called for the creation of a park on the eastern slopes of the Coast Mountains north of Bella Coola to honour the great explorer, Alexander Mackenzie. The government's response had been the creation of a five-hectare historic site sixty-five kilometers northwest of Bella Coola where Mackenzie had marked his name on a rock.

However, interest in a major park in that area had continued, and in 1936 the provincial government placed a reserve on a 320-kilometre-long, elongated triangle lying between the Bella Coola River in the south and Ootsa Lake in the north. The final impetus to formalize it as a park came when Canada's fifteenth Governor General, Baron Tweedsmuir of Elsfield, announced an investigative trip into the hinterlands of British Columbia. Tweedsmuir, who was better known as John Buchan—lawyer, newspaperman, politician, author of the secret-service thriller *The Thirty-nine Steps* (1915) and intrepid outdoorsman—arrived via Canadian National

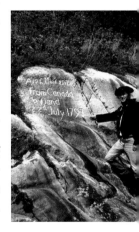

Nearly 200 years later, an actor re-annoints the rock where fur-trade explorer Alexander Mackenzie marked his name upon crossing the continent and reaching the Pacific Ocean. *Bill Merilees*

Tweedsmuir Park features incredibly diverse terrain, ranging from the rolling hills of the Fraser Plateau to the eroded lava domes and fragmented rock slopes of the Rainbow Mountains, which are dressed in brilliant red, orange, yellow and lavender hues.

in Burns Lake in August 1937 with his wife and nineteen-year-old son. Their plan was to explore the park reserve by horse and outboard motorboat but the party also had four RCAF float planes at their disposal. In the end most of their expedition into the park involved flying to good fishing sites and flying back to their deluxe lakeside tent camp in time for dinner. On August 23 they were flown over the park to Bella Coola where the party was joined by hereditary Nuxalk chief Sam King and driven seventy kilometres up the gravel road to Burnt Bridge Creek, the original site of "Friendly Village" where Chief King's great-grandfather had welcomed Mackenzie in 1793.

After receiving the Governor General's stamp of approval, on May 21, 1938, the premier of BC announced the creation of Tweedsmuir Provincial Park. The Governor General, responding to this announcement, wrote, "I have now travelled over most of Canada and have seen many wonderful things, but I have seen nothing more beautiful and more wonderful than the great park which British Columbia has done me the honour to call by my name." At an immense 1,398,594 hectares, it became the province's largest park. It features incredibly diverse terrain, from the rolling hills of the Fraser Plateau to the spectacularly coloured domes of eroded lava in the Rainbow Mountains. It contains the headwaters of two rivers, the Dean and Bella Coola–Atnarko, where grizzly bears feast on the large salmon runs. And because of its size and inaccessible ruggedness, this park provides undisturbed habitat for viable populations of woodland caribou, mountain goats, mule deer, moose, black and grizzly bears, and wolves.

The only road access to Tweedsmuir Park was constructed by the residents of Bella Coola. Prior to World War I they had begun asking the provincial government for a road from their isolated community east to Anahim Lake in the Chilcotin, but in 1952 after their requests had been repeatedly denied, the exasperated citizens decided to build their own. Local businesses paid the surveying and construction crews and by the fall of 1953 they had completed a simple, rough Cat track along the Bella Coola River, through the southern leg of Tweedsmuir Park and over Heckman Pass (1,524 metres)—generally known as "the hill"—to link them to Williams Lake. Two years later the provincial government took over responsibility for the road and it became Highway 20. The Parks Branch acquired private in-holdings along the river, which is a critical salmon stream, noted for attracting numerous grizzly bears, and developed a campground. In 1970 the Rainbow Nature Conservancy was designated to protect the huge upland area just north of this highway link.

A year after the creation of Tweedsmuir Provincial Park, the legislature passed amendments to the Forest Act, possibly on the advice of chief forester Ernest C. Manning. These amendments moved all provincial parks, except for the three statute parks (Strathcona, Mount Robson and Garibaldi) that were administered by the Lands Department, to the authority of the BC Forest Service. The words "parks as use of forest lands" were added to the act, and the words "management and administration of parks" were inserted into the list of BC Forest Service responsibilities. This was an acknowledgement of "multiple use" as forest policy and confirmed the double role of the Forest Service in the protection and administration of forests and the protection and development of provincial parks. But the annual report for 1939 stated that these new program responsibilities did not mean that the Forest Service "intended to undertake any expensive program of park improvement at the time, but the present move will enable a long-term development plan and planned reservation of most desirable parks while they are still in public ownership and still available."

Tweedsmuir, now at 981,000 hectares, is BC's largest provincial park and is home to woodland caribou, mountain goats, mule deer, moose, black and grizzly bears and wolves as well as wolverines, hoary marmots and Siberian lemmings.

While this statement signalled that there would be no immediate development of facilities within the parks or even improved management, there was now at least a long-range development plan. This objective was derailed and delayed by World War II, but it would become the Forest Service's modus operandi for the next two decades.

Among the other 1939 Forest Act amendments was a section that outlined a new classification scheme for parks—classes A, B and C. Class A parks were afforded the highest degree of protection from exploitation. No mining was allowed and

Above: The extensive river and lake system of Wells Gray Park makes it a favourite destination for paddlers. With 100 kilometres of shoreline, beautiful Murtle Lake is the largest paddle-only lake in North America.

Right: Much of Wells Gray Park consists of high mountains capped with icefields that feed the glacial streams and lakes below. There are more than 20 major waterfalls in the southern part of the park.

timber cutting was only permitted where it "may be necessary or advantageous in developing or improving the parks or protecting and preserving the major values of the parks for enjoyment." This point was bolstered by the statement that no timber in a Class A park could be sold "for the primary objective of revenue." Class B designation allowed prospecting and mining within the park as well as timber sales "except where, in the opinion of the chief forester, disposal of such timber would be detrimental to the recreational value of the area." Small local use "picnic and play-ground" parks were categorized as Class C. Over time the government's intention was to transfer these Class C parks to local control, and in the coming years there would be blitzes to shunt them into regional park systems. However, none of these classifications were written in stone because another section of the amendments granted the provincial cabinet the authority to "constitute…extend, reduce or cancel" any provincial park. After passage of these changes to the act, the provincial government designated the brand new Tweedsmuir Park as Class B, which meant that pre-existing mining claims and forest tenures remained, and future alienation of land for mining, logging and hydro projects would also be allowed. As a result, within a decade and a half this park would be shrunk from its initial 1,398,594 hectares to 981,000 hectares, though it would continue to be the province's largest park.

Wells Gray Provincial Park in the Kamloops Forest District, announced on November 28, 1939, was the second mammoth provincial park to be created by order-in-council. It was named for Arthur Wellesley Gray who had been elected to the legislature as a Liberal in November 1933 and served as minister of Municipal Affairs and Lands until his death in 1944. Located in the Kamloops Forest District, this Class B park covered 471,378 hectares of forested wilderness, making it the fourth-largest in the province. (Two additions in the 1990s increased it to approximately 540,000 hectares.) Before Europeans arrived, the area was a valued hunting and fishing ground for the Shuswap and Chilcotin First Nations people.

Wells Gray Park includes the southeastern portion of the Cariboo Mountains, which were formed when the Pacific oceanic tectonic plate was forced beneath the continental plate. However, most of the rare geological formations in these mountains are the result of volcanic activity that occurred beneath thick glacial ice sheets that lay over this area as recently as 10,000 years ago. Later the ice gouged deep valleys into the soft lava flows, providing basins for bodies of water such as Murtle Lake in the southeastern portion of the park and Hobson and Azure lakes, which feed south into Clearwater Lake. The park covers most of the Clearwater River watershed, which features more than twenty major waterfalls, including the 141-metre-high Helmcken Falls on the Murtle River, and give Wells Gray the nickname of Waterfall Park.

Two more major Class A parks were created by order-in-council in 1941—E.C. Manning and Hamber. Manning Provincial Park, designated on June 17, was named for Ernest C. Manning, BC's chief forester from 1936 until his death in an airplane crash in northern Ontario on February 6, 1941. The park area, which lies just north of the US border in the heart of the Cascade Mountains, is at the transition point between the wet coastal ranges and the dry Interior plateau. The subalpine

Manning Park, established in the heart of the Cascades in 1941 shortly before this photo was taken, continues to be one of the most popular camping destinations in the province. *BC Archives, NA-11038*

The Lightning Lake chain in Manning Park provides fishing for small rainbow trout as well as canoeing and swimming opportunities.

meadows in this area were designated as the Three Brothers Preserve in 1931 in order to save them from overgrazing by sheep. Five years later the preserve was doubled in size and became known as the Three Brothers Wildlife Reserve. Its incorporation in 1941 into Manning Park, which would eventually cover 70,844 hectares, protects unique flora and fauna, including mountain beavers, wolverines, and Cascade golden-mantled ground squirrels as well as the threatened North Cascades grizzly bear.

However, Manning Park's greatest value to the Lower Mainland area was its potential for winter recreation. Public access was, therefore, an early priority. Back in 1929 construction had begun on a gravel road westward from Princeton using labour provided by men from the relief camps in the Princeton area, but lack of funds brought the work to a halt a few years later at a point sixteen kilometres west of Allison Pass. Construction resumed during World War II using labour from the Japanese internment camps, and the first car travelled over the rough, gravel road from Hope to Princeton in 1943.

Hamber Provincial Park was created on September 16, 1941, and named for Eric W. Hamber, BC Lieutenant-Governor from 1936 to 1941. Lying south of Mount Robson Provincial Park and west of Jasper National Park, the original Hamber Park encompassed some 1,009,112 hectares and included Mount Sir Sandford, which is the highest peak in the Selkirk Range, the Mount Clemenceau Icefields and most of the Big Bend area of the Columbia River. Access to the new park was provided by the Big Bend Highway, part of the Trans-Canada network across southern BC. Completed in June 1940, it began in Revelstoke and followed the Columbia River

Towering over Fortress Lake, the magnificent mountains of remote Hamber Provincial Park are part of the UNESCO Canadian Rocky Mountains World Heritage Site.

Many unique plant species, including the frog orchid, thrive in the micro-climate surrounding Liard Hot Springs. *Bill Merilees*

around the northern end of the Selkirk Mountains to follow the Rocky Mountain Trench south to the town of Golden.

However, although Hamber was a fully protected Class A park, logging interests succeeded in pressuring the government to downgrade it to Class B just four years after it was created; lobbying over the next twenty years was successful in having parts of it removed altogether from protected status, especially the heavily timbered western slopes. Canada's agreement to the terms of the Columbia River Treaty was the final blow; in 1961 and 1962 the park was reduced by 98 percent to a mere 24,518 hectares to allow flooding of the Big Bend. Fortunately, the small park that remained includes remote Fortress Lake, one of the largest and most beautiful natural bodies of water in the western Rockies.

Liard Provincial Park, the fifth immense park created during this period, was designated on April 2, 1944, as a Special Land Act Park covering some 730,000 hectares on the Liard River close to the Yukon border. This region around the Liard (the French word for "cottonwood tree"), which was the hunting grounds for the Beaver, Sikanni, Nahanni and Dog Rib First Nations people, included the treacherous rapids of the Liard Canyon but it also took in the Liard Hot Springs and the surrounding warm water swamps that allow the growth of unique plant species, among them fourteen varieties of orchids.

The serene waters of Fortress Lake are home to brook trout. A rustic campground is located at the east end of the lake.

The history of this park is intimately associated with the American entry into World War II. In 1942 the American government, threatened by a Japanese invasion of Alaska and committed to supplying war materials to the Soviet Union, joined the Canadian government in constructing the Alaska Highway. The chosen route took the road builders past the Liard Hot Springs, and it was American army engineers who constructed the first boardwalk and pool facilities there for the benefit of their ten thousand army and six thousand civilian road workers. In 1944 the BC government declared this whole area a park then cancelled its park status just five years later. It was not until April 1957 that a 1,082-hectare area around the hot springs was reinstated as the Liard River Hot Springs Provincial Park. No protection was given to the remaining former park area as long as BC Hydro considered harnessing the river for hydro development, but in 1992 it was identified as a Protected Areas Strategy (PAS) Area of Interest (AOI). Subsequently it was split into the Liard River Corridor Protected Area and the Liard River Corridor Provincial Park with a combined area of 88,898 hectares.

The war years saw little progress in the construction of facilities in the provincial parks because of a shortage of both manpower and money. However, in 1942 the first two full-time park rangers were assigned to Mount Seymour and Wells Gray parks, and that summer the field reconnaissance of the new Manning Park was completed. Some help for parks was also made available under the federal program for "alternative service providers." In May 1942 the BC Forest Service concluded an agreement with the federal government to give alternative service work to hundreds of men, mostly Mennonites or Doukhobors, who had registered as conscientious objectors to military service. By April of the following year there were nineteen forestry camps set up in this province, and the men in two of these camps were employed on park projects. Although all of these men had been returned to their home provinces by March 1944, that summer the Forest Service was able to finish the field reconnaissance of Tweedsmuir Park started by Chess Lyons and Mickey True in 1943 and complete the formal gardens at Peace Arch Park.

Following pages: Although snow covers the nearby land, there is open water in Liard River Hot Springs, attracting both humans and wildlife. *All Canada Photos, David Nunuk*

3 :
Parks in the Post-war Years, 1945 to 1957

The Sloan Commission Report

The year 1945 saw the issuance of the landmark Sloan Royal Commission report on the forest resources of BC. This document, prepared by Mr. Justice Gordon Sloan of the BC Court of Appeal, proposed major changes to the manner of issuing forest tenures, but it also offered a few observations on the province's parks, which were administered under the Forest Act. Among those observations was Sloan's confirmation of the prevailing view that parks were not special places and that parks management was just another aspect of forest administration. He wrote:

Above: An alpine meadow of summer flowers provides the foreground for the sharp profile of Mount Robson with its distinctive horizontal multi-coloured rock strata.

Considerable support was given by a group of witnesses to the proposed creation of an autonomous Provincial Park Board which would assume responsibility for park selection, planning and development and general administration. With deference, I cannot concur in this recommendation. In my opinion parks should be administered by a Parks Branch of the Forest Service staffed by a selected personnel especially trained in this type of operation. By this form of control close integration between all forest uses in park areas may be anticipated.

The following February, consistent with Sloan's view, Don Macmurchie of the Forest Branch drafted an internal background paper outlining the challenges and opportunities that lay ahead for the Forest Service. He urged that "the Forest Branch shoulder its responsibilities to the public and put in progress that machinery which will contribute to post war stability the operation of an adequate park system…and set about the formulation of a long-term master plan envisioning a comprehensive and equitably distributed park system."

Morning mist rises from a lake edged by a forest of western hemlock in Tweedsmuir Provincial Park, BC's largest provincial park.

Opposite bottom: A visitor to MacMillan Provincial Park hugs a Douglas fir that has survived more than 800 years, miraculously escaping the logger's axe.

The Sloan Report also included a summary table of the park system in 1945. In the years since the creation of Strathcona Park in 1911 the system had grown to 4.4 million hectares held within fifty-eight parks, though 99 percent of this land was contained within only nine parks: the three statute parks (Strathcona, Mount Robson and Garibaldi), three of the largest Class A parks (Hamber, Kokanee Glacier and Manning), two Class B parks (Wells Gray and Tweedsmuir) and the ill-fated Liard River Provincial Park. The twenty-five Class C parks totalled only 1,673 hectares. However, neither the size nor the classification of any of these parks was fixed, and the status of all parks was subject to future political manipulation.

Park Development after the War

Manning Park was named in memory of Ernest C. Manning, BC's chief forester, who died in a plane crash in 1941. The forest ranger station, shown here in 1957, was the first building constructed in the new park. *BC Archives, I-28650*

With the end of World War II the capital budget for BC Parks was increased from $29,000 to over $75,000, and some of these new funds were used to purchase floodlights to illuminate Peace Arch Park, while the rest was invested in a truck and tractor, primarily for use in Manning and Mount Seymour parks. At the same time a new ranger position was created for Manning Park where a ranger station and fire lookout tower were built.

MacMillan Provincial Park in the Parksville–Alberni corridor was created in 1947. This park on Highway 4 close to Cameron Lake includes the spectacular Cathedral Grove of ancient Douglas firs, which was already a well-known tourist stop in the 1920s. At that time the timber was owned by the Victoria Lumbering and Manufacturing Company, and in 1929 the Associated Boards of Trade of Vancouver Island petitioned the government to buy it from them and preserve it for the public benefit. When nothing happened, public concern mounted over the inevitable loss of this old-growth stand. However, in 1944 after the timber licence fell into the hands of lumber tycoon H.R. MacMillan, he was persuaded to donate 136 hectares that still had unlogged forest cover for a park. It was not the first major land donation for park purposes but it was the first designed specifically to protect natural values of provincial/national significance rather than just local recreational use. Since that time the problems of preservation versus visitor use have plagued park managers and even became a political issue. The park also demonstrates the difficulties of managing natural cycles within eco-systems—in particular how to deal with over-mature forest cover, the risk of blowdowns and natural regeneration—and still provide public access.

Above: Earl Fletcher and his spaniel visit Cathedral Grove in 1945, a year after forester H.R. MacMillan donated the 136 hectares of land for a park. *City of Vancouver Archives, A-06341*

The John Hart Dam

Meanwhile, the improved economy in the immediate post-war years also allowed the BC government to go forward with plans that affected one of Vancouver Island's parks—the 1,137-hectare Elk Falls Provincial Park, created on December 20, 1940. The power potential of the Campbell River on which the falls lie had been recognized as early as 1909 and had inspired logger and entrepreneur Mike King to acquire the hydro rights. Then in 1926, when King's lease lapsed, Premier Duff Pattullo offered the rights to any company "ready to harness and use them." There were no takers at that time, but in 1945 with wartime austerity at an end the government was finally able to embark on its own Campbell River power project courtesy of the Forest Act amendments of 1939, which gave the cabinet the authority to "constitute…extend, reduce or cancel" any provincial park.

The government began by creating the BC Power Commission and giving it two mandates: meld the existing hodgepodge of power systems and extend service to all parts of the province. To accomplish the second goal more power was needed, so the commission's first project was a dam and generating system eight kilometres upstream from the mouth of the Campbell River. The site, however, stood inside the boundaries of Elk Falls Provincial Park. The government's solution was simply

Thundering Elk Falls is the centrepiece of a provincial park just north of Campbell River on Vancouver Island. In the fall visitors can watch salmon spawning in the nearby rivers.

to reduce the size of the park, and a 1946 order-in-council whacked close to one hundred hectares off the park. The John Hart Dam, named for the sitting BC premier (John Hart, 1941–47), was completed in 1947. Water from the new John Hart Lake behind the dam is carried through three penstocks to a six-unit generating station located downstream from Elk Falls; the lake also provides drinking water for the town of Campbell River. Fortunately, the dam did not change the scenic appeal of the falls and they are still a draw for tourists and recreationists.

The Parks and Recreation Division

In 1939 the Research and Forest Survey divisions of the BC Forest Branch had been merged to create the Economics Division, which was given responsibility for reforestation, forest surveys, aerial surveys, parks and recreation, and research. Very soon, however, these new sections grew so much in importance and workload that they had to be split off as separate entities. Parks and Recreation became a separate division in 1948 with E.G. (Cy) Oldham as the forester in charge. He had a staff of fourteen, including rangers in Wells Gray and Manning parks and a full-time parks officer for Vancouver Island. For the next few years the division would focus primarily on the development of Mount Seymour, Manning, Peace Arch, Wells Gray and Cultus Lake parks on the mainland as well as five Vancouver Island parks—Miracle Beach, John Dean, Englishman River, Little Qualicum and Elk Falls. All of them except Wells Gray were small, geared to recreation and easily accessible by nearby urban populations.

Cultus Lake, which was designated a provincial park in 1948, is just an hour and a half's drive from Vancouver and is one of the most popular day parks in the system.

Paths weave along the river in Englishman River Falls Provincial Park and provide access to the quieter waters below the falls.

When the Hope-Princeton Highway was completed through Manning Provincial Park in 1949, drivers were greeted with this sign commemorating a devastating fire just two years earlier.
BC Archives, H-04158

Shortly after the establishment of the new division, a circular letter that was issued to forest rangers, land officers and members of the fledgling Parks Division stated that the "primary objective of Parks Division is to reserve and develop as soon as possible the more urgently needed small parks for use of local public and travelling tourists."

The letter identified nine types of parks that would eventually form the provincial parks system: (1) campsites; (2) picnic areas, lookouts and roadside parks; (3) historical, geological and botanical sites; (4) primeval sites; (5) multi-use areas; (6) resorts; (7) wilderness areas; (8) community parks; and (9) hot springs. Unfortunately, the same letter went on to suggest there was no need for designated wilderness parks with the remarkable statement that: "in a province as large and as rugged as BC, there is some question as to whether wilderness parks are necessary." The list omits any mention of wildlife and the need to identify and protect areas of significant habitat, and oddly, given that BC is a coastal province, does not mention marine parks.

Opposite: The lower falls on the Englishman River, 13 kilometres southwest of Parksville, drops 6 metres into a crystal-clear pool, which makes a perfect swimming hole in summer when river levels are low.

However, this circular letter provided the Planning and Reconnaissance Section of the new Parks and Recreation Division with a clear statement of its future role, and its members quickly became modern-day explorers, visiting all the scenic wonders of this province by truck, boat, float plane or on horseback and documenting them for future reference. Along with lands officers and forest rangers, they identified and reserved waterfront beaches, interesting natural features, critical habitats and access points to numerous lakes and rivers. They submitted formal requests to the Lands Service to create and designate, under the Land Act, literally hundreds of sites for the use, recreation and enjoyment of the public (UREPs). Over the next twenty-five years, more than two thousand such UREPs would be identified and recorded on Crown land status maps, and these served as the backbone for a system that would provide recreational access to public lands and the core areas for dozens of future park proposals and forest recreation sites.

One of the Parks Branch's signature picnic tables awaits on the grassy bank at Bamberton Provincial Park near Mill Bay on Vancouver Island.

One of the sites identified for immediate park status was Cultus Lake, the largest warm freshwater lake in the Lower Mainland. This lake had always been a popular summer camp destination, and by 1930 there were some two hundred summer cottages on leased land along the shore. As a result, planning reconnaissance had been undertaken in 1944 and it became a park four years later. From the beginning this semi-urban park was overwhelmed by attendance that approached a thousand persons per day, and the facilities were totally inadequate. The new Parks Division was forced to expand the single-lane entry road and add more facilities along the lake to include Delta Grove and Maple Bay.

In 1950 the government purchased a 57 hectare parcel of beachfront at Miracle Beach, halfway between Courtenay and Campbell River. This became Miracle Beach, a Class A provincial park, and it immediately became one of the most popular parks in the system. In 1952 a game reserve was created over the foreshore area and this reserve was added to the park four years later. By 1972 with the purchase and donation of additional lands, the park reached its present size of 135 hectares.

Manning and Wells Gray Parks—A Tale of Separate Directions

Based on the difficulties encountered with the management of Mount Seymour Park, the Forest Service was determined to both develop and operate Manning Park's ski facilities without private contractors, although the capital requirements and operating know-how tended to place excessive demands on Branch budgets and staffing. As a result, development began in 1952 with the installation of a rope tow on Sugarloaf Hill, but it remained in operation for only four years as it stood in the

Left: Winter comes early in the high country of Manning Park in the Cascade Mountains.

Below: In 1964 a road from Manning Park headquarters to Gibson Pass was constructed and a year later twin rope tows were installed on a newly cleared ski slope. *BC Archives, I-28676*

way of a new Forest Service road to Blackwell Peak. In 1960 a new ski slope was cleared and a chair lift erected above the former Pinewoods Service Station.

In 1949, immediately after the completion and paving of the Hope–Princeton Highway, construction was started on three large buildings, including a café, an administration building and crew quarters to house twenty-five men. Construction also began on a motel, though this was not completed until 1958. (Fire destroyed the motel in 1969; it was replaced by a forty-five-unit building, Manning Park Lodge, the first and only commercial accommodation facility ever built in a BC provincial park.)

But the Parks Division had determined that this park was ideal for four-season use, especially for people from the Lower Mainland, and in 1957 Manning became the first park to see the introduction of a nature interpretation centre; a permanent nature house was erected in 1961. As Manning lacked a lake for swimming and the operation of small boats and canoes, members of the Parks Division identified a dry riverbed as a potential site to create one, but this first required a 5.6-kilometre access road. The Lightning Lake reservoir project was completed in 1961, after which the road was extended to a new ski area in Gibson Pass. Ski tows were installed there, followed by a chairlift in 1967.

Over the next twenty years, Manning would become the most developed park in the system. However, after the operation of park services was privatized in the 1980s, park development did not see any significant new growth except for the addition of an indoor pool attached to the motel. At the same time, park visitation numbers were declining, mostly because the new Coquihalla Highway rerouted a significant amount of tourist traffic but also because of competition from much larger ski resorts.

The role and development of Wells Gray Provincial Park, created in November 1939 as a Class B park, was different for at least two reasons. First, by comparison, Manning is not rich in wildlife values, while the Clearwater drainage system in Wells Gray is the wildlife haven of south central BC, matched only by the East Kootenay. Second, Wells Gray, while adjacent to the Yellowhead Highway, does not receive a high volume of park visits by people just passing through. As a result, in its early days the major emphasis of operations in this park was on management of its natural resources, particularly moose, caribou, grizzly bears and wolves, rather than on facility development. As both by policy and strong public support, recreational hunting was permitted in parks where there were no public safety or social problems, the division conducted extensive game surveys here, trapped animals for tagging and determined a conservative harvest surplus for a managed hunting season. The 1959 report for Wells Gray stated that in the previous year "over 1,200 hunters harvested more than 57 tonnes of high quality meat from the park, mainly from the moose herd, which had resource value of over $3 million." It also said that "technical papers were completed on caribou food, grizzly bear counts and the ecology of lichens important to caribou." The division also undertook the first trials of prescribed burning to improve habitat and increase populations.

Visitor access to Wells Gray was improved by the construction of a bridge over

the Murtle River, and then in 1949 work began on the eight kilometres of road needed to reach Clearwater Lake. A campground was laid out there in 1953 and the Clearwater–Azure lakes system was opened to motorized wilderness boating. A related project was the survey and construction in 1965 of a side road to provide viewing of scenic Helmcken Falls; many years later, an extensive viewing platform would be provided. Commercial lodges and guide outfitters services remain outside the park.

A forested point of land is reflected in the stillness of Murtle Lake in Wells Gray Provincial Park.

Park System Objectives

In 1948 the Forest Department's annual report had outlined six recreational objectives for the provincial parks system, and these objectives became parks policy in 1951 when Chief Forester C.D. Orchard published them in a formal public policy paper. The six objectives spelled out the Parks Division's mandate to provide for the recreational needs of non-urban British Columbians and the development of park areas to encourage these activities, but at the same time Parks was expected to perpetuate the recreational opportunities offered by the parks while controlling their use to prevent misuse. The objectives also included preventing the alienation of protected areas and the preservation of their natural "atmosphere."

The Parks Standards Manual

By 1952 the Parks budget had grown to almost $1 million, but the system now consisted of sixty-four parks, and all of them needed facilities such as signs, picnic tables, toilets, docks, fireplaces and change houses. This demand provided a major workload for the new Parks Division workshop at Langford on Vancouver Island. At the same time the division had begun compiling a *Parks Standards Manual*, the first half being a collection of detailed drawings and manufacturing and construction standards for park equipment. These designs were constantly amended; for example, the design for Pan-Abode pit toilets was continually revised to fine-tune air venting. One of the more interesting enterprises at the Langford workshop was the creation of fibreglass moulds to form the distinctive garbage containers known as the "Garbage Gobblers." Some items, such as the cedar picnic tables designed by Joe St. Pierre, became well known nationally as a symbol of the BC Parks system. Originally the tops were made from three large planks that could be removed, sanded and re-varnished every two or three years. The need for facilities to dry the planks and restore them led to the construction of large garage/workshop buildings in many of the major parks; these building also served as district headquarters. Years later the table design was altered to include a metal shelf for barbecues and much later the planks were replaced with polished concrete tabletops. The Langford workshop also produced the carved signs and large-scale carved animals that served as entrance portals to popular parks.

The second part of the *Parks Standards Manual* provided site design and layout specifications for campgrounds, parking lots, boat launches, sani-stations and information kiosks. Parks employee L. Brooks was responsible for the standard campground design with its angled driveway and offset campsite pad with a rock strategically placed to prevent vehicles from crowding the table. Initially, camping was encouraged in natural clearings, and the use of sites was rotated to give opportunity for rest and recovery. However, with regular heavy use this was not manageable, and it proved necessary to improve and reinforce individual campsite pads but retain vegetation screening between sites. Other standards in the manual dealt with parking lots and boat launches; for example, Al Fairhurst designed the standard park "dinghy dock."

Too many visits by bears led to the phasing out of the popular "Garbage Gobblers" that were introduced to BC parks in the 1960s.
Nick Tessman

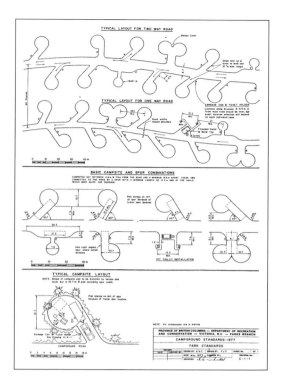

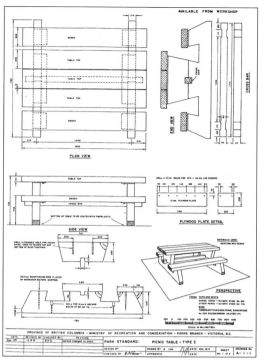

Far left: Although the final shape of each campsite was ultimately dictated by the terrain, in 1977 the Parks Branch standardized campsites and even prescribed the distance to the nearest toilet. *James D. Anderson collection*

Left: The Langford Workshop, established in 1948, built more than fifty kinds of park furnishings, including picnic tables, benches, Pan-Abode toilets, carved signage and animal figures. *James D. Anderson collection*

Hydroelectric Power Versus Parks

In contrast to the government's positive support of the recreation role of the park system, in the next few years political decisions would be made that challenged the integrity of park designations. Two decisions in particular would have dramatic consequences.

In the late 1940s the government of BC had identified the Eutsuk–Ootsa–Nechako drainage system in the northern portion of Tweedsmuir Provincial Park as a possible site for an enormous reservoir with hydroelectric power potential and invited Alcan Ltd, which was searching for a site for an aluminum smelter, to investigate its possibilities. Alcan approved of the site and in 1947 signed an agreement with the government for land and water rights. To accommodate the Kitimat–Kemano project that the company would undertake, the government made use of the Forest Act amendments of 1939 to reduce Tweedsmuir Provincial Park along the Nechako River corridor by 400,000 hectares. The project that Alcan then embarked upon involved the construction of a massive, earth-filled dam on the Nechako River, raising the water's depth by ninety metres behind the face of the dam and reversing the direction of river's flow so that it ran westward instead of east into the upper Fraser. The water was then directed from the western end of this lake system through a sixteen-kilometre-long mountain tunnel system under Mount Dubose to Kemano where a generating station was constructed.

The Kenney Dam, named for Edward T. Kenney, minister of Lands and

Summer clouds are reflected in beautiful Spectacle Lake in Bowron Lake Provincial Park, a canoeing and kayaking paradise east of Quesnel.

Forests from 1945 to 1952, was completed in 1952 and over the next five years the backed-up waters gradually inundated almost fifty thousand hectares of land within the traditional territory of the Cheslatta First Nation. It flooded Ootsa River and Lake, Whitesail Lake and Eutsuk River and Lake so that they formed two broad, curving arms running nearly two hundred kilometres from east to west. The southern arm, consisting of Eutsuk and Tetachuck lakes, bisects Tweedsmuir Provincial Park. Unfortunately, much of the flooded area was not pre-cleared and this created hazardous conditions for boaters trying to cross the reservoir to reach the park. Submerged trees still pose navigation hazards and visual eyesores on this lake.

In 1953 the BC Power Commission also gave approval for the construction of dams on the Campbell River that would raise the level of the water in Buttle Lake, a long north–south lake lying within Strathcona Park. This was an eventuality that had been provided for in the 1918 amendment to the Strathcona Park Act. In addition to the John Hart Dam that had been completed in 1953, the new Campbell River project involved the construction of two more large dams on the main river—the Ladore Dam at the foot of Lower Campbell Lake and Strathcona Dam that would impound Upper Campbell Lake and back water up into Buttle Lake—as well as smaller dams and diversions on three tributaries of this river system.

The announcement immediately raised a public outcry, and a protest was mounted by the Natural Resources Conservation League of Victoria, led by H.H. Stevens, and the Affiliated Fish and Game Clubs of Vancouver Island whose spokesman was the renowned conservationist and author Roderick Haig-Brown. When all their efforts failed to halt the project, the Parks Division developed a set of requirements for clearing the lakeshore and the borders of the new reservoir, leaving only flush-cut stumps, and they insisted that these rules be implemented. Thus, a standard was set for all subsequent reservoirs in hydro projects to avoid a fringe of flood-killed timbers; unfortunately, at low water the stumps of giant trees are clearly visible along the lakeshore. Construction on the dams began in 1955 and they were all completed by 1958, raising the level of the water in Buttle Lake by eight metres. One outcome of this increase was that the falls Price Ellison had named after his daughter Myra during his reconnaissance of the park in 1910 now emptied directly into Buttle Lake.

In contrast to these two inroads on provincial parks, in 1954 the BC Power Commission advised the government that it was not feasible to develop the Bowron Lake system for hydro, and two years later an area of 297,000 hectares was designated as a Use, Recreation and Enjoyment of the Public reserve. Park status came in 1962.

Creating Small Parks in the 1950s

Between 1955 and 1957, forty-six new and smaller parks were created, all of them made possible by the work of the Park Reconnaissance unit, which since the creation of the Parks Division in 1948 had been hard at work identifying sites. The precedent for this bundling of new parks was the cluster of new parks designated in 1940 that had included Elk Falls, Chasm, Englishman River, Little Qualicum, Premier Lake and Stamp Falls. This development was followed by a first wave of waterfront park development that included Cultus Lake and Miracle Beach.

In Crooked River Provincial Park, an hour's drive north of Prince George, visitors enjoy hiking along the willow-fringed river, which was part of the route taken by explorers Alexander Mackenzie and Simon Fraser.

Right: Successive lava flows have left brilliantly coloured layers of rock in the 300-metre-deep canyon walls of Chasm Provincial Park, northeast of Clinton.

Below: There are four freshwater lakes in Alice Lake Provincial Park and they all provide opportunities for swimming and fishing.

Bottom: Alouette Lake in Golden Ears Park is a popular spot for swimming, windsurfing, water-skiing, canoeing, boating and fishing, but the mountainous backcountry is extremely rugged.

Subsequent lakeshore developments in the mid-1950s included Wasa (1955), Kokanee Creek (1955), Alouette Lake (1955; now part of Golden Ears Park), Lac Le Jeune (1956), Lac La Hache (1956), Alice Lake (1956), Bear Lake (1956; now part of Crooked River Park) and Lakelse (1956). Some new parks such as Bear, Paul, Alice and Alouette lakes had ample waterfront areas but lacked natural sand beaches. In these cases, beaches were man-made or improved by importing sand to infill marshy or muddy foreshore and shorelines.

The next stage began in 1955 with Champion Lakes Park in the West Kootenay region then Okanagan Lake followed by Shuswap Lake in 1956. Several of the park developments—particularly Okanagan and Champion Lakes—involved major construction projects such as earthworks and access roads. At Champion Lakes ten kilometers of access road was constructed along with a two-hundred-car parking lot because at that time the Nelson–Trail area contained the third-largest population concentration in BC, and its residents needed to escape the heat of the valley bottom and find a swimming hole.

Projects of this kind served to recruit and train future field staff, but the fact that park operations were mainly seasonal, dispersed over a large province and located mainly along rural highways and in remote wilderness meant that the logistics and staffing of park maintenance services were significant considerations. Field crews were augmented by the Youth Crew program, formally established in 1956, which brought in young people for a six-week period, half spent working on a roadside

Alice Lake Provincial Park, north of Squamish, is a favourite park for families and provides the perfect trail for an evening stroll. More adventurous walkers will enjoy the nearby Four Lakes Trail.

project, half in the backcountry. The program lasted for over thirty years, and the hundreds of the youths who were lucky enough to secure a position with it found it to be the best summer experience of their lives. However, some field staff considered the participants a nuisance as they required training, extra supervision and provision of room and board in exchange for limited work output. Fortunately, for other field staff the experience of working with youth was a rewarding part of their careers.

When Cy Oldham left the BC public service in 1956, his place as forester in charge of Parks was taken by H.G. McWilliams, but Oldham's leadership had been responsible for a number of important park management initiatives that would be key to future progress. He had secured a specific budget for Parks and introduced a fledgling management structure for park planning and operations. He had installed full-time staff in field offices—park officers in Kamloops and Nelson and park rangers in Wells Gray and Manning—and established infrastructure services such as the construction section, the Langford workshop and wildlife programs. His capital works projects in Manning, Mount Seymour, Champion Lakes and Okanagan Lake parks had proved to be a great training ground for field staff, and his Youth Crew program brought young people into the parks program for the next thirty years.

4 :
Development
Versus Conservation,
1957 to 1969

The 1950s through the early '70s was the era of the "builders" when the majority of today's most popular parks were developed. While it was the job of headquarters-based professional planning staff to determine where new parks would be created, it was the task of a group of field staff to actually develop these parks and provide facilities for public use and later to manage these parks.

For two decades, the construction program was led by C.J. (Charlie) Velay, with C.C. (Tony) Hammond as construction superintendent and often Don Shaw as project engineer. They recruited thirty or so eager young men who started as

Above: Bromley Rock Provincial Park on the Similkameen River
is a popular swimming spot but also provides a starting point
for tubing downstream to Stemwinder Park.

seasonal labourers, truck drivers, powder monkeys (dynamite crews), heavy equipment operators and who over time had become foremen and project supervisors. By the 1970s, many became regional directors, district managers or zone supervisors.

A New Recreation and Conservation Act

The Southern Chilcotin Mountains Park, formerly known as the Spruce Lake Protected Area, features winding rivers, glistening lakes and rolling mountains, which invite backpackers and mountain bikers.

In 1957 the provincial government passed a new Recreation and Conservation Act that created a brand new ministry that brought together Parks, Fish and Wildlife, the Travel Bureau, the Photographic Branch and Commercial Fisheries. The Provincial Game Commission was disbanded and its responsibilities transferred to a new Fish and Game Branch, which became part of the new ministry. The Hon. Earle C. Westwood became the first minister of Recreation and Conservation, D.B. Turner his deputy minister and H.G. McWilliams became the first director of the Parks Branch. Apparently, this was the first attempt in Canada to combine all major elements of outdoor recreation—camping, hiking, tourism, hunting and fishing—in one department, although some argued that the Social Credit government of the day had just realized the potential of tourism and had created this new department to cater to the industry.

The Recreation and Conservation Act of 1957 incorporated the provisions already stated in the Forest Act concerning the administration of parks and retained the Class A, B and C classification system while at the same time rescinding those acts that had created parks by special statutes and placing those parks under the new

Opposite: A Squamish First Nation legend says that the two-headed serpent Say-noth-ka formed Shannon Falls by twisting his powerful body up the mountainside, wearing away a spillway for the waters.

ministry's control. The new act also kept in place the six objectives for provincial parks that were identified by Chief Forester C.D. Orchard in 1951, but it also stated that "the Lieutenant-Governor in Council may constitute any portion of the Province a Provincial park for the pleasure and recreation of the public," thereby confirming that the prime objective of the park system would continue to be recreation.

At the time this new act was passed in 1957 the park system consisted of 117 parks comprising 3.3 million hectares. Total assets included 3,635 picnic tables, 25 water systems, 755 pit toilets, 200 flush toilets, 2,405 fireplaces, 1,585 carved signs and 70 buildings. Some Pan-Abode pit toilets were being converted to flush toilets.

Recognizing Heritage Values

In 1959 the gold rush town of Barkerville, where Billy Barker hit the motherlode in August 1862, became the province's first historic park. The occasion was the 100th anniversary of British Columbia becoming a British colony. New funding was provided, and Chester P. (Chess) Lyons of the Parks Branch was given the responsibility for creating the master plan to restore the heritage townsite as well as coordinating a program of highway roadside stops-of-interest heritage plaques. Instead of bronze plaques, Lyons designed "a series of vivid, highly legible and thought-provoking signs."

The authentic heritage look of the townsite was greatly improved by removing all hydro poles and installing underground wiring. The restoration also included the conversion of the community hall building into the Theatre Royal, which was used for vaudeville performances and became a major visitor attraction. However, the increased number of visitors necessitated the upgrading of the water system to provide fire protection for the expanded Root Beer Saloon relocated to the Barkerville Hotel, and the Wake-Up Jake Café required kitchen improvements to meet the heavy demands for food services.

In 1967 Fort Steele on the banks of the Kootenay River in southwestern BC was given historic site status. This town, originally known as Galbraith's Ferry, was renamed Fort Steele in 1888 after the legendary North West Mounted Police superintendent Sam Steele resolved a murder mystery there. However, after

The work of reconstructing and preserving historic Fort Steele (photographed in 1967) in the East Kootenays began in 1961 after the townsite was acquired by the province.
BC Archives, I-07907

Cranbrook was founded at the end of the century Fort Steele lost most of its population and fell into decay. Restoration began after it was designated as a heritage site, and several of the original buildings, including a theatre, were refurbished to draw summer visitors. Although Fort Steele did not have a railway in its heyday, a four-kilometre-long track in a figure-eight loop was installed, and a vintage steam locomotive pulling a coach and several flatcars modified to carry passengers began operating during the summer months. In 1969 Premier W.A.C. Bennett opened these facilities as Fort Steele Historic Park, BC's second major heritage park.

It has been said that the senior executive of the Parks Branch never really made heritage parks a priority with policy, management and fiscal allocations equal to that given to outdoor recreation and natural history parks, relying instead on the ebb and flow of outside funding, particularly from the Provincial Secretary's office, to provide for their development and management. Like ski hills, the management of heritage parks and their collections—collecting, cataloguing, restoring, storing and displaying—has an almost insatiable appetite for capital maintenance and operating funds that the Parks Branch budget could never satisfy. Visitor services are also labour intensive. Meanwhile, for politicians, the appeal of both Barkerville and Fort Steele had little to do with the intrinsic value of cultural preservation and more to do with the tourism potential of the celebration of heritage.

The Roadside Park Program

In 1951 the Parks Reconnaissance staff had identified fourteen sites in the Hope–Princeton and Fraser Canyon corridors and another nine along the southern Trans-Canada Highway that would be ideal for the establishment of roadside parks. Over the next few years a number of these sites—including Bromley Rock and

A full moon rises as twilight falls on Bamberton Provincial Park and on the Saanich Peninsula across the inlet waters.

Right: Small Stemwinder Park, which lies beside the Similkameen River, provides a quiet spot for campers and picnickers beneath a canopy of Ponderosa pines.

Below: In 1950 when this photo was taken in Goldstream Park north of Victoria, it was still owned by the Greater Victoria Water Board. *BC Archives, I-26744*

Stemwinder on the Hope–Princeton corridor and Inkaneep, Kickininee and Boundary Creek on the southern provincial highway—became wayside campgrounds. However, it was not until 1958 that a program of roadside park development kicked into high gear. The impetus came from a national federal–provincial cost-sharing program to provide public recreational facilities along the new Trans-Canada Highway. The target was a campground every 160 kilometres and a picnic site every eighty kilometres. Funding would continue intermittently into the mid-1960s.

The focus was now on providing a system of day-use and campground facilities for both residents and tourists using the new highway system. Examples of the new roadside areas, include Goldpan, Pyramid, Soorimpt and Emory Creek. Some of these campgrounds—Skihist and Yard Creek, for example—were pleasant stopovers but lacked significant natural or recreational features. After the provincial government declared that the Trans-Canada route would continue from Vancouver by ferry to Nanaimo and south to Victoria, development of parks at Goldstream and Bamberton could also be funded under the program. Several more roadside parks were provided along the Alaska Highway.

Resources Versus Parks

Within months after Strathcona Provincial Park was created by special statute in 1911, the provincial government allowed mineral claims to be staked within the park's boundaries and in 1957 it was reclassified as a Class B park to permit mine development. Although no mining took place for many years, subsequent changes to Strathcona's status eventually encouraged mining companies to invest in this area, and in 1959 Westmin Resources Limited began developing a copper–lead–zinc mine on Myra Creek at the south end of the new Buttle Lake Reservoir. The company began full operation of the mine a year later, dumping the tailings into Buttle Lake. Following Westmin's lead, in 1964 Cream Silver Mines Limited began staking claims around Cream Lake, which is also within the park. To appease critics the government did attempt to protect the remaining roadless wilderness portions of the Class B park by designating three nature conservancies: Comox, Central and Big Den, which covered over half of the park.

Fortunately for Strathcona's development as a recreational area, in 1968 the government added another 12,000 hectares in the form of Forbidden Plateau, an alpine meadow area with numerous small lakes, and Buttle Lake Narrows to the park. They are all within easy access from the Courtenay–Comox or Campbell River area, and by the mid-'90s, the plateau had become a popular cross-country ski area as an adjunct to the Mount Washington ski resort. The Parks Division built Buttle Lake Campground along the road built on the western shore of Buttle Lake, followed by the Ralph River Campground at the road's southern end as well as a number of picnic sites. An east–west highway link through the park to Gold River was also completed in 1967.

There were already a few timber claims within Strathcona's boundaries at the time it became a park, and although it might have been logical for the government

The hiking trail system on the Forbidden Plateau at the eastern edge of Strathcona Provincial Park can be accessed from Courtenay via the well-marked Mount Washington and Piercy roads.

Amid the subalpine firs and mountain hemlocks of the Forbidden Plateau in Strathcona Provincial Park are small quiet ponds where water lilies flourish in summer.

to buy up these claims, this was not done. For a long time the park's remoteness deterred any major logging projects, but this changed in the 1950s when logging technology improved. The government also began removing areas of prime forest from the park as trade-offs for new parkland elsewhere. In 1962 timber rights in the Bedwell Valley of Strathcona were exchanged for waterfront at Long Beach. A separate timber exchange was completed to acquire ocean frontage at China Beach, which is now part of Juan de Fuca Provincial Park, and it was Strathcona timber that allowed the province to acquire parkland at Cape Scott in 1973.

The timber exchange that allowed the Parks Department to acquire Rathtrevor Beach came about through the personal connections of Ray Williston, the minister of Lands and Forests in W.A.C. Bennett's government. During the 1950s this property with its 2,100 metres of waterfront was owned by the Rath family, who operated it as a private campground, and the minister and his family camped there every summer. However, in 1961, after the death of one of the Rath sisters, the remaining

Left: Rocky promontories, or sea stacks, jut out from the white sandy beaches of Cape Scott Provincial Park.

Below: At low tide, hikers can descend from Cape Scott's inland trails to the beach and explore the rugged coastline.

Bottom: These sunny skies and wide calm beaches of Cape Scott on the northern tip of Vancouver Island belie this area's usual stormy weather.

Raths decided to sell the property; their price was $365,000. Williston saw this as a great opportunity to acquire it for a park, but when he approached Bennett for the money, he was turned down. In a determined effort to find the necessary funding, he began speaking to business people, service clubs and lumbermen, and one day he was approached by Jack Christensen of the Tahsis Company, which was logging in a river valley just west of the straight north–south line that was Strathcona Park's western boundary. Christensen offered to buy the Rathtrevor property in exchange for being allowed to continue logging the river valley right up into the park. Williston met with Stanley John (Jack) Squire, the NDP member for Alberni, and related what had happened. Squire agreed that it was a good deal and told him to "go get it," promising that "you'll never hear about it from the NDP."[2] Williston decided that it was worth the gamble. Christensen did log the valley and in October 1963 he pulled his equipment out of the park and handed Williston the deed for Rathtrevor property. A year later Liberal MLA Alan Macfarlane brought the matter up in the house, suggesting it had something to do with timber sales in Wells Gray, but the matter was soon dropped for lack of evidence. Rathtrevor Beach, which had been enormously popular as a private campsite, became even more popular as a public park in 1967.

The sign beside the highway at Okanagan Lake Provincial Park is one of the hundreds that were carved at the Langford Workshop.

Lakeshore Park Development

Back in 1955 a major acquisition of 260 hectares where Kokanee Creek empties into the West Arm of Kootenay Lake had provided a site for a major park development that would also serve as the headquarters for the West Kootenays Parks District. Two campgrounds—Redfish and Sandspit—were laid out here that would eventually provide 132 vehicle-accessible sites. As well as lakeshore recreation and hiking trails, Kokanee Creek Park provided an opportunity for visitors to witness the spawning of Kokanee trout, a freshwater form of sockeye salmon.

Two large campgrounds in Okanagan Lake Park provide family camping and picnicking sites amid Ponderosa pines and sagebrush.

Darkness descends on beautiful Lakelse Lake and the Kitimat Mountains.

The success of this park led to the development of three similar waterfront parks in 1962 in the Okanagan Valley. Okanagan Mountain Provincial Park on the northeastern shore of Okanagan Lake includes two hundred hectares of forested benchlands above a rocky shoreline. It attracts hikers, cyclists, climbers, scuba divers, canoeists and water skiers. Sun–Oka Beach Provincial Park, which has one of the finest beaches in the entire Okanagan, was acquired from Agriculture Canada's Summerland research station. The park provides outstanding beach, waterplay and picnic sites; it also protects a stand of old-growth cottonwoods. About the same time as these two parks were established in the north Okanagan, further south on Osoyoos Lake another remarkable piece of waterfront was developed at Haynes Point, a slim pencil of land that juts out into the lake just north of the US border. However, just a few years after it was designated as a park, it was almost lost to the Highways Department, which was looking at options for relocating the southern Trans-Canada Highway route across Osoyoos Lake. But when Robert H. (Bob) Ahrens, head of Parks Systems Planning at that time, was approached by ministry officials with the suggestion that the Haynes Spit would make a fine launching point from the western side of the lake, he was less than enthusiastic. As a result, the highway is still routed via the causeway through the centre of the community of Osoyoos. Though a mere thirty-eight hectares, Haynes Point was a very popular beach and picnic grounds for local residents before becoming a public campsite; it now has the highest occupancy rate of any campground in the parks system.

Meanwhile, at Lakelse Lake Park (created in 1956) near Terrace, headquarters for the newly created Skeena Parks Division, crews were hard at work in 1962 developing new sections of the day-use areas. But within days of the completion of construction, a mudslide undid all that hard work. Tom Moore, who supervised the job, had been quite pleased with the results of the project and had returned south only to receive a phone call that his newly installed picnic tables were floating in the lake. This was a tough lesson in the necessity of recognizing and providing for conditions of soil stability. Fortunately, a property donation by Alcan provided new waterfront for the park. But while this was the first major lakeshore park to suffer a natural disaster, a decade later a similar event would occur at Okanagan Lake Park campground.

Right: A thin band of beach on the eastern edge of Quadra Island, Rebecca Spit often accumulates large amounts of driftwood.

Bottom: The ranger station at the edge of Lakelse Lake, shown here in 1915, provided a rustic shelter for BC Forest Service staff.
BC Archives, NA-03887

Marine Parks

Apart from Miracle Beach, created in 1950, few of the early parks were focussed on the extensive ocean frontage or the myriad of island archipelagos just offshore. This oversight was partially a function of limited access because a ferry system was not yet in place but was also because many of the best beach frontages and anchorages were privately held. Rebecca Spit Provincial Park on the east side of Quadra Island and Skookumchuck Narrows at the entrance to Sechelt Inlet are not really marine parks as neither has moorage for boaters, but with their creation in 1957 the system had its first parks designated to protect unique marine environments and resource values. Like many parks on the coastal islands, they provide only walk-in access and no camping. Skookumchuck offers a view of the narrow passage to Sechelt Inlet with its dramatic tidal surge.

However, in the early 1960s the Yachting Council of BC, led by G.A. (Al) Fairhurst, who worked for Parks, completed a survey of popular coastal marine anchorages, and by 1964 the core of a marine parks system was in place. The following year after Fairhurst transferred to the Parks planning department, he purchased

Above: The tidal pools of BC's marine parks reveal a spectacular variety of colourful sea plants and animals.

Below: Sea kayakers from around the world have discovered the beauties of the dozens of undeveloped islands in Broughton Archipelago Park, BC's largest marine park.

Right: At low tide visitors to Newcastle Island investigate shells and debris deposited on the beach while in the background a BC ferry approaches Nanaimo.

Below: Botanical Beach, part of Juan de Fuca Park, is best known for its abundance of intertidal life, including hardy gooseneck barnacles and sea palms that have evolved to withstand the pounding of the surf.

Bottom: Visitors to Montague Harbour on peaceful Galiano Island can moor their boats to any of the 35 buoys in the sheltered bay.

While tent styles have changed since 1968 when this photo was taken, visitors to Sidney Spit can still expect to see huge numbers of shorebirds on the tidal flats and salt marshes during the spring and fall migrations. *BC Archives, I-03851*

the eight-metre sailboat *Grey Goose*, and he and his dog, Burgie, spent personal holidays and field trips over the next two decades on a coastal reconnaissance of the southern coast to document anchorages and special features. As a consequence, it is generally acknowledged that Fairhurst, by his personal leadership and motivation, is the founder of the provincial marine park system. The early emphasis was on what Fairhurst described as a good marine park—"a safe scenic harbour anchorage protected in its natural state." It would be another two decades before a similar emphasis was placed on establishing criteria for biodiversity and coastal landforms in marine parks.

Sidney Spit became one of Canada's first major marine parks. It provided a water access recreation system and safe moorage while at the same time protecting aquatic resources, bird foraging sites and unique marine landforms—notably, the spit and the lagoon. Its creation as a park was the first sign of the emergence of a truly diversified and comprehensive system encompassing mountaintops, lakeshores and seascapes.

Montague Harbour Marine Park on the southwest side of Galiano Island, established in 1959 and officially opened in 1962, is unique for the Gulf Islands because it includes both an auto access park and popular marine park anchorage. Typical of the Parks' construction projects of the period, it required a very difficult access road to be built through private property to access water frontage. Construction equipment had to be delivered by landing barge.

Newcastle Island, which had been a CPR resort, was bought by the City of Nanaimo in 1955 then donated to the provincial government in April 1960. Work immediately began to make it into a Class A park. It now has ferry service from the nearby mainland and heavily used marine docks; it also provided the first walk-in campground, now common in the Gulf Islands. In 1984 the original CPR dance pavilion was renovated as a visitor centre and canteen.

By 1966 there were eight marine parks, including Echo Bay, Smugglers Cove and the Copeland Islands, and this growth warranted a new Branch publication, *Marine Parks of BC*, which has been updated and reprinted numerous times.

Wilderness Parks and Nature Interpretive Programs

In 1963 a new document called *Purposes and Procedures: Parks Branch* was released, accompanied by twenty-four pages of updated Parks Branch policies. In contrast to the 1952 policy update, where the emphasis was on recreational objectives, this document stated that: "It is, however, a purpose of the Branch to devise and apply such forest and wildlife protection and management measures as are necessary to maintain, as nearly as possible, the conditions that would have prevailed had the Industrial Revolution not occurred and had the white man not come to British Columbia."

Concurrent with this formal broadening of the mandate to incorporate conservation was the recognition of the need and opportunity to enrich park users' recreational experience by providing provincial interpretive programs led by Yorke Edwards. In 1957 the first nature houses had been set up in tents in Manning Park, followed by Miracle Beach in 1958 and then Shuswap Lake. The first major public information and interpretive program, *Salute to the Salmon*, was held in 1958 at

Mitlenatch Island Nature Provincial Park is home to the largest seabird colony in the Strait of Georgia.
Bill Merilees

Adams River; in time this fall gathering to view salmon spawning would become the largest gathering of park visitors at one time. But interpretive programs began to blossom in 1962 with the start of the Campfire programs. A year later the division published a detailed manual, *Interpretation in Our Parks*, to provide guidance for the growing program for seasonal naturalists. The unique bird population and vegetation on Mitlenatch Island was the site for combined natural resources inventory and an interpretive program. At Wickaninnish Beach the first naturalist program on the west coast of Vancouver Island serviced increasing numbers of park visitors eager to explore the oceanside wonders, and by 1965 natural history programs were being introduced to the Okanagan District. A permanent outdoor amphitheatre for interpretive programs was built in Manning Park.

Parks Accounting

By 1962, in sharp contrast to the underdeveloped parks of the 1930s, 170 of the 202 parks in the system had facilities for public access and use, 83 were for day-use only and 87 had campgrounds. And in the four years between 1958 and 1962, over 400 campsites were added each year, to a total of 3,700 units. Picnic sites increased from 2,500 to 5,500. And by 1965 annual attendance had grown to five million. The public had discovered provincial parks.

Political Doublespeak

In 1964 the Social Credit government of W.A.C. Bennett approved Order-in-Council 659 to allow mineral claim staking in both Class A and B parks larger than two thousand hectares. For Parks staff, this was just another contradictory episode in a contradictory period: the government had created the Ministry of Recreation and Conservation in 1957, funded capital development in parks and created Barkerville, but at the same time reduced the park system by half, flooded portions of three parks and permitted mineral claim staking. They also issued logging tenures in existing parks as an expedient trade-off to acquire new parks.

On the other hand, just a year after Order-in-Council 659 was approved, a new Park Act was passed that added conservation to the purposes for which parks were created, specifically identifying conservation as "the preservation of [the parks'] natural environments for inspiration, use and enjoyment of the public." This statement officially broadened the mandate from previous recreation and tourism objectives and provided a set of principles and regulations by which parks would be managed. The act increased protection in Class A parks from all forms of alienation, but also provided for both nature conservancy and recreation area designations. These nature conservancies gave absolute protection to outstanding areas of scenic, flora and fauna value. This designation could also create "no go" areas within Class B parks, which had less resource protection. Also of significance in the new act was the fact that parks were not to be subject to the provisions of such statutes as the Water, Land or Forest acts, meaning that other agencies had no jurisdiction over lands and resources within parks.

Given that the past decade had seen a traumatic decline in the park system the new statute included a dramatic commitment: "The Lieutenant Governor in Council shall exercise the power to the extent and as often as may be necessary to ensure that the total area of parks and recreation areas is not less than six million three hundred thousand acres."

While the new Park Act did recognize different levels of resource development in parks—that is, differential degrees of protection—it also provided politicians with a rationale and means to simply reclassify parklands as it suited them. This loophole was made possible by the statement that permits for the "removal, destruction, disturbance, damaging or exploitation of any natural resource in parks" could be issued by the minister alone; thus, the minister would make the decisions on possible detrimental effects or the necessity for exploitation of resources in Class A parks. If the potential development didn't meet the classification criteria, the minister could simply reclassify the park to Class B or recreation area and issue the permit and allow the activity. The history of Wells Gray, Tweedsmuir, Kokanee Glacier and Strathcona reflect this protocol.

Alpine fireweed grows in Black Tusk Meadows, part of Garibaldi Park. *Bill Merilees*

Black Tusk Mountain, which is part of Garibaldi Park, became the first nature conservancy in 1964 right after the act was passed. Subsequently, a new Parks master plan would identify part of northern Tweedsmuir Park to be designated as Eutsuk Nature Conservancy; a second area in Tweedsmuir became the Rainbow Conservancy. Three conservancies were designated within Strathcona, although other areas of this park were still left with timber tenures and mineral claims.

Two parks, Strathcona and Kokanee, were reclassified from A to B, but road

access was improved—the Buttle Lake highway in Strathcona and improved alpine roads to Kokanee Glacier—to support exploration and development. However, other portions of these parks were to become nature conservancies and were thus exempt from resource claims. Murtle Lake in Wells Gray was designated as a nature conservancy in 1968, and today remains a roadless area. No further conservancies were to be created until after 1995.

In 1962 Hamber Provincial Park was reduced by 98 percent to allow flooding of the Big Bend. In 2011, the park measured 24,000 hectares.

The Columbia River Treaty and Its Effects on the Parks System

The 1960s could be described as the "H and H years" in BC as the prime economic focuses of the government were hydro and highways. Massive amounts of provincial and federal funding were directed toward enormous hydro dam projects on the Peace and the Columbia rivers and on three major new highways—the Trans-Canada, John Hart and Yellowhead. These years also saw the establishment of a new north–south railway route into Fort Nelson and the Peace region. All of these projects would either directly or indirectly affect the provincial parks system.

Neither the Columbia nor the Peace River projects were subject to the public hearings or environmental impact studies that were required for subsequent projects, but while the first dam on the Peace at Hudson Hope created the enormous Williston Lake as a reservoir (which to date has provided limited recreational opportunities), it did not flood any pre-existing parks. However, the economic boom that the construction of the dam engendered did create a demand for improved highway links and nearby roadside campgrounds. The result was the opening of a campground at Moberly Lake in 1969 and a campground and new Peace River District office at Charlie Lake. But this district remained difficult to manage because of the distances between parks north along the Alaska Highway and the difficulty of securing labour willing to work in such remote locations.

The Columbia River project, on the other hand, was a long time in developing and had a huge effect on the parks system. Even before World War II the Americans had been making plans to build a dam for power generation on the Kootenay River where it loops south into Montana. However, the only site suitable for a dam was at the southernmost bend of the river near the town of Libby, and the backed-up waters would flood Canadian territory. Such a dam would also have significant downstream effects on the lower Kootenay River and Kootenay Lake as well as the upper Columbia River, which the Kootenay joins at Castlegar. As a result, harnessing the power potential of the entire Columbia River system became the subject of international talks in 1944. The US wanted all upstream management to be in Canada—that is, the storage of spring runoff—in order to prevent downstream flooding and provide uniform water flow that would enable them to build additional dams for hydro generation and irrigation on their side of the border. However, it was 1956 before a political framework for power sharing was set up, January 1961 before a treaty was signed between the two countries and 1964 before it was ratified by the Canadian Parliament.

In the meantime, preparations had been underway in BC for the flooding that

The chain of six lakes and connecting waterways in Bowron Provincial Park is open from June to October to canoeists and kayakers eager to make the 116-kilometre circuit.

would ensue after the dams were built. The park primarily affected would be Hamber, created as a Class A park in 1941 and downgraded to Class B four years later. But this park had two strikes against it. First, by the mid-1950s the parks system had grown to 3,648,000 hectares, and within the Forest Service new proposals for more medium- and large-sized parks were not well received because there was a general feeling that the parks system was large enough. Second, nearly a million hectares of that parks total was in one park—Hamber—and some staff in the Parks Division were suggesting that, in proportion to its size, it offered little in scenic or natural values and, other than moose and waterfowl hunting in the Columbia Valley, few recreational opportunities. They made the case that the park system would be better served if Hamber was cancelled or reduced in size and replaced by other Crown land with more substantial natural features. In particular, they supported park status for the nearby but much smaller Bowron Lakes, which were much more accessible for recreationists.

As a consequence, in 1961 when international negotiations for power projects on the Columbia made it clear that the upper Columbia Valley would be flooded, the government reduced the size of Hamber Park to the 24,518 hectares surrounding Fortress Lake, while at the same time designating the Bowron Lakes as the province's newest park. This chain of lakes had been popular with fishermen, hunters and trappers in the early years of the twentieth century, but by 1925 the depletion of wildlife had raised alarms, and the area within the chain of lakes was declared a game reserve. After its designation as a provincial park in 1961, it became extremely popular as a canoe circuit—a 116-kilometre rectangle of lakes, rivers and portages. In the new Bowron Park, information signs were placed along the canoe circuit and marked the beginning of designated camping sites. Parks "wilderness management" principles for Bowron and also for Garibaldi were beginning to reflect lessons learned and being applied to visitor management by US National Parks and the US Forest Service.

The Big Bend Highway, which followed the Columbia River's huge hairpin bend around the northern end of the Selkirk Mountains, was also destined to be affected by the dam building and subsequent flooding, and in 1959 the government began work on a new section of highway. It would divert east–west traffic through the Rogers Pass, which lies in the middle of Glacier National Park (designated in 1886), instead of via the Big Bend. The new road was completed in 1962, cutting the route from Revelstoke to Golden by 160 kilometres. The new route significantly increased tourist visits to both Shuswap and Okanagan lakes and pushed the need for expanded park facilities in those areas.

The Duncan Dam, the first of the dams that the treaty required BC to build, was completed in 1967. It holds back a forty-five-kilometre-long reservoir north of Kootenay Lake, but as the area is sparsely settled, the dam did not have a major impact on settlements or on any existing parks. The remaining dams were built on the Columbia. The High Arrow Dam (later re-christened the Hugh Keenleyside Dam) lies twelve kilometres upstream from the town of Castlegar. After it became operational in October 1968, it raised the height of the Lower and Upper Arrow

Cummins Lakes Provincial Park, 60 kilometres north of Golden, features spectacular waterfalls and icy-cold lakes fed by the vast Clemenceau Icefields of Jasper National Park.

lakes so that they became one long reservoir stretching 232 kilometres north to the town of Revelstoke. Much fertile farmland was flooded and the lakeside settlements of Burton, Fauquier and Edgewood had to be relocated; on the plus side of the ledger, in subsequent years the Parks Branch received compensation funds to mitigate the impacts of this reservoir and create opportunities for public recreation. Syringa Creek Provincial Park was established just north of the dam in 1968 as a recreation area but increased to 4,417 hectares in 1995 to protect a larger ecosystem. Blanket Creek, just south of Revelstoke, was not created until 1982; it encompasses the remnants of a heritage farm and protects Sutherland Falls.

The Mica Dam at the northernmost bend of the Columbia River was completed in 1973. As the water rose behind it, it formed 214-kilometre-long Kinbasket Lake. This new reservoir has two reaches—Columbia Reach in the valley of the Columbia River and Canoe Reach, which occupies the valley of the Canoe River to the north of the dam, almost to the town of Valemount. The populations of five small settlements in this area—Mica, Big Bend, Downie, Boat Encampment and

Above: Hiking trails in Nairn Falls Park take a winding route beside the Green River to a point where the waters are transformed into a thundering 60-metre column of white water.

Left: Alice Lake provides a safe environment for family paddling expeditions.

La Porte—had to be resettled and the Mica to Golden section of the Big Bend Highway disappeared beneath the water. Unfortunately, this reservoir offers few attractions and has never become a major destination for recreationists. East of the reservoir a 21,728-hectare site, part of the old Hamber Park, was later established as the Cummins Lakes Provincial Park; access is only by helicopter or ski-touring across the Clemenceau Icefields from Jasper National Park. The Revelstoke Dam, halfway between the High Arrow and the Mica, was built to regulate water levels north of Revelstoke; it was not completed until 1984.

The Squamish-Whistler Highway—An Impetus for Parks

Completion of the highway from Squamish to Whistler in 1965 created a need for and provided access to a series of new roadside parks as far north as the Pemberton Valley. First, Alice Lake was developed as a major day-use and campground destination park, and almost from its opening it was subject to full occupancy. It also serves as the district's maintenance headquarters. Subsequently, roadside parks such

Above: When looking southwest from
the summit of Stawamus Chief, the
710-metre-high granite rock that guards
the southern end of the Sea-to-Sky
Highway, climbers are treated to this view.

Left: A 20-minute drive north of Whistler,
a 1.5-kilometre hiking trail leads to
60-metre-high Nairn Falls, long a spiritual
site for the Lil'wat First Nation.

as Murrin Lake, Nairn Falls and Green Lake were developed and later, Birkenhead Lake, north of Pemberton.

Immediately adjacent to the busy Squamish–Whistler highway are three scenic attractions that merited property acquisitions. The first was Brandywine Falls next to the Daisy Lake hydro project. Further south, Shannon Falls, an acquisition facilitated in 1982 by Carling O'Keefe Breweries, presents the third highest waterfalls (335 metres) in BC. Della Falls (481 metres) in Strathcona and Hunlen Falls (396 metres) in south Tweedsmuir are remote and seldom seen by most residents. This park soon became one of the most popular roadside rest stops in the province. The hiking trail—not the climbing route—to the top of the Chieftain begins in this park.

Shannon Falls is immediately adjacent to another dramatic natural feature, the Stawamus Chief, which is the world's second-largest granite monolith. It provides a readily accessible challenge to the novice and expert rock wall climbers whose cars and mountain bikes fill a sixty-three-unit campsite. Apart from the numerous routes up the wall, there is a trail to the three peaks above the face that provides stupendous views of Howe Sound and up the valley toward Whistler. As an added feature, the park contains nesting areas for peregrine falcons.

Highway improvement also provided the impetus for major development of the Whistler ski resort, the upper slopes of which originally extended into Garibaldi Park. Boundary adjustments to the park removed areas needed for ski lifts for both Whistler and Blackcomb resorts, but now hikers could use the ski lifts to access an alpine route south to the Singing Pass area. Over time Garibaldi Park would evolve as a popular near-urban wilderness park with highway routes terminating at the western park boundary, with four separate "foot-only" access corridors. In the south, a forest access road takes visitors up from the valley bottom to the Red Heather Meadows/Diamond Head area, popular with hikers and cross-country skiers. The well-known Rubble Creek/Barrier Trail route, after a short but vigorous climb, provides access to the heart of the park, Black Tusk Meadows and

Garibaldi Lake. The two northerly corridors, Cheakamus Lake and Fitzsimmons Creek, north and south of the adjacent Whistler ski development, link up to the Singing Pass area. Much of these latter trail links were developed or improved by volunteer groups, while trail work in Black Tusk area was done primarily by Youth Crews. In order to protect alpine meadows surrounding Black Tusk, camping has been focused at Battleship Island along the scenic lakeshore.

The Beginning of the Environmentalist Era

In 1968 when Cathedral Provincial Park was established southwest of Kere-meos, its park status was strongly supported by a new regional conservation group known as the Okanagan Similkameen Parks Society (OSPS), led by J. Woodward. They also gave their early support for Brent Mountain and Okanagan Mountain as parks and to heritage trails such as the Alexander Mackenzie (Grease) Trail. But in contrast to conservation groups on the Lower Mainland and Vancouver Island, the OSPS had a low profile because its battlefield was far from major metro area media coverage. On the other hand, two instances of formal organized protest during this same period would be accompanied by regular media coverage. Oddly, neither was directly related to park management or proposals for new parks but both raised the level of public awareness and led to the creation of two new provincial parks.

In 1968 a long-simmering dispute over the future of Cypress Bowl, above West Vancouver, became a major public issue after a private company, Alpine Outdoor Recreation Resources Ltd., applied to log the bowl in preparation for developing a multi-million-dollar ski resort there. Fortunately for Alpine, the Forest Service had just discovered that the trees in the bowl were infested with balsam woolly aphids, which were resistant to then-known sprays. Alpine was given permission to log and develop its ski facilities within specific boundaries. But the public became outraged by Alpine's logging practices—the company was taking out more timber than the per-mit allowed, the areas being logged were too steep for skiing and the clearing would affect water runoff. By 1969 it became apparent that even an access road and parking areas were beyond the financial capabilities of the company. Alpine tried to sell its interests to Benguet Consolidated, a Manila-based firm, and Benguet made plans for a massive housing development with peripheral ski facilities.[3] However, in the face

The tumbling waters of Shannon Falls originate on the slopes of mounts Habrich and Sky Pilot and fall 335 metres over a series of cliffs toward Highway 99, south of Squamish.

of massive negative press coverage, the government cancelled Alpine's lease, and the following year announced the Province would develop the ski area. Apart from the ski facilities, the project would need major funds to construct fourteen kilometers of a highly visible road across the face of the North Shore Mountains. (Road locations for Cypress were a class project for new concepts in "landscape logging" at the University of British Columbia, and pictures of proposed zigzag routes were regular front-page stories in the *Vancouver Sun*.) But between a lack of funds and protracted public hearings, the project commencement did not occur until 1975.

The second instance of formal protest involved a demand for power generation in the US, though separate from the Columbia Treaty. The problem had its roots in a 1924 treaty that gave Seattle Light and Power Ltd. the right to harness the Skagit River, which rises in southern BC east of Hope and drains southwestward through Washington state. The company built a series of power-generating dams and in 1949 completed a storage dam, known as the Ross Dam, about thirty-two kilometres south of the US–Canada border. But the treaty allowed the company the option of increasing the height of this dam if more power was needed, and within five years they began making overtures to the BC government for permission to raise the height by thirty-eight metres. The Social Credit government was in favour of this move as the water behind the dam would back almost thirteen kilometres into Canada and provide a recreational lake, and they signed an agreement in principle with the company. This raised a public outcry in the US as well as in Canada because the enlarged lake would flood cottage country south of the border. Protesters formed the Run Out Skagit Spoilers Society (ROSS) and the newspapers took up the refrain with photos and stories of the devastation the flooding would cause. In 1968, to complicate matters, the US created the North Cascades National Park on adjacent land. The debate and complicated legal proceedings would continue for several years and through two more governments so that the situation was not formally resolved until 1984. However, it has been argued that the organization of the ROSS group, with its broad-based public interest and support, marked the formal beginning of the environmental movement in BC. This may have been a direct result of the fact that the Skagit River is located in the Lower Mainland and the issue generated ongoing media coverage.

The year 1969 marked the end of an era and the emergence of the modern Parks Branch. R.H. Ahrens, the intellectual leader and planner of the park system, became Director and later Associate Deputy Minister. C.J. Velay, senior engineer in the roadside era, became Assistant Director. Over the next decade the park system would double in size, parks boundaries would be given statutory protection, staffing would double and capital budgets for park development mushroomed. Park facilities now included amenities like showers, flush toilets and paved roads. Much of the park system that the public appreciates and enjoys today was established and developed during the 1960s and '70s—including popular parks like Rathtrevor, Cypress Bowl, Porteau Cove, Bear Creek, Desolation Sound and important natural areas like Spatsizi, Kalamalka Lake and Tribune Bay—under the stewardship of Ahrens, Velay and their colleagues.

5 :
Growth Years,
1969 to 1975

A New National Park

By the late 1960s the federal government was very anxious to establish national parks on the Pacific Coast, and H. Paish and Associates were contracted to do an assessment of possible candidates. Their report identified several but in the end the focus settled firmly on the west coast of Vancouver Island, and in 1969 a federal–provincial agreement was finally negotiated to create Pacific Rim National Park, with three separate parts: Long Beach, the Broken Group Islands and the West Coast Trail. Marine parks generally have two components: an upland base and a foreshore strip usually accompanied by an offshore reserve, which often results in

Above: The spectacular beaches, dramatic coastline and lush rainforest of Pacific Rim National Park are divided into three distinct units: Long Beach, the Broken Group archipelago and the 75 kilometre West Coast Trail. *iStock*

a federal–provincial jurisdictional issue. Usually, the configuration of the shore-line, along with the offshore islands, provides a protected anchorage and beach access to the upland, but determining the extent and size of the offshore boundaries for parks can affect First Nations, moorage, navigation and vessel transport, recreational shellfish harvesting, commercial fishing and boat access to private upland. It became the BC Parks Branch's responsibility to acquire all of the numerous private in-holdings related to the proposed Pacific Rim Park, including timber rights.

Phase one of the project included the extremely popular former provincial campground at Greenpoint as well as the twenty-five kilometres of ocean frontage at Long Beach. Turning this area into a national park meant an immediate lifestyle change for the people who had spent long weekends there racing their vehicles on the wide, hard sand beaches and camping among the driftwood logs. Long Beach had also become popular with many counterculture transients who had built drift-wood homes in the forests bordering the beach. Efforts to evict them created public relations issues for park managers.

Phase two centred on the Broken Group Islands at the entrance to Barkley Sound, which was primarily Crown land. Phase three, the West Coast Trail, was part of a tree farm licence and needed to be extricated from it.

In 1971 in order to expedite the search for potential new national parks, Parks Canada published the *National Parks System Planning Manual*, which identified thirty-nine national park regions and developed a series of natural history themes based on the recognized landforms of Canada, one of which was "river systems and lakes." Eight BC rivers were identified in this initial document, but it would be many more years before any of them were designated as heritage rivers. The BC Parks Branch, however, found that identifying natural elements not protected as parks by using this national landform classification system was too broad. It was also inconsistent with the natural resource inventory methodology that was evolving in BC, a province that is characterized by extremely diverse landforms and plant communities and strong maritime influences. Here the study of traditional geophysical information—that is, soils, topography and geology—was being blended with climate and vegetation data to identify and classify "biogeoclimatic zones."[4]

The Ecological Reserves Act, passed by the BC government in 1971, formalized legal protection for the work of the scientists who had developed a system to identify and classify "representative and special natural ecosystems, plant and animal species, features and phenomena for scientific research and educational purposes." BC was the first province to do so, though by a government not noted for its support of environmental measures. The first twenty-nine ecological reserves were given protective status by order-in-council. Dr. Bristol Foster was appointed full-time reserves coordinator in 1974 and a year later regulations were in place to provide the framework for the use and protection of reserves.

Park Rehabilitation

By the end of the 1960s the trails in Mount Assiniboine and Mount Robson were suffering serious erosion, prompting a project to rehabilitate and relocate some of the trails. As well, the Branch moved to increase control and limits on trail rides sponsored by guide outfitters. Many of these trips originated in Alberta and linked up to the adjacent national parks.

The author remembers one occasion when he and two Parks staff were hiking in Mount Robson Park, along with Assistant District Manager C. Sadlier, when they observed a party on horseback crossing over from Alberta. Realizing that the guide outfitter in charge of the group was one who had refused to comply with the new rules for commercial use of the park, the ranger was inclined to evict them immediately. By coincidence, the author recognized some of the clients on horseback and pointed out that they would all have a lot of explaining to do back in Victoria when it became known who they had evicted—one of the riders was the Honourable Peter Lougheed, then premier of Alberta, who had paid the outfitter for a family trip into the park. The ranger was easily convinced to speak privately to the outfitter.

Just before arriving at the Whitehorn Campground, the Berg Lake Trail crosses a suspension bridge over the Robson River in Mount Robson Provincial Park.

The Environment and Land Use Committee

On July 15, 1969, a government order-in-council (OIC #2300) created a new cabinet committee called the Environment and Land Use Committee (ELUC), which would henceforth play a major role in approving park proposals and directing special reviews of contentious regional land-use issues. But while to a great extent it operated by consensus before matters were referred for a decision by the full cabinet, the ministers responsible for the resource sectors—forestry, agriculture and mining—could stonewall proposals made by the Recreation and Conservation ministry. As a result, the independence and leadership of the minister of Recreation and Conservation in support of new parks was often fettered by his colleagues.

Later, in order to accommodate the decentralization that was occurring in most of the resource ministries, the ELUC established Regional Resource Management Committees (RRMCs) with membership drawn from the senior regional staff of Mines, Agriculture, Lands, Parks, Highways, Forests, and Fish and Wildlife. New offices were established in Nanaimo, Smithers and Cranbrook in addition to the ELUC offices in Vancouver, Prince George and Kamloops. More remote regions such as Skeena and Kootenay were often successful in reaching consensus about local land-use conflicts because there were fewer competing demands, while the Lower Mainland and Vancouver Island were less successful because resource uses overlapped. However, some ministries, such as Forests, used their size and threats

Opposite top: "Landmark" meeting, 1973— headquarters and field staff meet to plan the Accelerated Park Development program after discretionary funding for parks grew to $15 million.

Opposite bottom: At low tide more than a kilometre of sand bars are exposed at Rathtrevor Beach, BC's most popular campground.

of sectoral unemployment to muscle their proposals through the process. And while the committee approach to resource sharing meant that Parks managers and planners had to be consulted by other ministries before they embarked on projects, it also meant that park development and proposals for new parks were subject to regional review by these other agencies, and they often met with resistance. As well, there were unrealistic expectations by other ministries that Parks should spend a share of its budget on their recreational programs. On other occasions, the RRMCs would agree in principle with a proposal for a new protected park area but would recommend recreation area status instead of Class A status because they wanted to retain their options for resource use or development there. Moreover, the new government's bias toward the logging industry was well known, and after numerous instances of the cabinet's resistance to further erosion of the forest land base, it became difficult for the Parks Branch and its staff to actively promote any new protected areas.

The Third Wave of Development

The 1960s ended with funding cuts that resulted in very little summer hiring by the Parks Department and large winter layoffs of regular personnel. Then again in late December 1970 the Branch was advised that fourth-quarter funding was being restrained. There were more layoffs and funds for out-of-province travel were frozen so that no representatives could be sent to the Federal–Provincial Parks Conference that year or the next. The irony was that, within three months, the financial situation would change dramatically: just prior to the provincial election of August 1972, the Social Credit government approved the Accelerated Park Development Fund Act, which increased discretionary funding for parks from under $500,000 to $15 million with the fundamental objective of creating employment opportunities. A "third wave" of park development was about to begin.

The new funds were to be used first to upgrade existing public day-use and campground facilities and access roads. Most had been built in the mid-1950s and early 1960s and were showing their age. Next, funds were to be used to greatly expand new visitor facilities, toilets, washrooms and change houses and to construct new and upgrade existing nature houses and replica historic structures in heritage parks. The Branch was also mandated to improve and greatly expand the trail system (including both day use and backcountry or alpine) and to expand regional administrative facilities (offices, workshops, equipment sheds, Youth Crew accommodations and kitchens). To do all of this it would be necessary to enhance seasonal staffing for specific program initiatives including interpretation, ranger services and security and to increase regular staff for all phases of planning and research. The only specific project on the list was the major new access road and ski area at Cypress Bowl, a project announced in 1969 but never funded.

With this large block of funding at hand, the Branch was subject to pressure from local MLAs who began lobbying the minister for park development in their constituencies, a factor that sometimes distorted priorities but did have the

general benefit of ensuring province-wide growth of the park system. There was also another factor at work here: between 1950 and 1971 BC's highway system had grown from 17,500 to over 36,000 kilometres, and politicians wanted new park facilities to serve all these new routes.

In-house staff did most of the basic construction within the parks—roads, parking lots and campground layouts—although contractors were hired for specialized structural, electrical and water works. Construction equipment and vehicles were now leased. The one exception to the use of the Branch's own workforce was co-operation with the Department of Highways to undertake paving projects in over forty parks, including Cypress and Seymour. Meanwhile, the maintenance of the now-enormous system of visitor facilities was to be done by a cadre of seasonal workers, which meant that over 1,600 seasonal employees had to be found. This expansion also meant finding supervisory staff and providing them with opportunities for future careers in the parks service.

But public expectations for visitor services had changed from those of the 1950s. No longer were gravel roads, pit toilets, water pumps and basic change houses acceptable. Now the public wanted paved roads, flush toilets, hot water and lighted buildings, all of which posed design and construction considerations in these mostly rural circumstances. They also added to present development costs and increased future maintenance costs. With such a massive works program underway, the survey section of the Branch's Engineering Division, which prepared all the topographic maps necessary for new construction as well as reconstruction of roads, parking lots, campsites, bridges and buildings, could not keep up with the number of priority assignments. Consequently, the Engineering Division was overwhelmed, site planning was constantly held up by the lack of surveys, office staff argued over control of projects while field staff were frustrated by the delays.

Twenty-three water system projects (either new, expanded or upgraded) and twenty-seven wells were researched and designed for the following year. Rathtrevor Beach was chosen for the first installations of hot showers, flush toilets and change houses, mostly because it was a recently acquired property located on the largest and most accessible beach on Vancouver Island. It was also the largest campground built in one stage, and it was heavily used from early May through Thanksgiving. In fact, Rathtrevor served as a vacation destination with many visitors who stayed up to ten days—hence the need for showers. Three very large day-use parking lots and picnic shelters were also required.

The upgrading of toilets from Pan-Abode at Shuswap Lake required ten new concrete block buildings for the campground and day-use areas. Similar programs in other parks resulted in the need for thirty-nine new toilet buildings, twelve change houses, two picnic shelters, four equipment sheds and the preliminary design for new nature houses for Golden Ears and Kokanee Creek parks. New residences were built for Bowron Park staff, as well as a dining room for Manning. Several Youth Crew kitchens were upgraded or replaced. Major road reconstruction and upgrading occurred in Mount Seymour, Wells Gray and Alice Lake parks. Many short park entrance roads were also paved. A staff ranger cabin was built at Berg

Lake Meadows in Mount Robson, and Goldstream received a large picnic shelter to allow year-round use.

Planning for Cypress Bowl was a major challenge in land-use and engineering design so the Branch's first priority was to create a master plan. It included three major elements: (1) road and parking locations, (2) slope analysis and lift selection, and (3) the design of a visitor lodge and service buildings. Unfortunately, the clearings created by private logging were not related to slopes suitable for ski runs and additional clearing was necessary as well as some slope rehabilitation. At the same time, it was necessary to balance access and parking with protection of the natural features of the bowl and valley and, more particularly, the scenic viewscape as seen from downtown Vancouver. A very large relief model of the park plans was produced and used for presentation to West Vancouver City Council and for several public presentations.

In 1975 after more than two years of major development and extremely large funding allocations and staffing commitments, Cypress Bowl opened with two chairlifts in operation. Subsequently, proposals for further expansion of lifts, lodges and parking areas would lead to debate about continued public funding and to the introduction of a role for private interests. After an initial emphasis on downhill ski facilities, a trail system was developed, first for Cypress Bowl and then extended

The sun shines on crisp new snow at the summit of the ski area on Cypress Mountain, designated as a provincial park in 1975.

Although Golden Ears Park sits on the rim of metropolitan Vancouver, it contains intact wilderness as well as an extensive system of easily accessible hiking trails.

across the entire North Shore Mountains to connect with Grouse and Seymour mountains. As a result, the growth of cross-country skiing and mountain biking would soon challenge the exclusive use of the park for downhill skiers and commercial operators. In 1981 park boundaries were expanded to include the Lions, the dramatic snow-capped mountain peaks seen from downtown Vancouver, and the Howe Sound Crest Trail, which provided access from the west.

Another major trail-mapping program in southern BC employed special crews to locate 170 kilometres of new trails and relocate another 116 kilometres of existing trails. The Centennial Trail, which starts at Simon Fraser University and takes hikers through the Fraser Valley to Manning Park, was extended a further 48 kilometres east to Cathedral Lake Park. The Simpson River Trail provided access up to Mount Assiniboine from Kootenay National Park via Ferro Pass. Other trails connected Clearwater to Murtle Lake, Cheakamus River to Helm Lake, Atnarko River to Helm Lake and Atnarko River to Turner Lake. Trails in Kokanee, Strathcona, Mount Robson and Assiniboine were improved, and a cable car was built to provide a crossing of the Cheakamus.

New day-use facilities were constructed for Paul Lake, Parrens Beach, China Beach, Big Bar, Porpoise Bay, Blanket Creek and Syringa Creek. Campgrounds at Mount Robson, Lakelse and Kokanee were expanded, and the Lowhee campground was constructed to provide more space for visitors to Barkerville. Very long

Top: The eight hot pools at Liard River Hot Springs flow into an intricate system of swamps where a unique vegetative community thrives.

Above: Once a pioneer homestead, Blanket Creek Park on the shore of the Arrow Reservoir, south of Revelstoke, provides easy access to 12-metre-high Sutherland Falls.

Left: The glaciers of Kokanee Glacier Park in the Selkirk Mountains feed more than 30 small jewel-like lakes.

In summer, visitors may stop at the information and concession centre at Shannon Falls Park. It is only a short walk from there to the falls.

boat launch ramps with extra turnaround pads had to be designed for the day-use facilities at Kikomun Creek and Syringa Creek to accommodate the twenty-four-meter annual fluctuation in reservoir water levels. Numerous lakeshore swimming beaches had to be either man-made or improved with gravel and sand to stabilize muddy bottoms. Often sand flingers were used or the sand was deposited on lakeshores in winter when they were frozen.

The production of display material for nature houses, self-guided trails and outdoor kiosks was shifted from the Langford workshop to on-site Parks workshops. The Interpretation Division developed their own display workshop, produced *The Naturalist's Handbook* and started spring training programs for new staff. Park interpretation programs were expanded to nine more areas, including Black Tusk and Bowron, tripling the number of seasonal naturalists hired. In 1972 specialized programs were begun in Newcastle Island, Horne Lake Caves and Mount Assiniboine alpine. By 1975 there would be nature programs in nearly thirty parks. At Liard Hot Springs Park, where increased tourist traffic was creating pressure to expand and upgrade the pools, an ecological survey was undertaken to document the unique plant life to save it from destruction.

A New Government and a New Era

The election of August 1972 brought in an NDP government, and the new minister of Recreation and Conservation was Bob Williams; he also held down the post of minister of Lands, Forests and Water Resources and served as the chairman of the Environment and Land Use Committee (ELUC), created in 1969. For the next

three and a half years, Parks was given strong support and consistent capital funding. The Branch also benefited from the new government's major policy emphasis on land preservation; this priority led to several landmark programs to identify and designate valuable land for special protection, the enactment of the agricultural land reserve (ALR) legislation to protect both Crown and private agricultural land and new legislation to provide statutory protection for both park status and boundaries. The government also strengthened the role of the ELUC cabinet committee by creating a full-time secretariat to examine the contentious issue of resource management and land allocation.

What had been the BC Land Inventory Group, funded by the Agricultural Rural Development Subsidiary Agreement (ARDSA), became the Resource Analysis Unit or technical arm of the secretariat. With more than one hundred employees, this unit specialized in identifying, mapping and presenting environmental resource values such as land use, vegetative cover, drainage, topography, special features and habitats, hazards and hydrology. Although many innovative resource mapping techniques were now becoming standard practice, much of the unit's mapping was done manually from field notes and air photos and posted on Mylar map sheets, an expensive and time-consuming process. (Later, when the secretariat was disbanded, this group became the Resource Analysis Branch [RAB] in the Ministry of the Environment, and the database they had amassed became the key building block in decision making for a new resource allocation framework.)

The secretariat was responsible for coordinating the application and approval process for all major energy, mineral, hydro, pipeline and transmission line projects,

Above: In Mount Robson Provincial Park a plump yellow-bellied marmot scouts the landscape for a meal of fresh berries and flowers.

Above left: A young mountain goat pauses in an alpine meadow to smile for the camera in remote, roadless Big Creek Provincial Park on the Chilcotin Plateau.

and they produced a planning manual and designed guidelines for a wide range of developments, though it would take several more years before a formal regulatory regime would emerge. Today it is a given that proponents of new resource projects, public or private, must fund and document environmental impact statements (EIS). Failure to do so can result in court challenges. Over time, the preparation of EIS statements and identification of impacts on various users and resources has led property owners, government agencies and Non Governmental Organizations to argue for "mitigation and compensation" as a condition of project approval. In particular, the terms and conditions of licences issued under the Water Act include recognition of recreational, wildlife and fisheries values. Parks and Fish and Wildlife branches have also regularly received funds and land as compensation for highway and hydro projects. The spawning channels at Meadow Creek were built with Columbia Treaty mitigation funds from the Duncan Dam hydro project. Park facilities at Blanket and Syringa creeks on the Arrow Lakes were also funded this way.

In 1973 the Okanagan Similkameen Parks Society (OSPS), with Branch support, proposed an expansion of Cathedral Park but the proposal met with strong protests from lumber and grazing interests as well as the Forest Service. To resolve the controversy, the Environment and Land Use Committee (ELUC) assigned the secretariat to review boundary options and assess economic implications. Their 1975 report concluded that park expansion from 7,300 to 33,000 hectares would have limited negative impact on commercial forest harvests. Still, the forestry sector would only agree to support a high elevation park there if the forested slopes and valley bottoms were retained for forest extraction. This theme of increased protection for valley bottoms would recur through the 1980s in numerous other locations, including the Stein, Carmanah and Valhalla valleys and finally Clayoquot Sound, and the debate would not be resolved until the 1990s.

Legislative Protection for New Parks

Bill 7, passed in 1973 by the new government, provided dramatic amendments to the Park Act. In particular, Schedule A of the amendments provided statutory protection to over seventy existing parks and Schedule B created nine new parks. (Unfortunately, because of several long-standing resource conflicts, Strathcona, Tweedsmuir and Kokanee Glacier were not included and their future protection was delayed by another decade of political discontent.) The amendments also gave precedence to the Park Act over all other statutes except the ELUC Act and the Pollution Control Act. More clarity was also provided on "resource use permits" authorized for non-recreation uses within recreation areas.

Fortunately, to facilitate this strong political support to create new parks, summer planning field reconnaissance two decades earlier had already documented numerous candidates that could readily be brought forward for parks status. They were all on file and simply awaiting a positive political response. A set of "green reports" was published, and nine major dramatic landscapes totalling 635,356 hectares were established as parks or recreation areas. They included Atlin, Carp Lake,

Left: Cape Scott Provincial Park on Vancouver Island is characterized by more than 115 kilometres of ocean frontage stretching from Shushartie Bay to San Josef Bay.

Below: The mountains of remote Atlin Provincial Park in the northwest corner of the province are mirrored in the clear, cold waters of Atlin Lake.

Elk Lakes, Top of the World, Kwadacha, Tatlatui, Naikoon, St. Mary's, Desolation Sound, Okanagan Mountain, Skagit Valley and Cape Scott. Mount Assiniboine was expanded from 5,000 to over 35,000 hectares, providing lowland access via the Simpson and Mitchell river drainages. But even more importantly, these new parks and dozens of existing parks were given statutory protection; in future their status could only be affected by an act of the legislature.

Carp Lake in the north central area of the province is unique in that its boundaries contain a large lake that offers a special fishing opportunity, while the extensive shoreline and small islets provide small boat recreational experience. The park includes portions of the historic trading trail that links Fort St. James on the Stuart River (part of the Fraser River system) to McLeod Lake on the Peace River system.

Naikoon Park in the Queen Charlotte Islands was named after the extensive natural features of Rose Spit ("long nose" in the Haida language) and protects a large portion of the coastal lowland portion of Graham Island where early settlers had tried to drain and farm the extensive bog areas. Remnants of a unique "pole railway" remain. The southern part of this park includes the estuary of the Tlell River, famous as a freshwater fishing site. The creation of Naikoon was not resisted by the forestry sector because this northeast quarter of Graham Island is mainly wetland bog with minimal commercial forest values, whereas parks proposals for the southern half of Moresby Island included part of a tree farm licence (TFL) and were strongly opposed. It would take nearly two more decades to resolve that dispute.

The creation of Cape Scott Provincial Park protected a long stretch of wild beach on the northern tip of Vancouver Island. By coincidence, this park, like the bogland of Naikoon, had been the site of early and unsuccessful attempts at settlement. Both

Nels Bight in Cape Scott Provincial Park is a popular destination for swimmers, but the surf conditions are sometimes intense and there are riptides as well.

parks offer cultural and historic features of both First Nations and early pioneers.

The new Tatlatui Provincial Park incorporates four major lakes at the head of the Finlay River that flows into the Peace River system and from there to the Arctic via the Mackenzie River. This park and Kwadacha, which is southwest of Fort Nelson, were among the first of the large wilderness parks to be created in northern BC. Atlin Park, wedged into the northwest corner of the province, is accessible by road from the Yukon; the large Llewellyn Glacier lies in the southern portion of the park. Elk Lakes, St. Mary's Alpine and Top of the World parks are all in the East Kootenay. Elk Lakes protects the scenic lakes and alpine areas adjacent to the southeast coalfields and the major industrial developments around them.

Desolation Sound is the largest marine park in the system with three separate mooring areas: Grace Harbour, Tenedos Bay and Prideaux Haven. A short walk to Unwin Lake provides a freshwater opportunity. Collectively, this region is a prime destination for hundreds of large and small vessels primarily from Vancouver and Seattle. By the late 1990s this area, along with the adjacent Copeland Islands and Okeover Arm and nearby Von Donop Inlet, Teakerne Arm and Roscoe Bay, also became popular with kayakers. Unfortunately, within the park area many of the best waterfront properties were already privately held and would require future land acquisitions.

Inclusion of a 32,000-hectare recreation area on the Skagit River was a strong political statement that showed that the new government did not support increased flooding by Seattle Light and Power. A new campground was opened there in 1975. The actual resolution of the obligations remaining from the 1941 hydro deal to permit flooding would not be resolved until April 1984 when the Skagit Valley Treaty was signed by the US and Canadian governments, putting an end to the raising of the Ross Dam. It was a major victory for the Run Out Skagit Spoilers (ROSS) organization and strengthened the resolve of other conservation groups.

The Libby Dam

When the Columbia River Treaty was signed in 1961, Canada had agreed that the US could build the Libby Dam on the Kootenai River in Montana, and this dam was finally completed by the US Army Corps of Engineers in August 1975. Lake Koocanusa, the reservoir created behind the 129-metre-high dam, extends 140 kilometres upstream, almost to Fort Steele. The terms of the treaty included a requirement for the US to provide mitigation and compensation to BC for the 68 kilometres of flooding on this side of the border, and once the dam was completed and the water rose, the Parks Branch received its share. The Branch's plan was to create three large-scale swimming lagoons on the new reservoir at Kikomun Creek, and apart from the terracing of the hillside at Okanagan Lake Park, this became the largest earth-moving project undertaken by the Branch in the development of any park in the system. Unfortunately, these facilities were excessive in scale and user demand estimates were never realized, although an adjacent park development at smaller Surveyors Lake proved to be very popular.

The Spatsizi

In December 1975, just three days before the provincial election that would see the NDP ousted and the Social Credit Party returned to power, the cabinet approved an order-in-council that created a 675,000-hectare park on the vast Spatsizi Plateau. Designated a Class A park, it lies between the Stikine Plateau and the Skeena, Cassiar and Omineca mountains and was the first large park to be created with the prime goal of protecting an extensive intact wildlife ecosystem. In most other parks—for example, Wells Gray and Tweedsmuir—the large ungulate populations and the animals that prey on them tend to migrate in and out of park territory. In Spatsizi, on the other hand, there are resident non-migrating populations of Stone's sheep, mountain goats and BC's largest herd of woodland caribou as well as the wolves and grizzly bears that prey on them. However, the new park was to be no exception to the BC Parks' policy of allowing hunting in larger parks (usually from Labour Day to the May 24 weekend), particularly for trophy game ungulates. (In a few near-urban parks on Vancouver Island and the Gulf Islands hunters are allowed the use of shotguns for waterfowl or upland birds.) As in Wells Gray, Cathedral and Edziza, hunting in the new Spatsizi was to be by "limited entry" permit only, a system that divides the allowable permits per species between guide outfitters for their non-resident clients and a public draw open to resident hunters.

In the case of Spatsizi, however, there was to be an exception in the west central portion of the plateau because protection of the wildlife values there had long been promoted by guide outfitters Tommy and Marian Walker. Branch staff suggested that a unique and broader application of ecological reserve legislation should be applied there, and as a result, in this core area of the park no hunting was to be permitted; it was designated the Gladys Lake Ecological Reserve. By coincidence, a short time after this designation, one of the licensed guide outfitters in the area was charged with major offences under the Wildlife Act, and conservation groups went to court to demand an end to all hunting there. Although they lost the case, this incident stimulated widespread public debate about the future allocation of the allowable big-game harvests between provincial residents and the out-of-province clients of guide outfitters; it also encouraged discussion about the rights of First Nations people to exercise their traditional harvesting activities versus the guide outfitters' expectations of game allocations for their exclusive use. Both of these issues are important as guide outfitters' operations are often sold for sums approaching a million dollars. These debates then moved to the question of whether any big-game hunting should be allowed to continue in parks.

In time Spatsizi would be expanded and combined with two adjacent northwestern parks, Tatlatui and Stikine, to cover millions of hectares. When an eighty-one-hectare parcel of land became available on nearby Cold Fish Lake, the Parks Branch partnered with the Nature Trust of BC to acquire it, turning one of the cabins at the former guide outfitters' camp there into park headquarters. Other cabins became available for use by park visitors, most of whom arrive by float plane or helicopter to hike or to canoe or kayak on the nearby Stikine River.

6 :
Parks Branch Restructuring and the Resource Wars, 1976 to 1983

Inventory

By 1976 the provincial parks system was nearly twice the size it had been in 1964—341 parks covering 4.5 million hectares—a total that exceeded the previous zenith of 4.4 million hectares before the cancellation of Liard Provincial Park and the loss of portions of Strathcona, Tweedsmuir and Hamber parks. More importantly,

Above: Smuggler Cove Marine Park provides a small, all-weather anchorage on the south side of Sechelt Peninsula near Secret Cove. Boaters can access it from the north end of Welcome Passage.

a dramatic shift had occurred in the degree of protection afforded to most parks. In contrast to the 1950s when two-thirds of the park system had Class B status, it was now reversed: over one-half of all parklands had been given Class A status and over 400,000 hectares within Class B parks had been designated nature conservancies. And by this time BC parks were seeing over ten million visitors per year.

A Major Branch Reorganization

In late 1974 Tom Lee had been recruited from Ontario Parks to become the new director of BC's Parks Branch. His hiring had been an attempt to inject some new leadership and experience into the Branch, and as Lee familiarized himself with the large and unwieldy system, he began posing questions about the level of park usage, length of stays, fees paid, capital and maintenance costs as well as the cost of visitor services. He assigned the research section the task of finding the answers, and the report they prepared, *Trends in Parks Branch*, was a compendium of facts that included a summary of annual budget allocations and supplementary funding, revenue as a share of operating costs, budget allocations between regions and estimates of the costs per user day for the entire period between 1961 and 1975.

After a year's experience in his new position and armed with this report, Lee issued a three-part report entitled *Parks Branch: A Collective Critique* in which he made it clear that massive changes would have to be made. His observations on the present state of the Parks Branch included the statement that the "relationship between Victoria and field offices can be characterized as ranging from subdued tension to open aggravation." He had found that regional offices were operating with agendas that didn't match those of the Branch, division heads were at odds with regional heads, important policies remained unwritten, programs were unrelated to the clearly stated annual Branch-wide objectives, the Branch really didn't know the cost of operating its parks, budgets were a nightmare of competitive bidding and site planning had become "something in which everyone believes he is an expert, a situation which leads to an interminable parade of on-site visits, prolonged discussion and organizational arguments."

It was a fair assessment of the Branch, its organizational framework, administrative practices and its personalities at the time, although most of Lee's comments also held true for the other resource ministries, most of which were in the process of reorganizing and decentralizing. The Parks Branch had evolved into a huge visitor service agency operating a park system that stretched to the most remote corners of the province, and as a consequence, there had been a tremendous increase in professional staff in the planning and interpretation sections, many of whom were not being effectively utilized, while the gulf between field and headquarters staff had become a bitter divide. Even within headquarters there was a "stovepipe" effect with few proactive exchanges between the planning, engineering and management sections. The Branch had experienced a huge increase in operating budgets, but expenditures were not being planned and there was no proper accounting for monies spent.

Members of the recently reorganized Planning Division at Nootka Court pose for a group photograph, 1975.

Lee's reorganization plan emphasized three elements: the decentralization of services such as system planning, master planning and interpretation from headquarters to regional offices; a sharpened focus on program delivery and accountability with an increased emphasis on resource management and plant maintenance; and a renewed emphasis on research and long-range strategic directions at Parks headquarters. The division of Parks regional administration that had been initiated in 1974 was also finalized. There were now six regional offices and twenty-one district offices, and nearly one-third of the Branch's 248 permanent employees were assigned new duties and/or relocated to regional offices. Headquarters staff were also regrouped into Information and Interpretation, Design and Development, Long Range Planning, Environmental Management and Plant Maintenance. Specialists from the former Engineering unit and site planners were combined in a new Design and Development Services unit that would focus on broader long-range planning. Park-specific planning was to be done by staff transferred to the regional offices. Another new unit, the Program Analysis Division, was given responsibility for providing the staff, skills and information for visitor/user research, program directions, costs and accountabilities that were needed to meet the increasing demands of central agencies, including the Treasury Board, for budget submissions and demonstrations of program accountability.

New Directions

In February 1976 the Long Range Planning unit of Parks produced an internal document called the *Recreation Land Purchase Program*, which contained a rationale as to why the province should fund an accelerated program for property purchases for parks use. Some proposed parks made the list because of regional needs rather than provincial priorities. When this document didn't stimulate immediate

Surveyor Lake was added to Kikomun Creek Park in 1975.

approval from the new Social Credit cabinet, director Lee turned to alternate funding sources. In 1975 he had encouraged the province to sign an agreement with the Devonian Foundation of Alberta to cost share the acquisition of several high-profile properties for development as parks. One limiting factor was the fact that the program had time restrictions, so negotiations had to be confined to those purchases that could be concluded in short order. The properties acquired included Winter Cove on Saturna Island, Tribune Bay on Hornby Island, the upland and lagoon portion of Sidney Spit, Porteau Cove on Howe Sound, Bear Creek Delta on Okanagan Lake and Surveyor Lake as an addition to Kikomun Creek Park. (Both Winter Cove and Sidney Spit were later transferred to the federal government for inclusion in the Gulf Islands National Park Reserve.)

The acquisition of Tribune Bay, including a small resort, was not entirely popular with local people who were concerned that park status would increase public visits to their island. The former resort is now used as an outdoor education centre by the school district. Porteau Cove provided a unique challenge for the negotiators because an active BC Rail line bisects it, and the Bear Creek Delta was the focus of a large log sorting operation for Crown–Zellerbach.

In June 1977 the Branch again tested the waters with an unpublished report called "The Park Proposal Program," which presented sixty-six candidates for the continued expansion of the park system. All of the sites met both the natural history and recreation objectives of the Branch, and the report was predicated on the expectation that the new government would continue to support an expanded parks mandate much as the previous government had. Results would prove the contrary to be true. And although the proposed parks had been presented only as "areas of interest," the report was generally viewed as a shopping list and caused considerable angst among the other resource ministries, especially Fish and Wildlife. This was not unexpected as Parks and Fish and Wildlife had a history of failing to recognize their mutual interests and common ground in conservation, habitat protection, wildlife management and public information and had generally operated as rival agencies. Now, increasingly, Fish and Wildlife staff and their public voice, the hunting and fishing interests of the BC Wildlife Federation, were opposing many new park proposals.

Meanwhile, the new government was making major changes in how ministry functions were assigned and grouped together, challenging the traditional linkages. In 1977 the department of Lands was separated from the Forest Service, and along with Water Resources and Fish and Wildlife, formed the core of a new Ministry of the Environment. And since the Environment minister chaired the Environment and Land Use Committee (ELUC), the ELUC secretariat was also included in the new ministry.

At the same time the Ministry of Recreation and Conservation was given a new Information and Education Branch to centralize all budgeting and publication services, including those of the Parks Branch, and within Parks, the natural history focus of the Interpretation program was broadened to incorporate recreation and First Nations heritage.

A restructured Recreation and Fitness Branch was tasked to deal with the questions of wilderness use policy, concerns for public safety—particularly the role of commercial recreation operators involved with river rafting and heli-skiing—and boating regulations, which, though a federal responsibility, was dependent on recommendations from the province.

Heritage Conservation

In September 1977 the legislature approved a broad-based Heritage Conservation Act, which created the need for a separate Heritage Conservation Branch that would be responsible for inventory, research and planning functions for all provincial heritage resources, including archeological and historic sites. Several Parks headquarters staff were transferred to the new branch, although until 1986 Parks retained responsibility for the operation, maintenance and interpretation of the existing heritage parks—Barkerville and Fort Steele. No one was well served by these changes as both Parks and Heritage Branch planners and managers were too often preoccupied by jurisdictional issues. The Heritage Act also created the Heritage Trust, which was given the power to provide cost-share funding for community heritage initiatives, allowing municipal governments to designate local heritage structures. This change, which shifted the emphasis away from regional growth and heritage theme parks to urban heritage architecture, was disappointing to Parks staff, but it did much to change public attitudes and give local governments the regulatory tools and funds to protect historic buildings at risk to redevelopment and urban growth. Downtown Victoria and the Revelstoke Courthouse were early projects that benefited from this new emphasis.

The Adams River: A New Kind of Park

One of the first tests of the role of regional Parks directors as members of a Regional Resource Management Committee (RRMC) had occurred in 1974 when the Branch proposed park status for the Adams River. The creation of this park was very important for two reasons. First, although chinook, coho, pink and sockeye salmon all spawn in this river, it is the spectacle of the dominant run of sockeye spawning here every four years that is—along with Stanley Park, Long Beach and Cathedral Grove in MacMillan Park—one of the most well-known natural features in BC. It was, therefore, vitally necessary to protect the water flows, quality of water and the spawning beds from adverse land use impacts. Second, the massive four-year spawning cycle attracts tens of thousands of visitors, which is remarkable considering that, although adjacent to the Trans-Canada Highway, the spawning area is not located near an urban centre. If the river was to be given park status, this nationally—even internationally—recognized area would have five major management issues: (1) acquisition of the several in-holdings and provision of funding, (2) protection and management of this valuable fish resource and its pristine habitat, (3) provision of recreational and parking facilities, (4) organization and delivery of large-scale public education/interpretation programs, and (5) rehabilitation of resource scars from gravel pits and hydro lines and management of traffic on nearby through roads.

The opportunity to observe spawning sockeye salmon attracts tens of thousands of visitors to the Adams River in Roderick Haig-Brown Provincial Park every four years. *iStock*

In the years since 1974 the RRMC had struggled valiantly to reach consensus on the Parks proposal for the Adams River site, but Lands, Forest, and Fish and Wildlife representatives had continued to argue the case for designating it a wildlife management area, similar to the Creston Valley Wildlife Management Area that had been created in 1968. But this was not a good precedent as the Creston site was managed by a local board with limited funds to provide visitor services or undertake capital works. This was not the model Parks had in mind for the Adams River. The Kamloops regional parks director fought a rearguard action by preparing a minority report to support an appeal to the ELUC deputy minister's sub-committee. This report finally tipped the balance in favour of Parks, and in

1977 the ELUC directed that the Adams River salmon spawning area should be designated a recreation area.

The Parks Branch reasoned that, if the habitat was protected, the salmon would generally take care of themselves so no active fish husbandry or enhancement measures were necessary. Instead, it was more critical to provide for and manage the impacts of the enormous gatherings of people who were coming to observe the spawning ritual. Therefore, it would be necessary to organize adequate parking and visitor services and properly located trail and visitor viewing platforms. Meanwhile, using funds from the Greenbelt Fund and a cooperative partnership with the Second Century Fund (founded in 1971 with a $4.5 million grant from the federal government and later renamed the Nature Trust of BC) and the federal government, the Branch acquired eighteen hectares of private river frontage that would otherwise have been developed for residential and commercial or tourist uses. One of these purchases required special sensitivity: the property in question was owned by a Japanese Canadian family who had chosen this location to re-establish their lives after being internees during World War II. Staff then worked hard to recognize and accommodate the interests of other agencies and local First Nations who controlled the southern bank of the river. As part of their commitment, Parks also prepared a detailed resource analysis of critical fish habitat areas.

The 988-hectare Adams River recreation area was dedicated in 1977 and named for Roderick Haig-Brown, the eminent salmon conservationist and writer. To celebrate the opening, the Parks Branch display studios produced twelve outdoor education panels to support the interpretation programs for visitors coming to view the salmon spawning, and the first Salute to the Salmon, conducted in cooperation with the Department of Fisheries and Oceans (DFO), was mounted in 1978. Subsequent Salutes have been attended by as many as 200,000 visitors. In 1991 Roderick Haig-Brown became a full Class A park. Today a joint management committee known as the Adams River Salmon Society, which includes Parks, Fish and Wildlife, the DFO, First Nations and community groups, is responsible for planning and delivering a range of visitor services, including public education, school programs and concession stands.

Environmental Management

By the late 1970s the Parks Branch had recognized the need to pay more attention to its role as landlord. However, even producing accurate legal descriptions of parks and boundary maps posed difficulties at this time since much of the Parks system was comprised of unsurveyed rural lands. The Branch's solution was a new Environmental Management Division with three units: Land Administration, Land Acquisition, and Resources (wildlife, water, forest cover and soils).

One of the tasks of the Land Administration unit was to deal with tenures and uses that predated park status. Many new parks of the 1970s came with traplines, grazing licences, foreshore tenures, access roads, railways, water licences and, of course, mineral claims. (At this time there were 730 valid mineral claims in parks and recreation areas in BC although no active exploration approvals were granted.) No central registry of titles, encumbrances and approvals existed at this time so that all licences, claims, leases, permits and even public road allowances had to be searched and dealt with separately. Imposing park status had not necessarily extinguished any of these uses and rights. For example, the road to Cypress Bowl was built by the Ministry of Highways using public funds, and thus was a public highway and technically not part of the park so the Parks Branch did not have full legal authority to limit public access or control roadside parking by hikers and cross-country skiers. The lower part of the highway system went through a private property whose owners wanted road access for a housing development, and this upset municipal officials. Resolving these issues required negotiations, exchanges, purchases and transitional use plans, and in some cases it took a decade or more to find a satisfactory resolution.

Bowron Lake Provincial Park is a wildlife sanctuary, where canoeists and kayakers can photograph moose, bears, caribou, deer and mountain goats.

Another responsibility handed to the Land Administration unit was the maintenance of the Branch's 2,800 files accumulated over the years that provided the details of all the parks and UREPs in the province, but since the planning staff had been regionalized, all these files and maps had to be updated and copied and sent to regional offices. The unit also created a standardized set of maps and land

Lakelse Lake Provincial Park preserves impressive stands of old-growth cedar, hemlock and Sitka spruce, which thrive in the moist air swept in from the Pacific Ocean.

status files—"green files"—for all 347 parks and recreation areas. They began this task with maps of the parks of Vancouver Island. The role of the Land Acquisition unit was very complex. Unlike real estate agents who usually represent the seller in private negotiations, Parks property negotiators are agents of the Crown tasked to purchase property, but they work within given fiscal limits and are subject to financial administration procedures and public accountability. And because they are spending public funds and the details of acquisitions and exchanges are subject to public scrutiny, freedom of information requests and internal audits, staff must be scrupulous in their negotiations and carefully document and exercise their fiduciary obligations.

The first task of the acquisition unit's negotiators was the completion of the land assembly for Long Beach and the Broken Group Islands of Pacific Rim National Park. When this job was completed, the land acquisitions group turned its attention to the more remote West Coast Trail portion of the park. Here, logging licences that ranged into the tens of millions of dollars in value were exchanged for cutting rights elsewhere. Owners of several small holdings in this sector were less amenable to selling, and these negotiations would take until the late 1990s to be resolved. A decade after the creation of Pacific Rim Park over $12 million had been spent on more than 250 parcels of land.

The Resources unit dealt with issues such as the management of forest cover in parks. In Bowron Lake Park a massive blowdown raised the question of increased fire hazard and pest infestation, and the Forest Service proposed a program of timber salvage to reduce the impact on adjacent commercial forest values. However, the new regional director and a professional forester reviewed the situation and recommended that no logging cleanup be undertaken; it was one of the first instances where the Branch tested the concept of parks as places for natural processes to occur without intervention. The same issue arose with regard to allowing wildfires to burn out without intervention unless they threaten facilities, visitors or adjacent forests.

The incidence of root rot in mature forests within parks raised concerns about the stability of large trees in high-use areas, particularly in campgrounds. Over time this would raise the question of the government's liability for events arising from known hazards. In Lakelse Park tree surveys suggested that almost the entire forest cover was in danger and should be removed, but when the initial clearing created a public outcry, staff implemented a more gradual annual pruning program. In Cathedral Grove, it was decided that the trees, while hazards, were not of sufficient risk to be pruned or removed since the park is a day-use-only area and visitor exposure is for shorter periods of time. Instead, park visitors face warning signs advising them to leave the park in periods of high winds. Selective tree removals were undertaken in the Ralph River campground in Strathcona after a visitor fatality occurred. In Goldstream several vehicles were damaged by falling trees. As a result, in 1978 a Tree Hazard Program was formalized, and a new handbook was published as a guide to evaluate possible hazards and risks.

The Ministry of Lands, Parks and Housing

In late 1978 yet another major re-organization of government departments brought together elements from Recreation and Conservation, Municipal Affairs and the Ministry of Environment in a brand new Ministry of Lands, Parks and Housing (MLPH). Parks was split off from its long-standing links with Tourism, Fish and Wildlife, Heritage, Sports and Leisure. In a sense, this restructuring marked the beginning of the breakup of a comprehensive Parks Branch, which had been a model of integrated services.

As part of the process of identifying its role, in May 1979 the new cabinet disbanded the Environment and Land Use Committee (ELUC) secretariat and gave its responsibilities to a new Assessment and Planning Branch in the new Ministry of Environment, instantly creating a fresh battlefield among the ministries to claim the lead for the management of Crown lands. MLPH also issued a major document called *Policy for Parks and Outdoor Recreation* that set out the Parks Division's role within the province's outdoor recreation activities and services sector. Among the new responsibilities for the Environment and Resource Management group was the management of all the historic artefacts and machinery scattered around the province's parks and heritage sites. Unhappily, it was almost a futile exercise as Barkerville and Fort Steele alone had become the recipients of enormous regional artefact collections with overwhelming requirements for cataloguing, storage and restoration.

The Resource Wars

By the mid-1970s the forest industry had become concerned about encroachment on and loss of forest lands, and the Forest Service had reacted by re-examining the manner in which it managed Crown forests and determined the annual harvest rates and how it issued forest tenures and cutting rights. At that time 80 percent of the provincial land base was owned by the Crown, with Vancouver Island being the only region with significant private forest land. But while the forest industry was worrying about its timber supply, there was also a growing public awareness of the effect of logging practices on other forest values such as wildlife, fish, water and scenery, and in 1976 the NDP government had responded by asking Dr. Peter Pearse, already well known for his review of the fisheries and water resource sectors, to lead his first Royal Commission on timber rights and forest policy. His report, as well as outlining a new system of timber supply areas and annual allowable cuts, urged an increased emphasis on the stewardship of forest and range lands, including watershed management and long-term timber supply.

The NDP, however, was defeated before Pearse turned in his report, so that the new legislation enacted in 1977 to replace the Forest Act of 1912 bore the imprint of the Social Credit Party's business and industry philosophy. Under the new act, the Forest ministry's mandate included the following purposes and functions: (1) to encourage maximum productivity of forest and range resources: (2) to manage, conserve and protect forest and range resources; and (3) to plan the use of the forest and range resources of the Crown so that the production of timber and forage, the

Right: Logging on Moresby Island, 1961. Although the southern half of Moresby was included in Gwaii Haanas National Park Reserve in 2010, loggers still make their livelihoods in the rich cedar, pine and western hemlock forests of the northern half.
BC Archives, NA-21333

Below: "Who cooks for you, who cooks for you all." Barred owls, common in British Columbia's densely wooded parks, are more often heard than seen.
Dean van't Schip

harvesting of timber, the grazing of livestock and realization of fisheries, wildlife, water, outdoor recreation and other natural resource values are coordinated and integrated, in consultation and cooperation with other ministries and agencies of the Crown and with the private sector.

In pragmatic terms, carrying out this third function meant a concerted drive to expand the amount of forested land designated as provincial forests and remove these lands from the jurisdiction of the Land Act. This drive included an aggressive campaign to prevent any further loss of timber supply to new parks. The ministry also adopted a policy of integrated resource management—a term introduced to replace the somewhat discredited term "multiple use"—by asserting the right to provide forest recreation opportunities as alternatives to parks. This new philosophy appealed to grazing and wildlife interests who felt threatened by exclusion from the growing park system. The mining sector also supported it, generally opposing any new parks until after exploration had confirmed only nominal mineral values within proposed park areas; by this means they successfully stalemated park proposals in Chilko, Taseko and Tatlayoka lakes for two decades. On the other hand, the Forest Service's proposal to extend provincial forest status over Moresby Island in the Queen Charlottes met strong opposition from public groups and First Nations who were promoting park status.

The jurisdiction of the Provincial Forest Service now greatly superseded the Lands Branch as managers of Crown land in British Columbia, and between 1979 and 1984 provincial forest lands were increased from thirty million hectares to over seventy million. Non-forest uses were now administered by authority of Special Use Permits (SUPs) that were issued under the Forest Act rather than by Land

The lakes and ponds of Kentucky Alleyne Provincial Park, 38 kilometres south of Merritt, are stocked annually with rainbow trout from the Summerland Trout Hatchery.

Act leases and licences. A number of blocks of Crown land that had been proposed either as parks or for disposition as private agricultural tenures were "deferred," a designation that meant their fate would be reviewed after December 1981. Some thirty-five of these deferred blocks would in time become the focus of special planning studies, but the majority were subsequently designated provincial forests. In the north Kakwa, Fiordland and Hakai became deferred areas, their designation only resolved after 1985.

By 1979 the Forest Branch was maintaining or had improved over 2,100 kilometres of trails in their 980 forest recreation areas, particularly on Vancouver Island and the Thompson Plateau, though they were confined to small sites easily accessed by road. Soon more and more provincial residents were turning to these sites in response to increased user fees and visitor security measures in parks, and some sites suffered from such heavy use that their primitive facilities needed upgrades to prevent degradation of the forests and ground cover. A typical case was Whiteswan Lake, which experienced garbage problems, damage to vegetation and parking area overflows, so that it became necessary to install traffic control, an enlarged parking area, more toilet facilities and a boat launching ramp. This scenario was repeated at other Forest Service and Fish and Wildlife sites where popular fishing spots were overwhelmed by heavy visitor-use pressures, and within a decade many of them—Kentucky–Alleyne, Pennask, Tunkwa and Trout lakes—would be turned over to the Parks Branch.

Long-Planned Parks

By the end of the 1970s, although the Parks capital budget was almost non-existent, several new parks were created. All had been in the planning stage for many years but fortunately none of them required a large outlay of funds. The first was a marine park system that was put in place in 1980 for Sechelt Inlet. This Sunshine Coast waterway, known locally as the "inland sea," is composed of three deep, narrow fjords—Sechelt, Salmon and Narrows—that provide 350 kilometres of sheltered, uninhabited coastline with a hinterland of steep, forested mountains. There was some urgency to establish marine parks here as this inlet system was the heart of the salmon farming industry at that time, and pens were in place in most of the bays and coves; however, within a decade all but one of the salmon farming companies were gone as the waters proved too warm for the successful raising of net-penned fish and prone to devastating algal blooms. The Sechelt Inlets Marine Provincial Park is a collection of eight marine camping sites covering a total of 155 hectares that have become enormously popular with canoeists and kayakers. In December 1992 the Artificial Reef Society sank the Canadian navy destroyer *Chaudiere* off Kunechin Point at the junction of Sechelt and Salmon inlets to provide a dive site for scuba divers.

Shuswap Lake Marine Provincial Park was also designated in 1980 to become the first inland lakes marine system of parks. It was the culmination of aggressive leadership by the Parks Branch's Kamloops regional office to obtain park status for

This view of Gambier and Keats islands was taken at sunrise from the top of Panther Peak in Tetrahedron Provincial Park on the Sunshine Coast. *Dean van't Schip*

Right: Each of the old Kettle Valley Railway tunnels in Coquihalla Canyon Provincial Park was bored through solid granite.

Below: The Coquihalla River flows through a deep, twisting granite channel, dropping 1,000 metres in 53 kilometres and creating an incessant roar.

numerous reserves that had been set aside for the Use, Recreation and Enjoyment of the Public (UREP) along the extensive shoreline of this popular lake. Today these sites are a central feature of a boat access system that services a large fleet of commercial houseboats rented in Sicamous. Later Parks would extend this multi-site concept to other large lakes such as Kootenay, Babine and Arrow.

During that same year the Lands Branch was able to expand on its "rails to trails" policy by acquiring the rights-of-way for three more sections of the abandoned CPR Kettle Valley rail line from Penticton east to Grand Forks and Castlegar. A decade earlier Lands had bought the rights to the western section of the line, running from Hope via the Coquihalla through to the Okanagan, and hikers and a few bikers had made good use of it. Now, with the route extended into the Kootenay–Boundary district, the trail would become even more popular, especially for the rapidly expanding sport of mountain biking. Unfortunately, the southern branch line running from Penticton south to Oliver and Osoyoos had been sold to private landowners.

Other park developments that year included a seventy-unit campground at

French Beach Provincial Park, which fronts on the Strait of Juan de Fuca, is a great place to watch the spring gray whale northward migration.

Previous pages: The beautiful Gwillim Lakes in the Valhalla range of the Selkirk Mountains offer canoeing and kayaking opportunities. *All Canada Photos, J.A. Kraulis*

French Beach on the road to Port Renfrew, the first new family destination park along the bottom end of Vancouver Island. Large near-urban parks were opened at Porteau Cove and Bear Creek. On the West Coast at China Creek an access road, boat launch and high density campground was opened for salmon fishermen using the Alberni Inlet. The 32,000-hectare Monkman Park became the first new mid-sized park in several years. It is unique in that it was promoted by the province in support of the British Columbia Resources Investment Corporation's creation of Tumbler Ridge, the townsite that was established in 1981, along with new highways and road connections, to service the northeast coal industry. However, some viewed the new park as a cynical move by cabinet to defer criticism of the sector's economic prospects.

The year closed with Anthony Island (now known as SGang Gwaay) at the southernmost end of the chain of Queen Charlotte Islands being designated a World Heritage Site by UNESCO. Back in 1957 this island, the site of Ninstints, a Native village with remnant totem poles, had become the first provincial park to protect aboriginal heritage. While a positive step, this early designation had merely focussed public pressure for a much larger park in the southern Queen Charlottes, possibly with national status. This campaign did not receive political support until 1987; Anthony Island is now part of the much larger Gwaii Haanas National Park.

On March 3, 1983, Valhalla was given park status. This 49,600-hectare area that encompasses most of the Valhalla Range of the Selkirk Mountains and stretches for more than twenty-five kilometres along the west shore of Slocan Lake, was one of the province's first large valley bottom-to-mountaintop parks. It was also one of the first major park proposals where leadership came entirely from outside the Parks Branch. The Valhallas had been first proposed for protection in 1970 by the Kootenay Mountaineering Club, but it was not until they were joined by the Valhalla Wilderness Society, a conservation organization formed in 1975, that they had their first success: a logging moratorium for the mountain slopes. The campaign that followed, which included a series of controversial agency and public planning processes, marked a significant new direction in public debate regarding the future use of Crown land. Using music and scenic video productions, these groups argued that regional tourism was a valid reason for new parks, and they prepared a study that predicted tourism would triple in the area, generating $3 million in economic benefits and 175 jobs.

Unfortunately, the Slocan Valley, while not remote, is off the main highway system and not even a minor tourist destination, and the park does not offer ready access or recreational opportunities that are likely to attract large numbers of park visitors. A 1989 report called *Economic Impacts of Land Allocation for Wilderness: A Retro Analysis of Valhalla Park*, prepared by Clayton Resources for the forest industry, concluded that the projected indirect "economic gains to the region from park status and tourism" (not including park visits) had not occurred. However, given that the Slocan region as a whole has not become a major tourist destination, it is not surprising that the economic impact of the park has fallen short of expectations and has seen limited regional development spinoffs. It is a result that suggests more caution should be used in arguing the economic case for new parks.

(In 2008 the Valhalla Society supported an initiative by the Land Conservancy of BC [TLC] to purchase a sixty-three-hectare parcel of private land known as the Valhalla Mile that is a vital shoreline movement corridor for wildlife and would protect the ecological integrity of the adjacent park. On April 8, 2009, the provincial government announced the acquisition of the Valhalla Mile property, which was appraised at $1.625 million. The partnership that funded this purchase was coordinated by the Land Conservancy of BC; funding included $700,000 from the BC government, a $325,000 Ecogift from the vendor, Burkhard Franz, under the Ecological Gifts Program of Environment Canada, and $600,000 raised by TLC and the Valhalla Foundation for Ecology and Social Justice.)

Valhalla Provincial Park includes habitat for a variety of large mammals, including mountain goats as well as cougars, grizzly and black bears and mule and whitetail deer. *Bill Merilees*

7 :
Changing Government and Policy Shifts, 1983 to 1991

Restraint and its Aftermath

In May 1983 in the midst of a province-wide recession Bill Bennett's Social Credit government was re-elected and began an immediate program of budget cuts and downsizing. The Public Sector Act and Public Sector Labour Relations Act, which allowed the implementation of dramatic changes to financial commitments and collective agreements with government employees, prompted a great outcry by organized labour that resulted in civil unrest, but the government persisted. In the

Above: Encompassing more than 120,000 hectares of land and sea north of Port Hardy, the Hakai Luxvbalis Conservancy is the largest provincial marine protected area on the BC coast.

downsizing that followed, the Ministry of Highways had to replace its own-force maintenance with five-year regional service contracts, the Ministry of Forests' seed nurseries were privatized and the Ministry of Agriculture closed both Colony and Tranquille farms.

The Parks Branch was not spared. Vince Collins, who became the executive director for Parks at this time, led the implementation of "significant initiatives that streamlined program delivery, reduced operating costs and maintained levels of service."[7] Among the "significant initiatives" was the contracting out of services. Although parklands would remain under public ownership and control, the private sector would be invited to operate parks and campgrounds. In addition, the private sector would be used exclusively for site design of all capital improvements to parks and the manufacture of park furnishings. This final initiative meant the closing of the Langford Workshop that had provided park furniture and signs for thirty-four years.

The Kootenay, Nanaimo and Skeena regional offices were closed, leaving Parks with three regions and twelve districts, plus two historic parks. Between September 1983 and the summer of 1984, using a combination of layoffs, early retirements and re-assignments, full-time staff numbers were reduced from 411 to 288 and seasonal full-time employees cut from 300 to 269. The engineering unit was disbanded, the entire draughting section was re-assigned to mapping duties in the Crown Land Registry, and the outdoor recreation section was disbanded and its staff disbursed. As summertime visitor services would now be handled by independent contract, there was an immediate end to the hiring of hundreds of seasonal employees. It was a sad note that the last of the original park "elders" Director CJ Velay was forced to give early retirement or layoff notices to many of the field staff he had recruited in the 1950s .

The Growth of Private Service Delivery

The Branch gradually adopted the government's policy of private delivery of park visitor services, though at first the changes were felt mainly in the North and the Kootenays and did not include full-scale park management. Instead, contracts were let for specific services such as the provision of firewood, garbage collection and toilet services. However, by the end of the 1984 season, 40 parks were managed under visitor service contracts, while 101 contracts were for specific services. The cost of these contracts exceeded $1.3 million. Volunteer hosts served in another 12 parks. By 1985–86, the number of parks under private contract was up to 76, with another 112 receiving specified services.

In an attempt to monitor the performance of the new service providers, the Branch began measuring success factors such as cost per visit and campsite occupancy. As a result, a rather brief 1984 Parks annual report made the first use of "resource management" and "visitor services" indicators with comparisons going back to 1980–81. The report also revealed that the current cost of service per visitor was $1.60. The following year the Branch instituted a formal program of visitor satisfaction surveys.

New Ski Area Policy

The new directives meant that all of the lifts and lodges in Cypress Bowl and the Gibson Pass ski area of Manning Park were to operate as private enterprises under commercial contracts, and in 1986 in order to encourage investment in upgrades and expansion, the operators were issued fifty-year park use permits (PUPs). As a result, all of the existing facilities in Cypress Bowl and Mount Seymour and the right to operate them for fifty years were sold for approximately $500,000. In Manning Park, even with private operators, Gibson Pass remained a minor operation.

A cross-country skier enjoys the backcountry trails of Manning Park, easily accessible from the Hope-Princeton Highway.

Of the ski hills originally within parks, only Apex, Silver Star, Hudson Bay Mountain and Red Mountain have grown beyond their roles as community ski hills to regional status, and of these four only Silver Star is considered a major destination ski resort. After increased skier use at Silver Star created pressure to expand the service facilities and provide "on the mountain" overnight accommodation, plans were approved for an expanded village, and the land base needed for residential units was removed from the park. This facilitated investment from the private sector, but also made it accountable for management and infrastructure, water and sewerage. However, extensive surrounding natural areas that are used for snowmobiling and cross-country skiing remain under park status.

The Lands Branch also approved leasehold agreements for four new private ski areas—Blackcomb, Mount Washington, Big White and Tod Mountain—and henceforth, except for heli-skiing in Wells Gray and the Bugaboos, pressure for new resorts on Crown land has been for areas outside of provincial parks. On Vancouver Island, the privately operated Mount Washington Alpine Resort replaced the Parks Branch's Forbidden Plateau/Wood Mountain as the major regional ski hill. Over the next three decades all of the major destination ski hills in BC—Whistler/Blackcomb, Mount Washington, Sun Peaks, Big White, Panorama, Mount Fernie and Kimberley—would be private developments outside of parks.

An interesting parks visitor issue arose for Mount Assiniboine Park when the adjacent Sunshine Ski Resort area was expanded. Improved access and the introduction of summer lift operation meant hundreds of visitors began making day visits to the alpine meadows, and this required significant improvements to trail systems by the Parks Branch.

Opposite: A backcountry skier airs off a crevasse in Mount Assiniboine Provincial Park. *All Canada Photos, Ryan Creary*

Climbers from around the world are drawn to the glacier-sculpted granite spires of Bugaboo Provincial Park in the Purcell Mountains.

The Wells Gray Mineral Claims

In 1985 the Supreme Court of Canada ruled on the validity of mining claims in Wells Gray Park that were held by a prospector named David Tener. Since the BC government had amended the Parks Act in 1973 to make it illegal to mine within a park without a park use permit (PUP), Tener had been unable to develop his claims because he had been refused a permit. After five fruitless years of trying to force the government to give him a permit or compensate him, Tener had sued the province for the capital value of the mineral resources within his claims, his wasted expenditures and his anticipated profits. The case had wound its way through the lower courts, ending up in the Supreme Court of Canada where the ruling finally provided some clarity on the question of mines in parks. The justices ruled that Tener's property rights had included not only the mineral rights but also sufficient access to develop a mine on the property and that the effect of the Park Act's amendment had amounted to "expropriation without compensation." The holders of valid mineral claims in parks, the Court asserted, could not be denied the right to explore them and, if the holders had been refused a park use permit, they would have to be compensated.

The previous provincial policy of permitting mineral claim staking in parks had now placed the government in the position of either approving exploration and development of those claims or buying up all the claims within parks. This decision was particularly distressing to the author, whose acquisitions unit had in the late 1970s negotiated a "quit claim" settlement for a nominal sum on a group of claims in a park but had not received executive approval to pay the money out. Subsequently the claims holder took legal action, and with this new court decision the process of acquiring his claims became very expensive. Over time the province would pay out in excess of $100 million to acquire the mineral rights in numerous parks.

Expo 86

Although it was well known that Expo 86—the World Exposition on Transportation and Communication—coincided with the centennial of Vancouver's founding, it passed almost unnoticed that 1986 was also the seventy-fifth anniversary of BC's first provincial park. But the previous decade had been traumatic for the provincial parks system and the Parks Branch. Fiscal restraint had caused a significant decline in funding and staffing, new park proposals had met concerted opposition from other agencies and their resource sector clients, and parks facilities had been poorly maintained. Then suddenly in the run-up to Expo and in the midst of a "Beautiful BC" campaign to encourage visitors to Expo to stay longer and see more of the province, someone in the government recognized the significance of provincial parks as a central element of beautiful BC. In contrast to several years of reduced funding, suddenly there was $6.5 million in special funds to upgrade parks facilities. Funding for parks publications was also increased to encourage tourists. This was the first new capital funding in almost ten years and provided the first signs of an improved climate for parks.

As part of the Expo tourist blitz, the brown and white lettering of parks highway signs were replaced with blue ones. A parks marketing campaign included portable mall displays and filming in eighteen parks for the *BC Moments* series, still shown on Knowledge Network two decades later. All of this promotion resulted in a very heavy tourist season and a record increase in provincial park attendance—over 17.48 million visits.

The Wilderness Advisory Commission

While Expo had increased tourism in BC and a new ski hills policy had increased winter recreation possibilities, there was still a growing movement within the general public for more protection for wilderness areas, especially those threatened by logging and mining companies. In 1980 a new group known as the Western Canada Wilderness Committee (WCWC) had registered as a society with the aim of building broad public support for protecting ecosystems and biodiversity. By researching, publishing and distributing information about threatened wilderness and collaborating with other environmental groups, such as the Haida Nation, the Islands Protection Society and the Valhalla Wilderness Society, they soon became an important element in the parks versus resource exploitation battles.

By the mid-1980s conflicts were escalating between conservation and resource development factions over the wilderness areas of BC. At the same time there was a growing public awareness that these lands had values for both recreation and resource uses and that planning processes needed to be changed to manage the conflicts between the two sides. Late in 1985 the government finally responded by appointing a special independent Wilderness Advisory Commission (WAC), which included blue ribbon representatives from conservation groups and academia as well as the mining and forestry industries. The WAC was tasked with "considering the place of wilderness in a changing society," and its mandate was to hold public hearings on sixteen proposals for wilderness protection (both within and outside of areas that were already protected), the modification of the boundaries of eight existing protected areas, including Pacific Rim National Park, and "general land use principles, allocation guidelines and administrative practices, whether existing, experimental, or proposed in the province and elsewhere."

The commission received over one thousand written submissions and two hundred oral presentations. Among the former was a Parks Branch submission that outlined the history, objectives and plans for provincial parks and ecological reserves and included specific recommendations regarding boundary changes to eight parks. This presentation was unusual in that during most public commissions the government seeks independent outside advice and seldom are government staff or agencies allowed to go "on public record" and make a submission. The presentation by the Canadian Parks and Wilderness Society (CPAWS) was also a positive contribution in support of parks. This non-profit group, which had founded a BC chapter in 1979, devotes its members' energies exclusively to conserving this country's wilderness heritage. Its rational and comprehensive submission along with that of the Parks Branch was enormously important in shaping the WAC's final recommendations.

The WAC report, entitled *Wilderness Mosaic*, delivered to the government on March 7, 1986, did not resolve all of the issues related to parks because the commissioners were constrained by the specific terms of reference and the fact that two contentious proposals—the Stein Valley and the Carmanah/Walbran area—had not been assigned to their review. But despite the disparate interests of its members, the report provided a united voice and specific recommendations for resolving the issues presented to it. This remarkable consensus was followed by a generally compliant government response to implement the recommendations. Over 850,000 hectares of new parks were to be created including Brooks Peninsula on the remote northwest coast of Vancouver Island, Akamina–Kishinena in the farthest southeast corner of the province next to Waterton Glacier National Park, and Khutzeymateen, which is located at the end of a remote inlet on the north coast and just south of the Nass Valley and is intended to protect intact habitat for the grizzly bear. Additions to Strathcona, Wells Gray, Kokanee, Tweedsmuir, Manning and Stone Mountain parks were also approved, although in some cases these were balanced by deletions. For example, in Wells Gray, the Trophy Mountain area was added to the southern tip of the park and the Flourmills area to the western boundary while an approximately equivalent area in the Pendleton Lakes region was deleted because it had lower park values. Portions of Tweedsmuir and Strathcona were upgraded from Class B to Class A status.

Fourteen new protected areas were approved for recreation area status where

The glacially gouged inlets of the Fiordland Conservancy, which includes Kynoch and Mussel inlets, are surrounded by dense forests that are home to both grizzly and black bears.

Previous pages: The Grand Canyon of the Stikine River, seen here from the air, is 75 kilometres long and 300 metres deep.
All Canada Photos, Gary Fiegehen

no logging would be permitted but mineral exploration would be allowed. The largest of these was the Stikine River corridor, which links Mount Edziza and Spatsizi parks. However, this designation failed to satisfy activists because the greatest danger to the Stikine was not logging but mineral exploitation. It would be another decade before full protection was granted.

The new 123,000-hectare Hakai Recreation Area, which covered an important access to the south end of the Inside Passage adjacent to the world-famous Rivers Inlet salmon fishing area, instantly became the largest marine park of the coast. The new Fiordland Recreation Area protects a north coast inlet that abuts the Kitlope and actually provides a continuum of protected area from the north end of Tweedsmuir Park west to tidewater. The Parks regional office staff in Prince George now found themselves responsible for several coastal parks with large estuary habitats, where visitor management and safety had to be balanced against protection of a dynamic salmon–grizzly interface. Two other WAC recommendations were positive steps but failed to meet expectations of environmental groups and First Nations: the WAC proposed that only a portion of South Moresby Island in the Queen Charlotte Islands should be recommended for national park status and that Windy Bay on Lyall Island only be designated as an eco-reserve.

The upper reaches of the heavily glaciated Stein watershed are dotted with small mountain lakes or tarns.

Apart from recommendations for specific new parks, the WAC report offered administrative solutions to end the bickering over other park proposals. First, it suggested that the government adopt a policy whereby new park proposals disputed

by the mining sector would be initially designated as recreation areas. If mineral reserves were not proven within ten years, these areas were to be reclassified as Class A parks and given legislative protection. This compromise satisfied no one but was implemented. Second, the report recommended it was unnecessary to designate all scenic backcountry areas as provincial parks; instead, as in the US model, they could remain under the jurisdiction of Forest Service as "wilderness areas." How this designation would be the same as or different from nature conservancies was uncertain. Both were defined as roadless areas, with the only evident distinction being that hunting was not permitted in the latter.

In August 1987 the Forest Act was amended to recognize "wilderness [areas] as distinct resources and legitimate land use" in the integrated management of provincial forests. The opportunity to use the new "wilderness area" designation arose shortly after this change in the act. It happened that naturalists, guide outfitters and environmentalists had long been promoting the Height of the Rockies for protected status because it would complete the network of parks along the Great Divide, including Banff National Park, Elk Lakes Provincial Park and Peter Lougheed Park in the Kananaskis. Access to this area was limited and its forest industry values low, so it was a prime candidate for the Ministry of Forests new wilderness recreation policy; as a result, the Height of the Rockies became the first Forest Service wilderness area.

Meanwhile, as recommended by the WAC, the province had designated the upper and lower portions of the Stein River valley, which lies between the Fraser and Lillooet rivers, as a recreation area with no logging allowed; the middle, most heavily timbered section was still open to logging. This decision satisfied neither activists nor the Nlaka'pamux First Nation, for whom the Stein was traditional territory. Evidence of the centuries of their habitation—the depressions where their storage houses once stood, culturally modified trees, and numerous pictographs on ledges and in caves and natural grottoes throughout the valley—tell their history there.

The Stein, as well as being the last intact watershed in southern British Columbia, is also geologically unique. The main valleys have the characteristic U-shape of glacially eroded riverbeds, and as a result, many of the tributary streams have "hanging" valleys. The drainage area ranges in altitude from 210 metres where the river empties into the Fraser to 2,925 metres at the summit of Skihist Mountain, and this watershed encompasses three small glaciers, four major lakes and about 52,000 hectares of alpine meadows. These important natural features should have been enough to make it a candidate for full park protection, but the area also has high timber values: ponderosa pine characterizes the forests of the lower valley, Douglas fir is predominant in the mid-valley and hemlock, cedar, spruce and fir become predominant in the western end of the valley. When the New Zealand-based multinational corporation Fletcher Challenge announced plans to log the valley in the early 1980s, the Sierra Club of BC mobilized to protect it with protests and demonstrations. Fundraising rock concerts held in the Stein during the 1980s morphed in time into the famous Stein Valley Festival.

After the WAC decision, the Sierra Club and the Nlaka'pamux First Nation

continued to demand protection for the middle and the most heavily timbered part of the drainage. In the fall of 1987, in an attempt to defuse the controversy, the Forest Service redesignated the combined upper and lower Stein valleys as its second wilderness area. As this move still ignored the middle valley problem, the dispute continued, although it was less voluble after Fletcher Challenge announced a moratorium on logging in 1988.

Opposite: These weathered mortuary poles stand at the abandoned village of Ninstints (Nan Sdins) on Anthony Island in Gwaii Haanas National Park Reserve, a UNESCO World Heritage Site. All Canada Photos, Chris Cheadle

South Moresby

The WAC was ahead of the times in recommending that the province should improve its consultation with First Nations on matters of land use, including new parks. Parks Branch staff was also prepared to do so in regard to the new Khutzeymateen, Hakai and Fiordland recreation areas, but the government did not encourage this because the official policy was to not recognize Native land claims. It would be another decade before such dialogue was accepted as a necessary practice.

When it came to South Moresby Island, the WAC had attempted to resolve the impasse by recommending that a portion of the island should be ceded to the federal government to become a national park. This decision was no more satisfactory to logging companies, First Nations or the Western Canada Wilderness Committee (WCWC) than the *Moresby Report*, which had been accepted by the government back in January 1984. That report had taken an interagency working committee four years of study and investigation and had provided four options for the island's future. None of them had satisfied the interested parties, and during all those four years of study, logging had proceeded on the island despite numerous court challenges, protests by First Nations and an ongoing campaign of support by the WCWC.

In the intervening years the province's stand had not changed, but the federal government was very anxious to deal with the concerns of the Haida First Nation and continued to encourage discussion. As a result, in July 1987, after more than a decade of public reviews and confrontations, a federal–provincial memorandum of understanding was signed to designate Gwaii Haanas as a new 147,000-hectare national park reserve with an additional 305,000 hectares as a foreshore marine park. Included in this area were both South Moresby and the former Anthony Island Provincial Park. This agreement was precedent setting because it included a provision for co-management with the Haida First Nation, thus preparing the way for other First Nations in future tripartite relations. The area had no private in-holdings but did require termination of valuable timber harvesting tenures. As a result, the federal government agreed to provide over $31 million to compensate forest companies, primarily Western Forest Products, as well as another $50 million for regional economic development, and $25 million for park management.

Strathcona—The War is Won!

It is likely the provincial government had realized for some time that park status for Moresby was inevitable, and by agreeing to a national park, much of the cost of mitigation and compensation would be paid by the federal government. And, as in the case of Pacific Rim Park, the operational costs would become a federal responsibility as well. However, many conservation groups were upset at the extent of the compensation to forest companies and were worried this would set an expensive precedent elsewhere in the province before any other new parks, either federal or provincial, could be created.

As a focus for the seventy-fifth anniversary of BC's first park, the Branch had prepared a master plan for Strathcona. Consistent with advice from the WAC, several portions of the park where mineral claims had been staked were reclassified as recreation areas, in particular to allow mineral exploration of claims held by Cream Silver. The Ash River drainage—that is, the southeastern tip of the Strathcona triangle, which had been partially logged—was removed from the park with the inten-

Below: The provincial government has over time removed areas of prime forest from Strathcona Park as trade-offs to establish new parks in other parts of the province.

Below right: Diversion dams and tunnels have regulated and changed the direction of flow of many rivers and streams within Strathcona, BC's first provincial park.

During periods of high water the stumps around the shores of long, narrow Buttle Lake are hidden from view.

tion of using its remaining forest values to acquire other areas with greater park values. A decade later it would be transferred to Weyerhaeuser in exchange for parkland in other Vancouver Island locations.

However, the master planning process for Strathcona Park was suspended after the public became concerned over mining claims in the parks, particularly the issuing of park use permits (PUPs) for the exploration of the Cream Silver claims. In fact, public protest became so extreme that some sixty protesters were arrested. In response, the government instituted a formal public inquiry chaired by Peter Larkin, an eminent fisheries biologist, well known and respected for his expertise in the areas of conservation, resource management and environmental impact assessment. His report, entitled *Restoring the Balance*, which was submitted in September 1988, offered the following comments:

> *It is widely accepted policy in North American jurisdictions that industrial activities in general and mining in particular are incompatible with the concept that parks are intended to conserve large areas of the national landscape...to the public a park is a park...The euphemistic redesignation to "recreation area" of areas that have long been thought of as "park" is seen by the public to be a legalistic convenience for not defending park values.*

The report recommended that holders of all existing mineral claims in Strathcona be denied exploration permits, that these claims be acquired by the province and, except for the existing Westmin mine, that there should be an end to all future mineral claim staking and an end to all mining. It also recommended that many of the portions of the park that had been previously removed—in particular, the Bedwell River drainage area—should be restored and the park expanded further by acquiring parcels of land adjacent to its boundaries including Wilmar, Pearl and Forbush lakes and Mount Adrian as well as additional ocean frontage on the Moyeha River in order to enhance and protect the estuary. Some lands were also identified that could be removed from the park and exchanged for parcels that had higher park values. And finally it was recommended that a formal advisory group be formed to facilitate the master planning process.

The cabinet accepted the report and it became government policy, ending a seventy-five year era of park resource exploitation and inadequate protection. The issue of how to deal with existing mineral claims remained unresolved but would soon be clarified. In retrospect, it is probably true that, apart from the flooding of Buttle Lake and the continued operation of the Westmin mine, the final outcomes of all the boundary changes in Strathcona were positive, and the park now offers a rich range of natural features and recreational opportunities. In particular, the addition of Forbidden Plateau and Marble Meadows and numerous small lakes provides the best alpine hiking and cross-country skiing on Vancouver Island with the road and parking lot for the adjacent Mount Washington ski resort providing ready public access. In 1987 most of Strathcona was re-established as Class A park and in 1989 an area of 3,400 hectares surrounding the mine site was established as separate Class B park known as Strathcona-Myra. Whenever the mine closes and the site is decommissioned the area will be restored to the main park. The addition in 1995 of the Megin/Talbot drainage area and extension to the tidewater on the Pacific now protects the largest undisturbed watershed on the Island. Other notable additions include McBride Creek, White Ridge and Rossiter/Divers lakes. Oddly, the major attraction of Della Falls still remains inaccessible to the general park visitor.

The Battle for the Carmanah/Walbran Area

The Carmanah and Walbran areas had not been included in the mandate of the Wilderness Advisory Commission (WAC), and soon after the Wilderness Mosaic report was issued, environmental groups began mobilizing to have these sites on the west coast of Vancouver Island protected as well. The tactics they used were guaranteed to generate public attention and included an announcement by the Western Canada Wilderness Committee (WCWC) on May 30, 1988, that volunteers were building trails in the Carmanah Valley so that the public could see the clear-cut logging practices for themselves. At the same time the WCWC lobbied the federal government to support a logging moratorium; this matter was, of course, outside Ottawa's jurisdiction, but the Carmanah Valley lies close to the West Coast Trail, which is stage three of Pacific Rim National Park, and logging in the valley would affect park values there. By August 5, 1989, the WCWC had staffed a research station in the valley to document its unique natural history. The group also published a poster with the rallying cry of "Big Trees, Not Big Stumps!" In October the WCWC published a coffee-table book to support their demands, and the following April they supported a First Nations attempt to get a court injunction against logging in the area. They were very successful in gathering public financial support,

Clear-cut logging has taken a toll on the landscape just outside the entrance to Carmanah Walbran Provincial Park on the west coast of Vancouver Island. *All Canada Photos, Chris Cheadle*

and they used their new funds to finance even larger publicity campaigns, storefront offices and the hiring of full-time staff. These tactics, along with a change in the political climate in the spring of 1990, finally produced results, although not the total protection of the Carmanah/Walbran valleys the WCWC had demanded. Unfortunately, Carmanah Pacific Provincial Park, announced in the summer of 1990, consisted of only 3,592 hectares of the lower valley to protect the tallest Sitka spruce in the world. Environmentalists were not at all satisfied and strongly expressed support for expansion of the park to include the upper Carmanah Valley and the adjacent Walbran Valley, but it would be another four years before any additions were made. At that time only the upper Carmanah and lower Walbran were added.

Parks Plans for the '90s

In April 1990, in the midst of the massive changes in the status of parks across the province, the Parks Branch was suddenly given full ministry status. Many believed that this was the result of cabinet ministers Terry Hubert and then Ivan Messmer (who both served as Parks minister for brief terms) working to convince the government to adopt a more pro-parks stance. With full ministry status came a budget increase and Parks was now ready for a major growth in the system. (Unfortunately, in December 1990 just as support was growing for Parks' future plans, the pro-parks minister Ivan Messmer was replaced by Dave Parker, who had been minister of Forests and was not known as a strong supporter of an expanded parks system.)

June 9, 1990, was a red-letter day for Parks. It marked the first formal recognition of Parks Day, a national campaign to celebrate all of Canada's parks. Dozens of visitor programs were featured across the province. (Parks Day is now a national event celebrated on the third Saturday in July.) June 9 was also the day that the Parks Branch released *Parks and Wilderness for the 90s*, which outlined plans for future growth and management. This document identified candidates for potential park status under two conservation goals (landscapes and special features) and four recreation goals (tourism and travel routes, holiday destinations, backcountry adventures and local recreation). To solicit feedback from the public, an oversized format map was published and widely distributed; this map along with two technical supplements represented nearly two decades of preparatory work by Branch staff. Over ten thousand people attended a series of province-wide public meetings to review the maps and plans, and the participants proposed many other candidates for park status. But for the first time Parks had produced documents that were acknowledged by, and acceptable to, the Western Canada Wilderness Committee and other environmental groups.

Carmanah/Walbran Provincial Park is home to some of the world's largest spruce trees, some reaching heights in excess of 95 metres.

The definitive policy document *Striking the Balance, 3rd edition* (originally issued as a draft in 1988) was amended and re-issued to confirm that parks would no longer be available for resource development. The first version implied a goal of 6 percent (up from 5.3 percent) which would have only provided for 60 percent representative landscapes. A revision raised the near term objective of including 70 percent of the landscapes. This document has survived several changes in premiers and governments and is still the pre-eminent policy document in use over 15 years later. Buried on page 16 was a small box with simple but concise text: "New Policy (1989) The policy concerning pre-existing mineral claims has been changed. The new policy is that there will be no more mineral exploration or development in parks."

Striking the Balance also confirmed the park system's dual mandate: to protect both recreation ("protect key recreation sites and outstanding scenic features") and conservation goals ("protection and experience of representative natural landscapes"). The new policy also formalized a zoning system to be identified in master plans to identify and categorize acceptable visitor uses and levels of park facility development. The five zones are: Intensive Recreation, Natural Environment, Special Feature, Wilderness Recreation Area and Wilderness Conservation.

Opposite: The Stoltman Grove, which includes the world's tallest Sitka spruce trees, was named for Randy Stoltman, author and outdoorsman, who discovered them and fought for their protection. The grove is now part of Carmanah/Walbran Provincial Park. *All Canada Photos, Chris Cheadle*

Over the next year twenty-two recreational areas, including important marine areas such as Desolation Sound, were reclassified as Class A parks, and the boundaries of twenty-nine more parks were established by legislation. The expanded

Kalamalka Lake Provincial Park, virtually at the city of Vernon's back door, is surrounded by groves of Douglas fir and Ponderosa pine.

budget allowed the creation of several new marine parks, including Kekuli Bay on the western shore of Kalamalka Lake, which provided a major boat launch site for the region. Okanagan Mountain Park was increased by the addition of the few accessible sites along a mostly steep shoreline. The parks system now covered 5.95 million hectares of the province and 72 percent with statutory protection.

In 1989 in order to implement the new policy of no more mineral exploration or development in parks, funds were made available to purchase all of the existing mineral claims; thirty claims were bought out in Tweedsmuir Park, fifteen in Kokanee Glacier and another four in Strathcona. The following year three more claims were purchased in Kokanee Glacier and five in Strathcona. In addition the mining sector failed to pursue the ten-year window of opportunity that the WAC had allowed them for exploring for minerals within recreation areas and no claims were registered during that period.

By 1990 parks visits exceeded 19 million annually. The original intent of the 1973 legislation reforms to give parks legislative protection had finally been given strong political commitment. The next era would see a grand expansion of the park system.

8 :
The 12 Percent Solution, 1991 to 2001

A Change in the Wind

The 1980s ended with serious public confrontations and political discord, and apart from other social or economic issues, the fate of the provincial government rested on its capacity to demonstrate its commitment to dealing with several outstanding resource issues. First, it would have to show a willingness to support park status for several areas that had been the focus of high-profile campaigns led by environmental groups. Second, it would need to establish a new comprehensive and participatory land-use planning framework to review new park proposals and prepare overall regional plans. Third, it would have to institute and enforce new

Above: In summer when the waters of Kalamalka Lake are warmed by the sun, the calcium carbonate in the water forms crystals that reflect the light and create its distinctive blue-green colour.

regulations governing logging practices, including an "old-growth strategy." Critics were, in fact, calling for an entirely new forest practices code. Fourth, it would need to institute a positive ongoing dialogue with First Nations in matters of aboriginal rights relating to land use and even recognize the need for tripartite treaty negotiations to resolve land claims.

The New Democrats were offering a political commitment to deal with and resolve these issues, and despite the Social Credit government having implemented the recommendations of the Wilderness Advisory Commission and approved policy changes to protect existing parks, environmental groups were able to convince the voting public that this government was not willing to end its alliance with the corporate forestry industry. At this point, virtually all environmental and outdoor recreation groups—the Outdoor Recreation Resources Council, BC Fish and Wildlife Federation, Canadian Parks and Wilderness Society, the Valhalla Wilderness Society, Greenpeace, the BC branch of the Sierra Club and the Western Canada Wilderness Committee—generally shared a common cause in support of a greatly expanded park system, the need for consultative regional land-use planning process and logging reforms. As a result, the provincial election of October 1991 saw the defeat of the Social Credit party, and the introduction of a New Democrat government under Premier Mike Harcourt. With the change in the political climate, a parks system that had taken eighty years to evolve would double in size within a single decade.

Federal Leadership

The federal government has a very limited role in resource allocation and land-use planning, its role being mainly confined to issues such as national and historic parks and migratory waterfowl. However, federal regulatory powers under the Fisheries Act can be used to restrict forestry, mining, agricultural and hydro use impacts on fish habitat. There is also some joint overlap with the jurisdiction of the provinces in environmental matters, and in some instances both levels of governments act in concert. In the case of parks, it was the federal government that first set standards that would raise public and international expectations of environmental performance, but these standards could only be realized by cooperative provincial actions. On June 17, 1991, Parliament accepted the resolution recommended by the UNESCO/Bruntland Report that the government should consider the advisability of preserving and protecting in its natural state at least 12 percent of Canada by working cooperatively with provincial and territorial governments, assisting them to complete a protected area network by 2000.

As evidence of its commitment to this 12 percent goal, within the following year the federal government established the 1.2 million-hectare Aulavik National Park on Banks Island in the Northwest Territories and proposed several others, including a park in the Georgia Basin Lowlands of coastal BC. And before the end of the decade federal statutes created Vuntut, Wapsuk, Tuksut, Saquenay and Sumilik parks, adding seventeen million hectares to the national park system. Canada had clearly demonstrated its international leadership in the creation of protected areas.

The Earth Summit conference in Rio the following year confirmed an international awareness regarding the environmental health of the planet.

When BC's new provincial government was briefed on these initiatives in November 1991, the cabinet embraced the 12 percent target for protected areas in this province and in the spring of 1992 appointed the independent Commission on Resources and the Environment (CORE) to develop a framework for future land-use decisions. When announcing its creation, Premier Harcourt said, "We can't continue the valley by valley confrontations that have plagued our province for too long, and the instability and uncertainty that it brings." So the promise of the 1990s was to find and implement an interactive, consultative process in which all parties would concur. CORE was expected to develop a province-wide strategy that would provide a general set of policies and priorities and options for legislation, but in order to avoid agency turf wars, decisions on how these policies were to be applied would be left to stakeholder consensus. Representatives from public interest groups and resource sectors such as guide outfitters, ranchers, recreationists, forest companies, First Nations and local governments were to sit around a table and systematically prepare land and resource management plans for each region of the province and identify areas that should be protected. Government staff were to serve as low profile, behind-the-scenes advisors, although in reality, as they had the most knowledge of remote areas of the province, they had the most influence on the outcome of the deliberations. However, since the 12 percent target was to serve as the cap on the total for all new and existing parks, each roundtable would be forced to make difficult choices.

Meanwhile, to guide policy direction, all affected government ministries were to be involved in the development of a Protected Areas Strategy. To coordinate these processes and to undertake the technical analysis required for the new strategy, regional interagency management committees were created. By 1994 the cabinet also recognized that a central agency inside government was required to coordinate all of the interagency processes, and a Land Use Coordination Office (LUCO) was established for this function. Initially the role of LUCO was to set strategic directions, coordinate work plans, monitor and report on ministry responses to the implementation of plans and manage effective public participation processes. It also facilitated land-use decisions by ensuring that all values, issues and impacts were presented to regional decision makers objectively. As time went on, LUCO also took on the task of ensuring that land-use planning and resource inventory programs were integrated with First Nations entitlements and treaty rights.

All of this work was made easier by the fact that the bureaucracy had been readying itself for a new regime and during the past decade had been doing preparatory and behind-the-scenes work to draft a new paradigm and policy framework. The Ministry of Forests had already quietly created a new forest practices code, *A Provincial Old Growth Strategy*, which included guidelines for logging that emphasized the retention of biodiversity values rather than the clear-cutting of single species forest stands. Parks staff were able to access files based on three decades of reconnaissance and system planning and had already produced the document *Parks and*

Wilderness for the 90s. Thus, ministry staff were prepared to move forward as soon as they received the political green light.

The Protected Areas Strategy

There were three components to the Protected Areas Strategy. It was, first of all, a political commitment to increase the park system to 12 percent of the provincial land base by the year 2000. Second, it provided a list of candidate study areas based on the document *Parks and Wilderness for the 90s.* And third, it established the framework for the comprehensive land-use planning process for the stakeholders who were participating at the regional level.

The target of 12 percent was to be applied both regionally and provincially although it was assumed that some regions would end up with more or less than that percentage since the opportunity still existed within the province to designate some large, dynamic ecosystems to protect predator–prey relationships. In other areas, human modifications had left no large untouched representative landscapes. The new protected areas were to be inalienable and there would be no mining, logging, hydro dams or oil or gas development. These restrictions were not new but rather a confirmation of the major policy shift that had occurred at the end of the 1980s. Of course, there were still recreation areas, wildlife management areas and Forest Service wilderness areas that did not exclude other resource uses. But the new policy required that, where these parcels were low in mineral or energy potential, they were to be given protected status against mining or forest harvesting. (Eventually, most were reclassified as Class A parks.)

A thirty-nine-page policy manual called *PAS—A Strategy for BC,* which provided the background for the objectives, structure and processes for the Protected Areas Strategy, was distributed to government field staff in all of the resource ministries and to the citizen representatives who served on the regional planning tables. The manual identified the government rationale for expanding the park system and outlined all the values of protected area status. These included the natural benchmarks for long-term scientific research, reservoirs of genetic information, contributions to the preservation and understanding of cultural heritage, support for aboriginal people's traditional use and spiritual relationship with the land, provision of outdoor classrooms and opportunities for the public to experience, appreciate and enjoy nature and a range of outdoor recreational facilities, and contributions to the long-term viability and growth of the tourism industry.

The Regional Land-use Planning Process

To help identify and prioritize possible candidate areas for parks status, the stakeholders at each regional table were asked to assess all of the "eco-sections" within their planning areas. First, they were to look for representative examples of the major terrestrial, marine and freshwater ecosystems, characteristic habitats, hydrology and landforms, and the backcountry recreational and cultural heritage values. Criteria to be used in evaluation included the land's representativeness, its degree of naturalness, viability, diversity and vulnerability, the opportunity for public use, appreciation and scientific research. Next they were to consider the protection of special natural, cultural heritage and recreational features, including rare and endangered species and critical habitats, outstanding or unique botanical, zoological, geological and paleontological features, outstanding or fragile cultural heritage features, and outstanding outdoor recreation facilities such as trails. Criteria to be used in evaluation included rarity, scarcity and uniqueness, diversity, vulnerability and cultural significance. In contrast to the previous decades of fractious debate, the benefits of such a structured planning process were expected not only to ensure careful consideration of all social and economic effects before park decisions were made but also help provide certainty about present and future land-use allocations that would stabilize local investment and development.

Initially three regional land-use planning tables were convened: Cariboo–Chilcotin, Kootenay–Boundary (later split into east and west) and Vancouver Island. Clayoquot Sound was not part of the mandate of the Vancouver Island table because a task force was already dealing with the issues in that area. In early 1993 the Commission on Resources and the Environment released the first draft of the *Vancouver Island Land Use Plan*. As the list of parks contained in it had been severely constrained by the 12 percent cap, certain sectors of the public were very unhappy, and protests were mounted. A review a year later of the final boundaries of twenty-three Vancouver Island parks made changes that exceeded the 12 percent limit but still failed to satisfy conservation groups. Eventually the government approved parks to the 17 percent level.

Clayoquot Sound

In the years before the Protected Areas Strategy initiative was announced, conservation groups and local First Nations had identified an area north of the new Pacific Rim National Park and extending up the west coast of Vancouver Island to include Clayoquot Sound as key "old-growth" forestland that should not be logged. Unlike the campaigns for Haida Gwaii and the Stein, where the focus had been on special landscape features and recreation opportunities, these groups were championing the preservation of the old-growth cedars and firs in order to maintain biodiversity.

The first protests in this area had occurred in 1979 in response to logging by MacMillan Bloedel on Meares Island near Tofino, but the Nuu-chah-nulth First Nations resolved that problem in 1984 by proving that the island was traditional territory by identifying its culturally modified trees and getting an injunction from the BC Court of Appeal to prevent further logging there. The company moved its logging operations, but their new sites were also within the Clayoquot drainage area and resulted in renewed protests, although at first they remained local. Then, as the problem came to the attention of a wider public, the protests began to grow in scope, and in 1989 the government was finally forced to establish a Clayoquot Steering Committee, later known as the Sustainable Task Force, to provide a forum for local representation and discussion. But nothing this committee did could resolve the wide differences of opinion between forest industry supporters and environmental groups on the future of the Clayoquot area. In 1992, as the battle lines hardened, BC's environmental groups nominated Clayoquot Sound for UN Biosphere status, urging the necessity to protect and preserve mature coastal rainforests. The Western Canada Wilderness Committee (WCWC) followed up by distributing 100,000 copies of a tabloid entitled *Wild and Beautiful Clayoquot Sound*, which featured a satellite photo of a large clear-cut; it received worldwide attention. The following spring the Valhalla Wilderness Society published a thirty-six-page book called *The Brazil of the North*. Advertisements in the *New York Times* took the campaign to the international level. In response, the logging industry and members of resource communities formed Share BC and mounted their own campaign. In the meantime MacMillan Bloedel continued to log, an action that inspired protesters to blockade remote logging roads.

Then on March 18, 1993, a small group of environmental protestors invaded the legislature, demanding the Clayoquot area be saved. This was a level of militancy that did not receive widespread support, but it did generate more international publicity, and on April 13, 1993, the government admitted defeat. The Sustainable Task Force was disbanded and, as a compromise designed to satisfy the competing interests, the cabinet announced protection for about one-third of the forests in the Clayoquot drainage area, at the same time granting approval for the remainder to be logged. The new protected lands included four sites in the Clayoquot area that totalled 48,000 hectares and another 23,000 hectares in the Megin–Talbot drainage area, which effectively extended the boundaries of Strathcona Provincial Park westward to the Pacific. The outer coastline of both Vargas and Flores islands and the Hesquiat Peninsula also became protected areas.

However, neither First Nations nor environmental groups, led by the WCWC, were satisfied. In fact, the cabinet's decision only escalated the "war in the woods." That summer the WCWC established a "peace camp" on the road to MacMillan Bloedel's Kennedy River logging camp, and hundreds of protesters made it their base of operations to continue the campaign. They were joined by international personalities such as Robert Kennedy Jr. and the members of the Australian rock band Midnight Oil, and as a result the site received worldwide media coverage. Arrests were made, but for every protester hauled away by police, there seemed to be two to step in. In all, more than eight hundred people of all ages were arrested. By September the protesters' publicity campaign was featuring a flatbed trailer on which was mounted a huge four-hundred-year-old red cedar stump; it graced the legislature lawn during rallies and was even transported to Ottawa.

In October 1993 the government tried to further appease protesters by appointing a scientific panel to assess logging practices and future land use in Clayoquot Sound, but the cabinet made it clear that while they would support the reform of logging practices, there would be no more wilderness areas designated on the island. They also got tough on further blockade tactics by militant protestors. Public opinion polls seemed to support this position. In November the government issued

an "old-growth strategy" and the first draft of a new forest practices code. Again neither satisfied the expectations of environmentalists, and this posed a dilemma for the NDP, which had been elected by two diverse interest groups—the "greens" and public sector and industrial unions. Some relief for the embattled government came in December when First Nations representatives agreed to sign an interim measures agreement that created a central regional board to oversee future resource decisions in Clayoquot Sound. This diffused the issue to some extent as it put local groups, particularly First Nations, partially in control of logging practices there.

Ironically, the apparent loss of forest lands in Clayoquot Sound for logging purposes had strengthened the resolve of loggers and resource communities, and in February 1994 after the Commission on Resources and the Environment released its final report on Vancouver Island, a report that expanded parks and reserves to 13 percent of the land base, the government learned that the battle for Vancouver Island was not over. On March 2 a massive protest march on the legislature was staged by some 25,000 members of Share BC and the Forest Alliance, a forest resource coalition that supported improved logging practices but called for more balanced timber allocations. Their battle cry was "12 percent and no more." In response the WCWC released *Vancouver Island: Paradise Lost* and insisted the cabinet must add as much as 30 percent more to the protected areas.

The government was now forced to develop a strategy that appealed to both groups. In particular, they promised forestry workers they would be compensated for job losses and provided with special assistance. The tool for this new initiative was to be Forest Renewal BC, an new arm of the Forest Service that would be financed by creating a dedicated funding source from increased stumpage rates and used for reforestation programs, road upgrades, silviculture, stream rehabilitation and retraining. A fund of over $2 billion would be made available over five years.

Then, despite all the protests and confrontations—and possibly to divert attention from the conflicts on Vancouver Island—in July 1994 the cabinet announced that the Protected Areas Strategy (PAS) would be expanded into a province-wide initiative. The government also demonstrated its commitment to the goals of the PAS by announcing several major new parks in the Interior and the North. Seven months later it followed this up with the announcement of its own final version of the plan for Vancouver Island that included a major expansion of Carmanah Pacific Park to include both the upper Carmanah and lower Walbran drainages. And to appease critics of the plan who still demanded more, they expanded Brooks Peninsula Provincial Park on the Island's upper west coast, added the Shushartie Bay–Nahwitti Valley areas to Cape Scott Park and designated the lower Tsitika Valley as a park in order to give more protection to the sensitive orca habitat of the Robson Bight Ecological Reserve.

In May 2000 Clayoquot Sound was designated as a UNESCO biosphere reserve and a $12-million fund was established to promote research and education there.

Southern Interior Parklands

When the Okanagan—Shuswap plan was finally approved in 2001, nearly 123,000 hectares of new parklands were designated. The new Anstey–Hunakwa Provincial Park, which can only be accessed from the north end of Shuswap Lake, has no amenities but includes an extensive old-growth fir, cedar and hemlock forest. Snowy Mountain Protected Area, just north of the US border and adjoining Cathedral Lakes Provincial Park, presents the greatest range of protected vertical ecosystems in Canada, going from semi-desert to grasslands to subalpine forest to alpine meadows. Snowy Mountain and Cathedral Lakes, along with South Okanagan Grasslands Park, all of which may eventually become part of a new national park, are all situated along the US–Canada border. Together with the Pasayten Wilderness Area and North Cascades National Park in the US and Manning and Skagit provincial parks in BC, these properties form a 1.2 million-hectare complex of protected wilderness.

The new Myra–Bellevue Provincial Park, which lies along a stretch of the old Kettle Valley Rail line and includes sixteen of the famous Myra Canyon wooden trestles and two steel trestles, had been acquired by the BC Lands Branch back in 1980, but no maintenance had been done on the trestles or the old railbed, and they gradually fell into disrepair. As hikers and bikers were using the trail in

A major American cycling magazine has rated the Myra Canyon trail in Myra-Bellevue Provincial Park as one of the 50 best bike rides in the world.

Previous pages: Height of the Rockies Provincial Park includes routes traditionally used by the Kootenai Native peoples to access North Kananaskis and Palliser passes. *All Canada Photos, Russ Heinl*

growing numbers in spite of the neglect, the Myra Canyon Trestle Restoration Society, formed in 1992, repaired the trestles and the trail, installed toilets and benches and built viewpoints. By 2000 it was rated as one of the fifty best cycling routes in the world, and the society realized that the best way to keep it protected and maintained was to have it declared a provincial park. Society members joined the land management planning process, and park status was granted in January 2003, just nine months before a forest fire destroyed twelve of the sixteen famous wooden trestles and damaged the two steel bridges. Fortunately, reconstruction costs were eligible for Federal–Provincial Disaster Relief Fund assistance, and the work of rebuilding began. The last trestle was replaced in early 2008, and the Myra Canyon Trestle Restoration Society entered an agreement with BC Parks to maintain the trail and trestles from the ties up.

The establishment of the Stein Valley Nlaka'pamux Heritage Provincial Park on November 22, 1995, marked the end of twenty-five years of debate and acrimony over development versus protection. The upper and lower Stein had been granted Forest Service recreational area status in 1987, but the middle section of the river valley had been left open for timber extraction, and while Fletcher Challenge had cancelled its plans to log there in 1988, other logging companies were again eyeing it. The new park, co-managed by BC Parks and the Nlaka'pamux First Nation, includes the entire 106,000-hectare Stein drainage area, the largest unlogged watershed in southwestern British Columbia. It provides 150 kilometres of hiking trails; neither horses nor motorized vehicles are allowed within the park's boundaries.

Directly to the south of Stein Valley Nlaka'pamux Provincial Park lies another of the new protected areas, Mehatl Creek Provincial Park. Created in July 1997, the 23,860-hectare Mehatl provides a link between

From the safety of a viewing platform two visitors check out the construction of one of the remarkable Kettle Valley Railway trestles in Myra Canyon.

the Stein and the Nahatlatch Protected Area to the southeast, creating enough high-quality habitat to support at least fifty species of mammals, from shrews to grizzly bears.

The first regional management table for the Kootenays included representatives from twenty-four sectoral groups, but while such diversity was laudable, it made for an unwieldy process and consensus building was extremely difficult. However, the eventual approval of the Kootenay land management plan resulted in the creation of the Akamina–Kishinena and Goat Range parks, the redesignation of the Height of the Rockies from Forest Service wilderness area to Class A park, and the enlargement of the Purcells and Bugaboo parks.

Parks for the North

Prior to 1990 there were very few parks in the half of the province lying north of Highway 16, the exceptions being Edziza, Spatsizi, Atlin and Kwadacha, which were all designated in the 1970s. Amazing natural features, representative landscapes and large populations of wildlife and their habitat were unprotected. All this was to change in the 1990s, but in contrast to the land-use allocation conflicts on Vancouver Island and in the Kootenays, the planning processes in the North were carried out with little conflict because, except for the Peace District, much of the area remains roadless, unsettled and minimally committed to resource extraction.

Other factors that were in play during the processes here were embedded in the rules handed to the planning tables. First, each table was given specific targets and procedures that limited the scope of debate and forced members to focus on reaching an acceptable land-use plan that accommodated all the diverse interests. Second, most of their debates took place in rural regions somewhat removed from

The ultimate purpose of the 44,300-hectare Khutzeymateen Grizzly Sanctuary, north of Prince Rupert, is to preserve a part of the ecosystem in which grizzlies thrive.

the attention of the big city media, which usually emphasize opposing positions rather than shared interests. In fact, in urban communities, land-use planning committee members often left the table to do their bargaining via the media. Third, the local people around the table knew they had to live with the outcomes of their plan, but they were also aware that creating new protected areas only meant the loss of future opportunities and did not interfere with existing resource operations, licence commitments and jobs. As well, having a land management plan in place would remove many of the uncertainties for future development in the local resource sectors. Fourth, the members made good use of the government advisers because they had received help from them in the past. There was also a history of successful co-management agreements with First Nations in this area, and this minimized their outright rejection of the planning process and the proposed protected areas.

The members of the planning tables were also inspired by the fact that the cabinet had already clearly demonstrated its commitment to protecting land in

The topography of the Khutzeymateen grizzly sanctuary is diverse, with rugged peaks towering over a broad valley of wetlands and old-growth rainforest.

the North by its designation, outside of the Commission on Resources and the Environment process, of four new high-profile protected areas—Khutzeymateen, Tatshenshini–Alsek, Kitlope and Ts'il-os.

The Khutzeymateen

The Khutzeymateen, which lies forty-five kilometres northeast of Prince Rupert near the mouth of Portland Inlet, was the first of the four parks to be designated (1994) with the special objective of protecting about 44,000 hectares of the estuary and upland drainage to provide extensive habitat for a grizzly bear population of approximately fifty animals. It is jointly managed by the province and the Tsimshian First Nation in whose territory it lies. There are no roads and access is only permitted from the inlet; however, visitor use is not encouraged. In 2008 three conservancy areas were added in order to further protect the bears.

Tatshenshini–Alsek

During the early 1990s the far northwestern corner of the province was the focus of a debate concerning the "Windy Craggy" mine that was proposed by Geddes Resources Ltd. This open-pit copper mine was considered the most environmentally hazardous mining project ever proposed for Canada because the ore that the company wished to exploit was on average 35 percent sulphide, which when

Tatshenshini-Alsek Park, in the farthest northwest corner of the province, contains nearly a million hectares of glacier-cloaked peaks and wild rivers.

exposed to oxygen and moisture becomes sulphuric acid that would leach heavy metals from the bedrock. Once this process begins, there is no known technology to reverse or even to stop the reaction; this acid mine drainage, as it is called, persists for thousands of years and is lethal to fish. To make matters worse, the proposed mine site lies in an earthquake-prone mountain wilderness area drained by two salmon-bearing rivers—the Tatshenshini and the Alsek—that originate in the Yukon and flow southwest through BC and the Alaska Panhandle and into the Pacific.

Windy Craggy was subject to the most intensive environmental review of any mine ever proposed in Canada as Geddes Resources continued to submit applications for the mine, tailings ponds, a slurry pipe to carry waste to terminal facilities in Alaska. Environmentalists reacted by forming Tatshenshini Wild, an umbrella organization representing over fifty major groups in the US and Canada, to spearhead a high-profile campaign. For five long years Canadian, American and BC governments rejected Windy Craggy applications and finally, on June 22, 1993, Premier Mike Harcourt put an end to the reviews by announcing that the Tatshenshini–Alsek drainage area would be designated a Class A provincial park. This decision cost the government $32 million to purchase the mineral claims held by Geddes Resources.

The new park includes Mount Fairweather, at 4,633 metres the highest point in BC, and the largest non-polar ice cap in the world. The varied geology and great elevation changes within this 958,000-hectare area provide an exceptionally diverse range of habitat conditions; it is home to unusual plant communities, one-half of BC's Dall sheep population as well as large populations of grizzly and glacier bears (a colour form of the black bear). The combination of Tatshenshini–Alsek Park, the adjacent Kluane National Park and Reserve in the Yukon, Glacier Bay National Park and Reserve and Wrangell–St. Elias National Park in Alaska forms the largest protected area in North America and likely the world. In 1994 this whole area was designated as a UN World Heritage area.

The Kitlope Valley Provincial Park lies within the traditional territory of the Haisla First Nation and protects the largest intact coastal temperate rainforest in the world.

Kitlope

Kitlope Heritage Conservancy, located at the upper end of the Gardner Canal and west of Tweedsmuir Park, was also designated in 1994 after an inventory and park assessment was conducted in conjunction with the Haisla Band by Ecotrust Canada, a non-profit society dedicated to helping coastal BC First Nations, communities and private enterprises to "green and grow" their local economies. Subsequent negotiations with the West Fraser Timber Company, which held the timber lease for this area, resulted in the company relinquishing all its tree harvesting rights without consideration or compensation from the BC government. This set a precedent for successful negotiations with other resource companies along the coast and in the Great Bear Rainforest.

Kitlope encompasses the world's largest intact coastal temperate rainforest and has old-growth trees more than eight hundred years old. It also includes critical estuarial habitat for the grizzly bear, moose, mountain goats, marbled murrelets, bald

The Kitlope watershed provides a largely intact diversity of wildlife habitats ranging from estuaries to lakes, flood plains, steep-sided slopes and alpine areas.

In the fall, bald eagles are attracted to Ts'il-os Park as spawning salmon struggle up the Chilko River at the north end of Chilko Lake.

eagles and many species of waterfowl. All five species of Pacific salmon, as well as oolichan spawn in its rivers and streams. Kitlope and the adjoining Fiordland Conservancy provide a protected wildlife corridor from Tweedsmuir west to tidewater.

Ts'il-os

Ts'il-os Provincial Park comprises approximately 233,000 hectares of rugged mountains, clear lakes and waterfalls, glaciers and alpine meadows that are bounded in the west by the Coast Mountains and on the east by the dry Interior Plateau. The park's boundaries include Chilko Lake, the largest natural high-elevation lake in Canada. Ts'il-os Mountain, also known as Mount Tatlow, which dominates the park, has spiritual significance to the Xeni Gwet'in people and, according to legend, keeps watch over the people and their territory.

The park was established in January 1994 as a wilderness area to protect the diverse vegetation in this transition zone between dry interior and wet coastal landscapes. Ecologically sensitive animal populations found here include California bighorn sheep, grizzly bears, fishers, wolverines, bald eagles and several species of amphibians. Chilko river and lake support populations of sockeye, chinook, trout and steelhead.

Opposite bottom: Stunningly beautiful, due to its blue-green waters and dramatic mountain backdrops, Chilko Lake in Ts'il-os Park is popular with boaters, kayakers and anglers.

Above: Ts'il-os, the imposing peak also known as Mount Tatlow, dominates Ts'il-os Provincial Park. It is spiritually significant to the Xeni Gwet'in First Nations people.

Stikine River Provincial Park

In 2000 park status was given to the Grand Canyon of the Stikine River, thereby providing a fully protected corridor between Spatsizi Plateau Wilderness and Mount Edziza provincial parks. The Stikine rises within Spatsizi Park and flows north and then west in a broad arc. Just west of the point where the Cassiar Highway bridge crosses it, the river drops into a three-hundred-metre-deep, eighty-kilometre-long canyon that its waters have carved into the ancient volcanic rock. This section, which varies from two hundred metres to two metres wide, is not even navigable by skilled kayakers. At the southwestern end of the canyon sits the town of Telegraph Creek, which marked the head of navigation during the Stikine and Cassiar gold rushes. The final forty kilometres of the river lie within the Alaska Panhandle.

The Stikine River, which cuts a fast-flowing course through the Coast Mountains in northern BC, is considered one of the last truly wild rivers in this province.

Before European contact the river provided a trade route to the interior for the Tlingit people and in the nineteenth century prospectors followed it when heading for the Stikine, Cassiar and Klondike goldfields. It also figured in a number of failed railway schemes in the nineteenth century, but it was not until 1980 that the canyon itself was threatened; at that time BC Hydro began to study the feasibility of building two massive dams there and three more on the Iskut River that joins the Stikine just before it crosses into Alaska. Conservationists mobilized under the banner of the Friends of the Stikine River, but in the end the canyon was saved by

the fact that the scheme was totally uneconomic: this part of the province is so far from the industries that would have used the power that it would have cost more to build the necessary transmission lines than to build the dams. In 1986 the Wilderness Advisory Commission recommended that the upper river should be protected, and a broad corridor down the Stikine Valley almost to Telegraph Creek was given recreation area status.

However, this designation did not protect the canyon area from resource extraction, and the canyon was again threatened when mining interests at the Stikine Land and Resource Management Planning table attempted to have its recreation area status rescinded. Instead, a convergence of key environmental groups, including the Friends of the Stikine, BC Spaces for Nature and the Tahltan First Nation, fought to save it, and in 2000 it became a full Class A provincial park. At the same time expansion was also announced for the adjacent Spatsizi, Tatlatui and Mount Edziza parks, all created in the mid-1970s, thereby creating a park complex of over 1.5 million hectares.

The Northern Rockies

In October 1997 the government made the dramatic announcement that a massive new special management area had been designated in the corner of northeastern BC where the Northern Rockies separate the Peace River District from the rest of the province. The plan for the Muskwa–Kechika Management Area, which was to include new and existing parks surrounded by resource management areas, had been achieved through the dedication and hard work of land and resource planning tables in Fort Nelson, Mackenzie and Fort St. John, three contiguous land-use management areas that cover nearly one-quarter of BC, as well as input from local First Nations and representatives of the resource extraction industries. Together they agreed on a plan that balances continued resource development with the protection

Designated trails provide access to Northern Rocky Mountains Park. At 665,000 hectares it is the third-largest park in the province.

Above: Northern Rocky Mountains Park, established in June 1999, is the largest unit in the Muskwa–Kechika Management Area. It encompasses 665,709 hectares of wilderness.

Right: A packtrain climbs a slope in the rugged alpine backcountry of the Muskwa-Kechika Wilderness in northeastern BC. *All Canada Photos, John E. Marriot*

of important wildlife and environmental values. Interests that were once in competition had found a way to co-exist. (The November 2008 issue of *National Geographic* magazine includes photos and an article on the cooperative planning process that resulted in the designation of the Muskwa–Kechika Management Area.)

The protected core of this special management area consists of 1.1 million hectares of parks and recreation areas, some of them established decades earlier, some new, but all of them fully protected from resource exploitation. Northern Rocky Mountains Provincial Park is the largest of Muskwa–Kechika's original components, and its size was increased in 2008 when it was combined with the Wokkpash Recreational Area; at 665,000 hectares it is now the third-largest park in the province. But the Muskwa-Kechika has very small components as well: the provincial park at Toad River Hot Springs is just 400 hectares; that at Hornline Creek 300 hectares; and that at Prophet River Hot Springs 180 hectares. The plan also enlarged some existing parks—the Liard River Corridor was expanded by 90,500 hectares—and some areas were designated specifically for the protection of old-growth forests—the Dall River and Scatter River Old Growth provincial parks.

This collection of fully protected parks, sometimes called the "Serengeti of the North," is home to the only Plains bison population in the province as well as approximately 3,500 black and grizzly bears. There are also coyotes, wolves, wolverines and cougars, about 22,000 moose, 4,000 caribou, 15,000 elk and 7,000 Stone's sheep. There are fur-bearing animals such as mink, weasel, marten, lynx and beaver here, and the wetlands provide habitat for Canada and snow geese, trumpeter swans and a variety of waterfowl.

These fully protected areas of the Muskwa–Kechika are surrounded by 3.24 million hectares of special management areas where logging, mineral exploration and mining and oil and gas extraction are allowed under stringent, best-practice standards. This provision for resource industries is extremely important as the Muskwa–Kechika borders on the richest area in BC for known oil and gas reserves while its central and western sections are high in metallic and non-metallic resources. Other portions have high timber values, a fact not lost on the population of the Fort Nelson area where 40 percent of the economy is driven by the forest sector. Careful exploration and development of resources here will, as a result, have significant social and economic benefits for the whole province.

Establishment of this area and its innovative management regime required new legislation, the Muskwa–Kechika Management Area Act, which was passed into law on July 30, 1998. The act also provided for the creation of a thirteen-member inter-sector board, charged with administering a large trust fund created to support special projects such as conducting research into wildlife biology and ecology, preparing wildlife inventories, mapping and enhancing habitat, supporting planning initiatives for resource development and producing public education programs. The provincial government is required to contribute to this fund annually and private sector donations are also encouraged. In 2001 an additional 1.9 million hectares were added to this special management area.

Urban Parks

Given the high degree of urbanization in the Lower Mainland, the Victoria area and the Okanagan, the regional land-use planning process was not applied. Instead, the province set up land acquisition partnerships, which resulted in the preservation of important greenbelts and offered outdoor recreation opportunities in near-urban "pocket wildernesses." However, the funding and land swapping and trading of land parcels that occurred in order to finalize these new protected areas was complex beyond imagining.

The Lower Mainland Nature Legacy, negotiated with the Greater Vancouver Regional District (GVRD), now Metro Vancouver, in March 1995, was financed by $23 million from the province and $12.5 million from the GVRD. The agreement saw the province transfer dozens of land parcels with high natural values to the district, including Minnekhada and Colony farms, Belcarra, Surrey Bend and Derby Reach on the Fraser River and Douglas, Crescent and Barnston islands. An extra 145 hectares were added to Boundary Bay Park to extend the regional trail system around the bay. Later the purchase of the 91-hectare Blaney Bog, which had been destined for development as a cranberry farm, was shared between the GVRD and the municipality of Maple Ridge, and the 2,200-hectare Burns Bog in Delta was acquired through a three-way partnership between the province, the GVRD and Parks Canada.

Say Nuth Khaw Yum Heritage Park is a conservation area that protects the shores of Indian Arm, the 18-kilometre fiord that extends north from Burrard Inlet.

The province also agreed to create Indian Arm Provincial Park, a unique area that provides a marine wilderness as an extension of Vancouver Harbour and protects an eighteen-kilometre urban fiord. Amassing the land for this park was an extremely convoluted process that involved slowly acquiring properties along the inlet, including the purchase of the Weldwood holdings on the estuary of the Indian River in 1999. In 2004 the Land Conservancy partnered with the GVRD and the municipality of North Vancouver to buy Thwaites Landing to serve as a launching point for kayakers, and the final elements were added in 2005–06 when Granite Falls was acquired for $3.4 million and Croker Island for $1.7 million. The province also created Pinecone–Burke Provincial Park on the North Shore to fill a gap between Mount Seymour, Garibaldi and Golden Ears parks.

The province and the Capital Regional District negotiated a composite provincial–regional plan called the Commonwealth Nature Legacy—so-named because the signing happened to coincide with the running of the 1994 Commonwealth Games in Victoria. The province began by acquiring 1,300 hectares along the south shore of Finlayson Arm to create Gowlland Tod Provincial Park, and then negotiating with Western Forest Products to exchange land for the company's cutting rights on Mount Finlayson in order to add it to Goldstream Park.

Fintry Provincial Park, south of Vernon, includes 360 hectares of the former Fintry Estate, created by the innovative Captain James C. Dun-Waters. *James D. Anderson collection*

Private forestlands belonging to Timber West were acquired to continue the Juan de Fuca Marine Trail from Botanical Beach to Sombrio Beach. More private property in Mystic Vale and Glencoe Cove was purchased to preserve urban open space there, and the land surrounding Sooke Mountain was bought to form the core of a new "Sea to Sea Greenbelt" from Sooke Harbour to Finlayson Arm.

In the Regional District of Central Okanagan (RDCO), the Nature Legacy of BC focussed on the purchase of the Fintry Estates on the northwest shore of Okanagan Lake. Here, a subdivision proposal had come to the brink of bankruptcy during a downturn in the real estate market a decade earlier. As only a small portion of the property had been sold for housing, the province was able to purchase 360 hectares of water frontage that provided a much-needed public beach area. The price was $7.68 million, funded partly by the Devonian Foundation and a contribution from the RDCO. By the addition of another 520 hectares of Crown-owned upland, the new park was also able to protect Shorts Creek Canyon, waterfalls and kokanee spawning channels as well as the adjoining California bighorn sheep habitat.

Within a decade all of these new urban-area parks would see significant increases in visitor use, diverting user patterns away from rural-based provincial parks.

Park Operations in the 1990s

Despite philosophical differences with the Social Credit Party, it is notable that the NDP government that took power in October 1991 maintained that regime's

Left: The marine trail in Juan de Fuca Park on the west coast of southern Vancouver Island offers scenic beauty, roaring surf, and marine and wildlife viewing.

Below: The landscape across the water from Okanagan Lake Provincial Park is part of Okanagan Mountain Park, accessible by road from Kelowna or by boat.

The 4,000-hectare Burns Bog at the mouth of the Fraser River is the largest peat bog on the west coast of North America. It purifies the air, produces oxygen, stores carbon and absorbs excess rainfall.
All Canada Photos, Russ Heinl

basic framework for park operations, including service delivery by the private sector. However, Cypress Bowl provided a real test of both government and Parks staff's resolve to stay committed to this policy. When the park was created in 1972, the government had funded construction of a major access highway, provided water and sewer facilities and installed two chairlifts, but adequate funding for a major day-use lodge and more lifts was continually delayed. As a consequence, in 1984 the Social Credit government had been very happy to approve Cypress Bowl Recreation Ltd. as the park's private operator and to give the company a lease on the land, infrastructure and ski lifts. About the same time the new operator also purchased the nearby historic Hollyburn Lodge (built in 1926), which was accessible by a short walk from the new road.

In the mid-1990s the operator sold his business, and the new permittee proposed major expansions that included a gondola, mountaintop restaurant and the expansion of ski lifts eastward to Hollyburn Mountain. Unfortunately, Cypress and Hollyburn were now part of a master plan under the Protected Areas Strategy, and that master plan did not call for such a massive scale of facilities; the plan had, in fact, reserved Hollyburn for cross-country skiing and snowshoeing. Permission was denied, and the operator subsequently complained to the ombudsman for "abuse of process." The government appointed an independent four-person review panel headed by Brian Williams, the former chair of the Wilderness Advisory Commission, who recommended against the major expansion proposed by the permittee and compliance with the basic provision of the park management plan. Subsequently, with prospects for the Winter Olympics looming on the horizon, the operations were again sold. However, although new facilities for aerial skiing and snowboarding and a new day lodge were built for the Olympics, they were located near Black Mountain instead, not Hollyburn.

In both winter and summer, the use of the park is now facilitated and promoted by two popular major trail systems, including the Howe Sound Crest Trail, which provides a wilderness route north on the ridge that parallels Howe Sound and down to Porteau Cove. The Baden-Powell Centennial Trail extends forty kilometres east across the North Shore Mountains, from Horseshoe Bay to Deep Cove on Indian Arm, and serves as a link in the Trans Canada Trail. In the summer, the Yew Lake Trail provides a short and barrier-free self-guided interpretive family experience through subalpine meadows. Given its near-urban location, year-round use and role as the most heavily visited park in the province, Cypress Park seems to be able to provide a balance of both intensive recreational use and protection for the natural environment.

Marine Parks

There are a number of safe anchorages available in the long, narrow Ha'thayim or Von Donop Inlet, one of the new marine parks designated under the Protected Areas Strategy. Located on the northwestern tip of Cortes Island in the Discovery Island group, this 1,277-hectare undeveloped marine wilderness park encompasses lakes, estuaries, a saltwater lagoon and the old-growth forest that the Coast Salish First Nations call Ha'thayim. Most of the population of this twenty-five-kilometre-long island lives on its drier southern end; evidence of past settlement and logging on its wet northern end are fast disappearing as nature reclaims the landscape. This park is jointly managed with the Klahoose First Nation.

Broughton Archipelago Provincial Marine Park, established in September 1992, is composed of a multitude of islands that offer sheltered waters and anchorages with a backdrop of magnificent coastal mountains to the east and the waters of Queen Charlotte Strait to the west. These islands are within the traditional harvesting territory of a number of coastal First Nations people, who developed clam terraces and villages here. There was some European settlement here during the nineteenth and early twentieth centuries, and remnants of overgrown homesteads are still visible. The park contains one of the most under-represented terrestrial ecosystems in the province, the Outer Fiordland Ecosection Coastal Western Hemlock forest, giving it a critical role in the parks system.

Several species of marine animals, including orcas (especially along the park's western boundaries), harbour porpoises, sea lions and sea otters, are found within the waters of the Broughton Archipelago, and river otters, mink and raccoons can often be seen playing along the shoreline. Black bears can occasionally be spotted rolling boulders on the shore in search of food. There are several sea lion haul-outs within the park.

Out with a Bang

On June 29, 2000, with less than a year to go in its mandate, the NDP government was still adding to its record of major environmental protection legislation. On that day parks and eco-reserves were consolidated under one statute, the Protected Areas Act, that gave statutory authority to 14 Class A parks and 4 eco-reserves, established 29 new parks and 6 eco-reserves, and made additions to 16 Class A parks. The provincial total now stood at 530 Class A parks and 148 ecological reserves.

In early 2001 during the final months before the call for a spring election, Ian Waddell, the minister for Environment, Lands and Parks, issued a press release on the success of the protected areas strategy. With over ten million hectares designated as protected parks or reserves, the 12 percent target had been met and exceeded. On March 31, just six weeks before the election, Waddell joined Premier Ujjal Dosanjh and the federal Environment minister, David Anderson, to announce that a joint federal–provincial agreement had been formalized to establish a national park in the southern Gulf Islands and to provide joint funding with the Greater Vancouver Regional District to acquire Burns Bog.

In retrospect, it can be acknowledged that the 1990s was the most dramatic decade in the history of the BC provincial park system.

9 :
Approaching the Centennial, 2001 to 2011

The Lillooet Land and Resource Management Plan

On May 16, 2001, a Liberal government was elected in British Columbia with Gordon Campbell as premier. While the previous government had experienced difficulty promoting consensus for several regional plans such as the Vancouver Island Land Use Plan, the new government inherited one of the most contentious: the Lillooet Land and Resource Management Plan (LRMP), which covered an area in the South Chilcotin north of Gold Bridge and the pioneer mining town of Bralorne. This planning table had begun meeting in 1995 and, in order to ease the members' concerns about future local job losses, the surrounding area had been one of the

Above: Churn Creek Protected Area, just south of the Gang Ranch at Alkali Lake, was established to conserve the unique grassland ecosystem.

first regions in the province to receive funding from Forest Renewal BC. However, even with this impetus, the members of the table had been unable to develop consensus, and environmentalists, First Nations and resource extraction industries had been pitted against each other for control of the process, especially the fate of Spruce Lake.

Historically the Spruce Lake region had been the shared hunting territory of the Lakes Lillooet and Tsilhqot'in First Nations. Conservationists had begun focussing

on protection for it as early as 1937 when the Vancouver Natural History Society, led by wildlife filmmaker Charlie Cunningham, had proposed a provincial park for this region. However, World War II had intervened, and it was not until 1970 that another group began pushing for a Spruce Lake–Eldorado Park, and in 1975 a government-funded study finally recommended the establishment of a Class A park to include the headwaters of Tyaughton, Relay and Big creeks as well as Spruce Lake and the Eldorado Basin to the east. But no action was taken on this recommendation, and over the next decade and a half several of the valleys were clear-cut; logging only came to an end when the government imposed a moratorium

A mule deer blends into the surrounding aspens in Charlie Lake Provincial Park, north of Fort St. John at the junction of the Alaska Highway and Highway 29.

in 1990. By the time the LRMP process was initiated, the northern half of the proposed park had already been placed within the jurisdiction of the Cariboo–Chilcotin planning table and incorporated into the Big Creek Provincial Park, leaving Spruce Lake to the Lillooet table.

In the spring of 2001 the NDP government, seeing no possible consensus developing on this plan, had announced as one of its final acts (before going into the election that would result in its defeat) the establishment of a new, 71,000-hectare protected area, which was to centre on Spruce Lake. This decision was not well received by local groups, especially the mining companies who were not keen on having such a huge area removed from future exploration. As a result, the new Liberal government sent this decision back to the LRMP table for more review and in 2004 they concurred on the formal designation of just 56,000 hectares as the Southern Chilcotin Provincial Park. The remaining 14,000 hectares would be available for commercial recreation, tourism and mineral exploration though not logging. Environmental groups accused the planning table of listening only to the resource and commercial interests. Skeptics accused the government of lacking support for the Protected Area Strategy and LRMP processes, without noting that, even with its reduced boundaries, the total designated protected areas in the Chilcotin had reached 17 percent, including the previously expanded Stein Valley Park.

Opposite top: Chase Provincial Park with its undisturbed mixed forests and rolling mountains was established in 2001 to protect critical habitat for the Chase-Sustut Woodland caribou herd.

Opposite bottom: Morning mists rise on beautiful Spruce Lake in the wilderness of spectacular South Chilcotin Mountains Provincial Park.

The Southern Chilcotin–Spruce Lake Wilderness, located where the coastal wet ecosystems meet those of the dry Interior, is a spectacular area of winding rivers, glistening lakes and rolling alpine meadows. Its extensive trails continue into the Big

Creek Chilcotin Provincial Park to the north, providing opportunities for hiking, backpacking, horseback riding, cross-country skiing and mountain biking. (In 2007 Southern Chilcotin Park was downgraded to a protected area; in 2010 it was raised to Class A park status and renamed South Chilcotin Mountains Provincial Park.)

Meanwhile, although the furor over Spruce Lake finally died down, controversy continued over final cabinet decisions for the Lower Mainland's parks as well as over the Western Canada Wilderness Committee's unfulfilled expectations for more and larger parks, particularly in the upper Elaho River drainage or "Stoltman Wilderness." However, in general, as more LRMPs were completed, it appeared that the decades of vigorous debate and large-scale protests were largely over, an indication that forest, mining and energy companies, environmentalists, community interests and First Nations could and would work together to reach agreements on land use. In that sense the hopes and expectations of Premier Mike Harcourt to develop a province-wide land use plan and end the "war in the woods" had been realized.

A New Role for First Nations

Although the Wilderness Advisory Commission's report in 1986 had recommended that the province acknowledge the interests of First Nations when making land-use decisions, especially in the creation of new parks, the provincial government was reluctant to do so, having taken the position that First Nations were primarily a federal responsibility. However, the 1990s were marked by the strong assertion of First Nations land claims, and soon the ongoing treaty negotiations had become a prime obstacle restraining provincial land allocations. As a compromise, the provincial government began creating new parks "without prejudice" to the Native land claims, which in essence postponed formal dialogue and resolution on whether park management would recognize a role for First Nations.

Meanwhile, environment groups such as the Western Canada Wilderness Committee and the Valhalla Wilderness Society had long recognized the legitimacy of First Nations interests and formed coalitions with them in jointly led protests against the issuing of logging tenures in such locations as Haida Gwaii, the Stein, Clayoquot and later the Central Coast. Native leaders had become regular faces in the media's coverage of blockades and legal challenges in support of proposed protected areas. At the same time the federal government was also determined to recognize First Nations rights and, when creating national parks within BC, built the recognition of aboriginal interests and opportunities for economic development and park management right into its agreements with the province. As a result, Pacific Rim, Gwaii Haanas and later the southern Gulf Islands national parks became park "reserves" pending resolution of Native land claims.

It took several significant court decisions before the provincial government made an official change in policy, at last recognizing some degree of Native entitlements and the need to negotiate new treaties. Foremost among those decisions was that of *Delgamuukw v. the Queen*, handed down by the Supreme Court of Canada in 1997, which confirmed that aboriginal title does exist in British Columbia and that it is a communal rather than individual right to the land itself and not just the right to hunt, fish or gather. Further, it confirmed that, when dealing with the disposition of Crown land, the government must consult with and may have to compensate First Nations whose rights are affected. Shortly after this decision was handed down, the non-profit society Ecotrust Canada published a well-researched report entitled *More than the Sum of Our Parks: People, Places and a Protected Areas System for British Columbia*, which advocated for a government-to-government relationship with First Nations and the use of those relationships to facilitate the development of joint management and stewardship agreements. It also spelled out the need for government to recognize aboriginal entitlements when dealing with new protected areas proposals.

The Ecotrust Canada report set the scene for a complex internal dialogue within the government to find policy solutions. In the decade-long dispute over the Clayoquot, acknowledgement of First Nations entitlements had been one of the foremost issues in the public campaign against logging. But as a result of the *Delgamuukw* decision, First Nations began to be major players in the development of economic strategies for each region, and Parks staff at the regional level, realizing that park management would require cooperative initiatives with local First Nations, held unofficial discussions with them about their future roles, particularly in the management of Kitlope, Khutzeymateen and the Stein. Even more significantly, written into the Nisga'a Treaty, which was signed into law on April 13, 2000,

Hakai Luxvbalis Conservancy, encompassing 123,000 hectares of land and sea north of Port Hardy, challenges sea kayakers with reversing rapids and an intricate network of coves and inlets.

is the provision for the Nisga'a people to have a formal role as partners in the management of the Nass Valley lava beds, now known as Anhluut'ukwsim Laxmihl Angwinga'asanskwhl Nisga'a or Nisga'a Memorial Lava Bed Park. This unique feature is the youngest (just 250 years old) and most accessible volcanic landscape in BC, and visitors can hike through the forest to a viewpoint where they can look down into the dormant crater.

A little further south an agreement had been reached in 1995 that provided for tourism and conservation co-management with the Heiltsuk people in their traditional lands adjacent to the village of Bella Bella (Waglisla) on Campbell Island. About one half of the territory would be protected as "natural and cultural areas" with the remainder designated as "ecosystem-based management" areas. In particular, the province designated the Hakai Luxvbalis as a protected area (later a conservancy area) of 122,000 hectares, which includes the southern half of Hunter Island and northern half of Calvert Island, just north of the world-renowned sport fishing destination of Rivers Inlet. It is the largest marine park and one of the better-known paddling areas in the province.

The original Park Act, however, did not sanction arrangements of this kind with First Nations. Although it allowed the contracting out of visitor services within parks, the act assigned all responsibility for park management to the minister and did not permit the delegation of this responsibility to any party other than public service staff. It was, therefore, necessary to change the act, and an amendment, announced in 2003 but not approved until 2006, created a new classification of parkland, the conservancy area, specifically to allow co-management and stewardship arrangements with First Nations. Conservancies differ from other parks because they prioritize the protection of biological diversity and First Nations values related to social, ceremonial and cultural uses. They allow First Nations to pursue low-impact economic activities that do not undermine ecological values, but commercial logging, mining and hydroelectric generation are prohibited, except for small run-of-the-river projects to service local communities. Evidence of this policy change can be seen in the fact that all management contracts signed after 2006 have required close consultation with First Nations and a role for them in management. In several cases, Native people became the sole contractors for the provision of visitor services. The new legislation also offered a solution to a decade-long impasse in reaching consensus-based land and resource management plans (LRMPs) for the North and Central coasts and provided a tool to help end the international boycotts orchestrated by environmental groups.

The Great Bear Rainforest

In February 2006, after a decade of protests, publicity campaigns, land-use planning and negotiations, an agreement was reached between environmentalists, logging companies, First Nations communities and the BC government on LRMPs for the North and Central coasts. This combined area, now generally known as the Great Bear Rainforest, stretches from just north of Knight Inlet to the Alaska

border and covers some 6,400,000 hectares. It is one of the largest tracts of temperate rainforest left in the world, although years of clear-cut logging have left vast holes in the landscape and logging roads have cut deep swathes across watersheds, permanently destroying wildlife habitat. The forest is characterized by some of the oldest and largest trees on Earth, including thousand-year-old red cedars and ninety-metre-tall Sitka spruce. Its ecology is marked by dynamic and complex interactions between terrestrial, freshwater, estuarine and marine systems so that 350 bird and mammal species, 25 tree species, hundreds of species of fungi and lichens, and thousands of insects, mites, spiders and soil organisms are found here.

The two roundtables for this remarkable area produced plans that recommended three protection zones, the first being fully protected parks. Within twenty-one smaller "biodiversity" areas, mining and tourist development would be permitted but no logging or hydro development. Within larger "ecosystem-based" management operating areas, logging could proceed but was to be subject to special "lighter touch" rules; there is also an expectation that these areas will serve as buffer zones around or corridors between protected areas. The plans also support conservation-based economies in coastal communities and strengthen First Nations involvement

The Great Bear Rainforest, a 6.4-million-hectare protected area on BC's Central Coast, is home to a unique subspecies of black bear. The Kermode's bear is named for Francis Kermode, a former zoologist at the British Columbia Provincial Museum. *Dean van't Schip*

in decisions affecting their traditional territory. In accepting these two plans, the government was agreeing to add 1.2 million hectares to this area's protected lands, a remarkable decision, given that there were already 600,000 hectares of protected lands within this land-use area, specifically in Kitlope and Fiordland conservancies and Khutzeymateen Provincial Park.

Beginning in July 2006, a series of press announcements proposed 114 new conservancies and parks within the Great Bear Forest area, and a series of collaborative agreements were signed with First Nations that dealt with economic opportunities in forestry and tourism as well as a commitment to share land-use decision making. Among the first twenty-four areas to be designated in 2006 was the 200,000-hectare Kitasoo Spirit Bear Conservancy, with 103,000 hectares of it centred on Laredo Inlet on Princess Royal Island, the remainder on Swindle and Price islands to the south. This conservancy's old-growth forests, wetlands and floodplains, tiny sheltered bays, pocket beaches and reefs provides protected habitat for the famous Kermode bear. At the same time the Khutzeymateen Grizzly Sanctuary, designated in 1993, was increased threefold. Much like the creation of the Muskwa–Kechika Special Management Area in 1997, the decision to designate the Kitasoo Conservancy and increase the grizzly sanctuary was widely publicized to attract and appease an international audience. Then to complete this dramatic commitment, in 2007 the government designated another forty-one conservancies and a further forty-nine were set aside in 2008.

This landmark legislation, similar to those enacted for Gwaii Haanas and the Muskwa–Kechika Special Management Area, was accompanied by the establishment of a $120 million Coastal Opportunities Fund, with $30 million coming from federal government, another $30 million from the provincial government and $60 million from charitable foundations, including Ecotrust Canada. Half of the money will be used to fund conservation management projects and half to support economically viable and ecologically sustainable business ventures for First Nations. With funds from Forest Renewal BC to stimulate a cooperative approach, the province committed to helping workers, contractors, communities and companies whose jobs and interests had been affected by these new land-use decisions. This was especially true of forest companies that had been threatened with international market boycotts and now needed to modify their logging practices. The fund also facilitated the negotiation of protocol arrangements with First Nations to provide economic opportunities and park co-management agreements.

In March 2009 the province and First Nations confirmed implementation of a resource management framework for ecosystem-based management zones including low-impact logging regulations. The government also announced that the near-white Kermode's "Spirit Bear" will be designated as the official animal of BC.

Gulf Islands National Park Reserve

On March 31, 2001, just six weeks before the election that swept out the NDP government, the federal and provincial governments made a joint announcement that a national park reserve would be established in the southern Gulf Islands to safeguard one of the most ecologically at-risk natural regions in southern Canada. The new Gulf Islands National Park Reserve lies within the Garry oak ecosystem, but with less than 5 percent of that habitat still in a near-natural state, there are more than one hundred species at risk of extinction, including plants, mammals, birds, reptiles, butterflies, dragonflies and insects of all kinds. The plan for the new 3,600-hectare park would include the designation of whole islands, sites on the larger islands, numerous islets and reefs; another 2,600 hectares of submerged land were also covered by the agreement. The federal government had already invested $31 million and agreed to a further $10 million to acquire private lands particularly on Saturna, Pender and Prevost Islands. Instead of contributing funds for cost-shared acquisition the Province transferred 9 provincial parks including Sidney Spit, Beaumont, Winter Cove, Portland Island and also McDonald Park , an eco-reserve and other Crown lands with value of $40 million. However, the Province also committed another $25 million to acquire parkland elsewhere on Howe Sound and the remarkable additions include Bodega Ridge, Wakes Cove and Burgoyne Bay.

The process of creating the park was not begun until 2003 when the federal and provincial governments signed a memorandum of understanding that launched a "feasibility study." But actually establishing the Gulf Islands National Parks Reserve took many more years and presented far more challenges than the creation of either Pacific Rim or Gwaii Haanas national parks. To begin with, the word "reserve" in the park's title indicates that aboriginal title to the land has not been extinguished by the establishment of the park; in fact, nineteen First Nations have expressed some level of claim to this land base. Evidence of their long history here can be found throughout this area. Mount Warburton Pike on Saturna Island, at 397 metres the second-highest point of land in the Gulf Islands, was used by First Nations for spiritual and sacred purposes, while the Outer Islands fronting on the Strait of Georgia provided a launching area for canoe travel to the Fraser River.

Princess Margaret Marine Park, which is on and around Portland Island, has a more complicated history. It was once the site of a Native village, a fact borne out by the shell midden beaches that ring the island, but in the 1880s it was farmed by Kanaka (Hawaiian) immigrants and some of the fruit trees and rose bushes they planted still remain. In 1958 it was given to Princess Margaret to commemorate her visit to BC, and when she returned title to it in 1967, it became a provincial park and was renamed in her honour. Now, as a component of the national park, the park is noted for its protected coves and sand beaches. It is also well known as a recreational diving area as the vessel *G.B. Church* was sunk off its northeast shore in 1991, the first ship to be deliberately sunk as an artificial reef in BC waters.

While some of the designated land for the park was Crown-owned, many of the islands were privately owned and had to be purchased. A number of them were also encumbered with resource allocations. Some of the properties designated are parts of the larger islands in this group: for example, Lyall Creek is a small park on Saturna Island. One of the few remaining salmon-bearing streams in the Gulf Islands,

Juniper trees stand sentinel on a tiny sandstone islet near Gabriola Island in the Gulf Islands National Park Reserve. *All Canada Photos, David Nunuk*

it became the focus of a group of volunteer stream restorers in the late 1990s. Its designation as part of the new national park reserve meant that funds and technical support were made available to them to restore the stream to a more natural state. A number of the smaller islands, such as Blunden and Brackman, have never been inhabited and have intact ecosystems including Garry oaks and Douglas firs with little evidence of invasion by exotic species; these islands can now only be accessed by authorized persons.

Parks Branch Reorganization

In 2001 the Parks Branch became part of a new Ministry of Water, Land and Air Protection, and the branch lost its identity in the new structure. Parks' headquarters unit was integrated into the larger Environmental Stewardship Division and, even with the enormous growth in its land base, shared the same assistant deputy minister as the Fish and Wildlife Branch. At the field level both regional managers and park planners became responsible for the combined roles and responsibilities of multiple mandates, including Protected Areas, Fish and Wildlife and First Nations liaison.

In 2005 the Land Use Coordination Office was disbanded and replaced by the Integrated Land Management Bureau in yet another new ministry, this time Agriculture and Lands. *A New Direction for Strategic Land Use Planning in BC*, published the following year, outlined a more streamlined and effective planning process that had been developed from lessons learned over a decade of extensive, expensive and time-consuming preparation of Land and Resource Management Plans (LRMPs). The report also laid out the next step in the process: the preparation of Sustainable Resource Management Plans as small areas within the LRMPs that would provide more detailed planning of old-growth harvesting or specific economic development for energy, agriculture and tourism. These smaller plans would also consider access corridors to protected areas and parks.

Ruckle Provincial Park on Salt Spring Island overlooks Swartz Bay and is the perfect vantage point to watch pleasure boats and ferries sail by.

The Final Step in Private Service Delivery

Between 1989 and 1991 the number of contracts for the provision of park visitor services increased from 47 to 197, meeting government objectives but creating administrative overload and inefficient operations, and because of the variations in facility size, seasonal use and weather risks in BC's parks, some contracts were providing only marginal financial returns to the Parks Branch and the contractor. The government was still committed to private service delivery, but it was obvious that the standard contractual arrangements would have to be restructured. Subsequently the number of sub-regional contracts was greatly reduced by pooling or "bundling" them into multi-year regional contracts. Park facility operators (PFOs) were now not only responsible for such specific services as facility maintenance, firewood and sanitation but also for all aspects of park operation, including security, public information, interpretation and revenue collection. And in selected parks they were also encouraged to provide small seasonal retail concessions such as horse and boat rentals and food services.

In the past PFOs had collected user fees, returned the funds to the province and were then paid a set contract fee for their services; they had no incentive to monitor attendance or to be diligent in collecting revenues. Under the new contracts the operator would collect and retain user fees to cover operating costs, although the fee structure would be set and approved by the province. However, in regions of the province where the summer park visiting season is short, the province would provide a "deficiency payment" to make up the difference between costs and income; for example, the short season in Skeena, Peace River and Alaska Highway districts means that park operators cannot recover costs from user fees. With the new system in operation, the financial report for 2007–08 showed that PFOs collected and retained $11.9 million in fees and received an additional $3.7 million in deficiency payments. By that time, bundling had reduced the number of PFO contracts to twenty-nine, which are held by twenty-two contractors as some PFOs held more than one regional contract. Successful operators received a five-year permit with provision for a five-year renewal. But to reassure the public about the privatizing of parklands, the government once again confirmed that no interests in land or resources would be sold. At the same time the province continued to administer park user surveys to assess visitor satisfaction and monitor operator performance.

New Partnerships

In the last decade of the old century and the first decade of the new one, a recurring feature in land acquisition for parks in BC became the Branch's successful cooperative endeavours with conservation groups that are legally structured as "land trusts." These groups do not necessarily hold and manage parkland but instead promote land stewardship and conservation, and they have, to a great extent, replaced the traditional environmental groups, such as the Western Canada Wilderness Committee (now known simply as the Wilderness Committee) and the Sierra Club, as the leading public voices advocating for new parks. Many of the environmental groups, on the other hand, have moved from appeals for new parks to much broader public policy issues such as global warming, alternative energy, forest management, endangered species and health of oceans. These concerns for biodiversity, of course, readily link them to a continued support for parks.

Although the first land trust groups were established a half century ago, their numbers and scope within BC have grown significantly since 1996 when Section 210 of the Land Titles Act was amended to permit individuals to register conservation covenants against a piece of property. These covenants often provide a means whereby public-minded citizens can protect their property (or a portion of it) for its environmental value without necessarily donating that property to the government or some public organization. Landowners sign voluntary agreements to protect the land in a specified way while still retaining title to it so that they can continue to live on it and use it within the terms of the covenant. The objective is usually to preserve scenic values, open space, a natural environment, specific habitat, wetlands or nesting sites, and covenants of this kind have been used to prevent subdivisions, restrict logging and farming, prevent access by motor vehicles, prevent harvesting of plants or animals or the diversion of water over all or a designated portion of the land. They remain in effect even if the land is sold, thus binding future owners as well.

Landowners must designate an organization to be responsible for protecting, monitoring or defending the covenant in perpetuity. The land trust that takes on this obligation can be an environmental organization or a government agency, but it must be recognized and registered by the Surveyor General. For example, the Islands Trust, which was established in 1974 as a land use and planning agency, operates in this capacity for the 13 major islands and 450 smaller islands between Vancouver Island and the Lower Mainland. Regional districts and even the Ministry of Environment can also serve as land trusts, but some agencies, for example the Greater Vancouver Regional District, have created separate land trust societies as a vehicle for fundraising and to encourage land donations. A land trust can also purchase a parcel and place a covenant on it to protect specified environmental values before transferring management to either the provincial Parks or Fish and Wildlife branch or to a regional district.

As conservation covenants often limit economic land uses such as farming or logging or the type of improvements or structures that can be built, the value of the property may diminish, but a variety of taxation benefits are available as incentives for the affected landowner. The Assessment Authority of BC may reduce property taxes by re-assessing the land, and since 2002, under the federal Ecological Gifts Program, donations to approved conservation charities and land trusts of "ecologically sensitive" land or easements have been eligible for special income tax assistance, both personal and corporate. To qualify, Environment Canada certifies that the land in question is eco-sensitive and an expert panel certifies the value of the donation. By April 2009 Environment Canada had approved 99 gifts in BC valued at $179 million and providing 63,865 hectares of parkland. This generosity by BC residents is remarkable considering that in all of Canada there were just 678 eco-gifts valued at $417 million protecting 117,000 hectares.

This combination of policies and programs has seen land trust organizations become major players in the protection and acquisition of land with environmental values. Certainly in the first decade of the twenty-first century they have provided active leadership in defining priorities for acquisition and forcing political response.

Wildlife viewing at Botanical Beach, which forms
the western end of Juan de Fuca Park, is best at
low tide when visitors can walk out over the flat
sandstone and granite outcroppings.
James D. Anderson collection

They have also been remarkably successful in securing the contribution of millions of dollars in fundraising campaigns.

Currently there are over forty land trusts in BC, four with province-wide mandates while the others have more local interests. Among those with provincial or national focus is the Nature Conservancy of Canada (NCC), founded in 1962, which seeks the direct protection of wildlife habitat through property purchases or donations and long-term conservancy stewardships. Of the NCC's fifty-four properties in BC, thirty-seven are freehold and seventeen are held through conservation covenants. Properties acquired by the NCC in conjunction with the BC Parks Branch include Brackman Island (acquired in 1975) and Cabbage Island (1978), which were incorporated into the Gulf Islands National Park Reserve in 2003. They contributed funds for the purchase of Botanical Beach (1984) near Port Renfrew; it became a Class A park in 1989 and part of the Juan de Fuca Provincial Park in 2009. The NCC also purchased land to add to existing provincial parks: 890 hectares to Gowlland Tod in 1994, 895 hectares to Princess Louisa Inlet in 2002 and 85 hectares to Francis Point on the Sunshine Coast in 2000. Other NCC holdings include the Campbell River estuary and ranchlands in the Tatlayoko, Columbia and Thompson–Nicola valleys.

In 2007 Environment Canada approved creation of a $225 million National Areas Conservation Program (NACP) fund and entered into an agreement with the NCC to secure environmentally sensitive lands across Canada. A year later the NCC, in partnership with the NACP, acquired 55,000 hectares of diverse forested slopes and mountaintops directly above the Kootenay Lake shoreline from Pluto Darkwoods, a German forest company, for about $100 million; $65 million came from the NCC. As part of the transaction, $50 million was sanctioned as an ecological gift. In 2002 the province had acquired 1,200 hectares along the northern block of these forestlands to add to West Arm Park on Kootenay Lake.

The Nature Trust of British Columbia began life in 1971 as the Second Century Fund. Its first president, Bert Hoffmeister, the chief executive officer of MacMillan Bloedel from 1949 to 1957, persuaded the federal government to provide an initial grant of $4.5 million, and the trust has never looked back after this auspicious start. To date it has invested $65 million to help acquire fourteen properties in conjunction with BC Parks. These include contributions toward the purchase of Francis Point, Botanical Beach, Burgoyne Bay, Marble River on northern Vancouver Island and Squitty Bay on Lasqueti Island, as well as additions to MacMillan Park, the Cowichan River corridor, the Adams River corridor and a parcel on Cold Fish Lake to add to Spatsizi Provincial Park. The Nature Trust is also active in support of numerous ecological reserves and wildlife management areas. Highlights include Addington Marsh, Boundary Bay, the Hoodoos and the Englishman River estuary.

In recent years the most visible and active partner for the Parks Branch has been the Land Conservancy (TLC) of BC, founded in 1997, which tended to focus at first on southern Vancouver Island and the Gulf Islands but expanded to province-wide scope in the new century. An extremely active group, they have acquired over a hundred properties for a total of more than 32,000 hectares. Their cooperative

The harbour seal is the most numerous and widespread marine mammal on the north Pacific coast. *Dean van't Schip*

A storm lashes the rocky shore near the entrance to Smuggler Cove Marine Provincial Park on the Sunshine Coast. *Dean van't Schip*

projects with Parks include Jedediah and Gerald islands and part of the Winchelsea Island group south of Gabriola Island. The acquisition of Skaha Bluffs near Penticton in 2007 was a joint initiative involving both federal and provincial governments and both the TLC and the Nature Conservancy of Canada.

Another major multi-party campaign with both senior levels of government plus regional districts resulted in the purchase of property at Burgoyne Bay on Salt Spring Island, which seems likely to become one of the most popular parks in the Gulf Islands. Most recently the TLC has taken a $1.5 million option to purchase a parcel of land that provides 1.7 kilometres of frontage on Slocan Lake, abutting Valhalla Park.

The Marine Parks Forever Society was formed in 1989 by the Council of BC Yacht Clubs, which has over fifty member clubs, to acquire marine-oriented properties within the province. The society has raised nearly $1 million to date. In the 1990s it led the campaign to acquire lands at Pirates Cove on DeCourcy Island, Smuggler Cove on the Sunshine Coast and Wallace Island in Trincomali Channel. In 1995 it participated with the Friends of Jedediah, the Nature Trust of British Columbia and many other individuals and groups to purchase Jedediah Island from Al and Mary Palmer, owners of the island since 1949. The estate of the late Daniel Culver also committed $1.1 million to Jedediah's preservation. More recently in conjunction with the Greater Vancouver Regional District, the society has helped to gain title to major pieces of shoreline that were necessary to the consolidation of a large marine park in Indian Arm, contributed to the purchase of Musket Island, which is situated off Hardy Island in Jervis Inlet, Wakes Cove on Valdez Island and Squitty Bay.

In addition, the province, with the Fish and Wildlife Branch as its agent, has funded numerous cooperative acquisitions with the provincial share coming from the Habitat Conservation Trust Fund. This fund receives a share of revenue from the sale of provincial hunting and fishing licences and is targeted on the acquisition and protection of critical waterfowl, wildlife and fisheries habitats. These are generally designated as provincial wildlife management areas rather than parks or ecological reserves.

The success of the land trusts in raising funds and increasing public awareness of land stewardship has resulted in changes to the role of the Parks Branch. First, the focus has shifted from the acquisition of large natural-area parks to smaller-scale natural habitats. Second, the new emphasis is on the acquisition of properties more noted for their natural history than for their recreation potential. Third, the competitive fundraising campaigns of these groups, each promoting public support for a different candidate property, are nearly all predicated on cost-shared government financial support. Consequently, they, rather than Parks Branch staff, have to a degree assumed leadership in determining priorities for government spending.

To cope with this demand for cost sharing, in 2004 the province provided $8 million to create a "public lands trust" as a source of matching dollar contributions to support conservation planning and management of private lands with unique ecological values. This fund will be jointly managed by the big four land trusts, which collectively belong to the BC Conservation Lands Forum. Funding of $3 million has already been directed to Stanley Park cleanup and $30 million to the Great Bear Rainforest Trust Fund. The province provided an additional $9 million in 2008 to be accessed by land trust groups to fund management of their property holdings. In 2009 the Land Conservancy announced a special $3.5 million fundraising initiative, Forever BC, in support of their needs.

Given the considerable success of land trusts and similar groups over the past ten years in raising funds, it appears the public may have shifted financial support to the less militant environmental groups who have developed a more positive image to achieve results through cooperative partnerships with each other and government. Groups such as Ecotrust Canada have worked closely with coastal communities, displaced forestry and fisheries workers and First Nations to co-fund cooperative arrangements that will stimulate "sustainable economic opportunities." ForestEthics has emerged as a collaborative force with the Canadian Parks and Wilderness Society and the Land Trust Alliance. And while it is evident there is still strong political dissent over government policy in matters affecting land use and resource management in BC, there are also numerous circumstances where groups have looked for solutions and built bridges between competing interests.

Marine Protected Areas for the Twenty-first Century

Montague Harbour Marine Park is the perfect place for a family camping holiday or an afternoon of birdwatching.

The first marine protected area in the BC Parks system was Montague Harbour on the southwest side of Galiano Island, established in 1959. At that time the primary role of the ninety-seven-hectare park was to provide recreational opportunities for the people of the Gulf Islands, but as the years went by it was clear that there were other important values within this small boat harbour. As a result, its secondary

Holidayers head for home as the sun sets on Montague Harbour Marine Provincial Park on Galiano Island.

role became the protection of a saltwater marsh, a tombolo, the intertidal marine life and the adjacent foreshore bird habitat. And finally, when it was belatedly realized that there are numerous Coast Salish archeological sites here dating back at least three thousand years, a third role was developed: the protection of cultural features.

By 2011 British Columbia, with its approximately 29,500 kilometres of coastline and an estimated 40,000 islands of every size, had designated over one hundred marine protected areas, many of them with all three roles to fulfill. However, the province's designation of marine parks is limited by the fact that the government of British Columbia only has control over coastal shorelines down to the low-water mark; the federal government has the primary jurisdiction for matters affecting the harvest and protection of fisheries, marine mammals and their habitat as well as for marine navigation and shipping—in fact, everything that lies beyond that low-water mark right out to the boundaries of Canada's two-hundred-mile offshore exclusive economic zone. However, control of the sea bed, particularly inland seas, is still subject to constitutional debate and court challenges. In December 1996 the federal government's new Oceans Act became law, providing a legislative framework for the management of the country's ocean areas. The act was followed in 1998 by a joint federal and provincial policy paper called *Marine Protected Strategies for BC*, which included a variety of mutual inventory initiatives to identify natural and cultural values on this coast, such as abandoned canneries, archeological sites, seabird colonies, anchorages, shellfish beds, fish habitat, kelp beds, marine mammals and fiord landscapes, all of which were candidates for marine protected area status.

Then in July 2002 the Department of Fisheries and Oceans (DFO) issued a policy paper called *Oceans Strategy* to implement the Oceans Act. This paper outlined an ecosystems approach to ocean resource management and environmental assessment based on the principles of sustainable development, integrated management and a precautionary approach. Even more importantly, it was a call to designate marine protected areas that recognize the economic, social, cultural and ecological values of marine resources. At the same time, it acknowledged the need for co-operative arrangements with both the provincial government and First Nations. Subsequently, the federal government created three core programs that would lead to the construction of a coast-to-coast-to-coast marine protected network.

The Oceans Act Marine Protected Areas program was established by the DFO to "protect and conserve important fish and marine mammal habitats, endangered marine species, unique features and areas of high biological productivity or biodiversity." In BC, three such areas have already been designated. The Endeavour Hydro Thermal Vents Marine Protected Area, created on March 7, 2003, was the very first federal marine park. An active seafloor zone 250 kilometres southwest of Vancouver Island, where tectonic plates diverge and the seawater is heated by the underlying molten lava, the vents support a rich ecosystem of microbes and animal life. The Bowie Seamount, which became Canada's seventh marine protected area on April 17, 2008, is a complex of three submarine volcanoes located 180 kilometres off Haida Gwaii. Then in June 2010 Gwaii Haanas National Marine Conservation Area Reserve and Haida Heritage Site was redesignated as marine protected areas. Race Rocks at the eastern end of Juan de Fuca Strait, which became a provincial ecological reserve in 1980, is also under active consideration for federal marine protected area status.

Marine Wildlife Areas were established by Environment Canada to "protect and conserve habitat for a variety of wildlife, including migratory birds and endangered species." In 2002 the department completed and implemented a plan for the Alaksen National Wildlife Area and the adjoining George C. Reifel Migratory Bird Sanctuary on Westham Island in the Fraser Delta; both are managed by the Canadian Wildlife Service. Another significant area under study as a possible marine wildlife area is the Scott Islands group off the northern tip of Vancouver Island; three of the islands are designated as ecological reserves and all five comprise Scott Islands Provincial Park. They are home to large populations of Stellar sea lions, sea otters and several species of whales and support a seabird colony of over two million birds.

Parks Canada has begun the creation of a series of national marine conservation areas to "protect and conserve representative examples of Canada's natural and cultural marine heritage and to provide opportunities for public education and enjoyment." As yet, only two have yet been designated: Fathom Five National Marine Park on Lake Superior and Saguenay–St. Lawrence Marine Park in Quebec. Two BC sites under study are the foreshore areas surrounding Haida Gwaii and the Gulf Islands National Park Reserve.

The province has not created a new category or special designation for the marine protected areas of the twenty-first century, but there are already over 175 Class A marine parks and ecological reserves, totalling 275,000 hectares of foreshore. And many provincial marine parks do more than just provide protected anchorages; like Montague Harbour, they also incorporate cultural values and coastal landscapes. Among them are Rebecca Spit, Mitlenatch Island, the Skookumchuck Narrows, Porteau Cove, Desolation Sound and Princess Louisa Inlet. It is likely that several of the new conservancies designated along the Central and North coasts will eventually be given some sort of marine protected areas status as the coastal Land and Resource Management Plan designated dozens of Crown land parcels as new protected areas along the Inside Passage. These include Penrose Island, Fiordland and the Hakai Conservation Area.

Of interest is a separate but related initiative to establish a series of safe harbours as a sort of "marine trail," primarily for kayakers. This would dovetail with the recent proposal to establish a "Cascadia Marine Trail" in San Juan Islands/Puget Sound area and along the Columbia River. In a sense, the multiple sites of Sechelt Inlets Marine Provincial Park in combination with nearby Princess Louisa Inlet already serve this function. Three other areas—the Broughton Archipelago, the Desolation Sound/Cortes Island area and the Southern Gulf Islands—may serve as similar nodes.

Kayakers pause in their exploration of the dozens of islands and islets that form Broughton Archipelago Marine Park, at the mouth of Knight Inlet on the west side of Queen Charlotte Strait.

The Trans Canada Trail

In 2004 the provincial government announced the creation of a Spirit of 2010 Trail Network to enhance tourism during Vancouver's Winter Olympics year. In one sense, this was simply putting a "Made in BC" label on the Trans Canada Trail project, which was organized by a volunteer-directed, registered non-profit society with the objective of creating a linear trail system right across the country that would link with trails to the North. While primarily a trail for hiking and cycling, in some parts of the country it also serves horses, all-terrain vehicles and snowmobiles.

In 1999 the BC government had announced a $960,000 program, funded by the provincial and federal governments and the Trails Society of BC, to assist in the upgrading of former railbeds to cycling trails. By this time the "rails to trails" initiative was well underway. The popular Lochside and Galloping Goose trails, connecting the City of Victoria with its rural surroundings and serving both as a commuter route and recreational trail, had become a tremendous success with thousands of users. The trail from Princeton through the Okanagan to Rock Creek and Midway had already been upgraded and, having been advertised by cycle tour groups for over a decade, had become a significant tourist attraction. The next challenge was to convert the eastern extension of the Kettle Valley Railway through Grand Forks to Castlegar, and six environmental teams were assigned to projects based in Rossland, Creston and Grand Forks.

On a map, a railway right-of-way appears as a simple unitary linear corridor that could be purchased with a simple deed of sale. In reality, the acquisition of abandoned railways is a frustrating and time-consuming project. Most of BC's railways were built a hundred years ago, and in most cases, the property they sit on is unsurveyed and consists of literally hundreds of pieces of rights-of-way crossing through other properties, many of them private. These pieces of railbed are seldom the same width. At numerous locations are blocks of land set aside for station structures, yards, junctions and double tracks for passing, so that just defining exactly how much property is involved and where it is located is a tedious land status task. As well, railway corridors have always invited other parallel linear uses, such as power and telecommunication lines, oil and gas pipelines. The early railways also granted numerous approvals and easements across the tracks for major highways, industrial roads and private access. In some places they included bulk-loading sites for chemicals or oil storage tanks, and although long abandoned, they left the soil contaminated.

These rail corridors also came with numerous liabilities—bridges, culverts, trestles, tunnels—many of which have fallen into disrepair so that they are unsafe for public access and use. The famous Myra–Bellevue trestles near Kelowna fell into disrepair and were upgraded by volunteers, only to have them destroyed by forest fires in 2003. Over the next five years they were rebuilt under the supervision of qualified engineers. Debate raged for years over the several millions of dollars needed for the repair or replacement of the Kinsol Trestle, also known as the Koksilah River Trestle, north of Shawnigan Lake. This bridge, a vital link in the Trans Canada Trail, had become unusable by hikers and bikers because of its dilapidated condition, but a feasibility study in 2008 put the cost of repairs and reconstruction at $5.7 million. The government finally promised to provide $4.1 million; a local fundraising campaign is attempting to raise the remainder. Official re-opening is scheduled for the early summer of 2011.

Within BC the Trans Canada Trail now consists of four sections of abandoned railway right-of-way acquired by the province in the 1970s through to the 1990s. Other key pieces of the trail are located in the Slocan Valley (fifty kilometres), Shawnigan Lake to Cowichan Lake (forty-six kilometres), and Nelson to Salmo (forty-eight kilometres). But although the right-of-way for the Spirit of 2010 corridor is usually held by the Crown, it has not been dedicated as a provincial park managed by the Parks Branch. Generally, the policy of the province has been that responsibility for trail management, upgrades, signage and promotion should be assigned to local volunteer community groups. The Spirit program, apart from its promotional aspects, is a means to provide funding to these groups to upgrade and maintain trails and promote their use. However, the Trans Canada Trail corridor has become a major feature where it crosses through two notable provincial parks—Cowichan River and Myra–Bellevue. Kettle River Provincial Park has also become an important waypoint

The forests of the Kitlope Valley nurture a wide variety of ferns, lichens and mushrooms, including this poisonous fly agaric mushroom (*amanita muscaria*).

for cyclists travelling from the Okanagan Valley to the West Kootenay. A major motivation for regional management is that this route has the potential to become a tourist attraction with local economic benefits, and it is actively promoted by communities such as Penticton, Princeton and Grand Forks.

Both nationally and provincially there was an earlier and rival proposal for a "National Hiking Trail," which competed for political, government, user group and public attention. Its organizers, who came together in the 1970s, proposed a historic trail route across the country; in BC it was to cross the central Interior from Banff and incorporate the Mackenzie Grease Trail with some linkages on Vancouver Island. It differed in two main respects from the higher profile Trans Canada Trail: it was to use a more southerly route, largely utilizing abandoned railway corridors, where it would be more accessible to urban populations, and it was to be a multi-use trail for both hikers and bikers, though in some sections it would be open to snowmobiles and all-terrain vehicles. Although currently within BC the Trans Canada Trail has received more widespread community support and government funding, certain links of the National Trail concept are still championed by outdoor clubs and are being realized with volunteer efforts. Since this trail does not generally utilize abandoned railway lines, it does not usually involve land acquisition on any major scale.

A recent initiative has been a proposal to add two new trail corridors on Vancouver Island: one a north–south route running the length of the Island; the other a mid-Island route crossing from east coast to west coast.

Yellowstone to Yukon

In 1993 lawyer and environmentalist Harvey Locke wrote the words "Yellowstone to Yukon" on a map while sitting beside a campfire in what is now the Muskwa–Kechika Special Management Area in northern BC. He remembered the story of a grey wolf that had been collared with a satellite transmitter in Kananaskis, Alberta, in 1991, and in the course of the next two years had travelled through two Canadian provinces and three American states, thereby covering an area fifteen times larger than Banff National Park. The wolf proved how far and wide carnivores roam and clearly demonstrated that small islands of protected parks are not enough; the islands must be connected by safe migration pathways. This experience marked the start of a project to establish wildlife corridors throughout the mountain ranges from Yellowstone National Park to the Yukon, and in December 1993 a group of scientists and conservationists assembled in Kananaskis to formulate a plan.

The Yellowstone to Yukon Conservation Initiative, created in 1997, is a joint Canada–US, not-for-profit organization dedicated to preserving and maintaining the wildlife, native plants, wilderness and natural processes in the Rockies from Yellowstone National Park to the Yukon Territory. It supports a network of organizations, agencies and individuals doing on-the-ground conservation work.

Opposite: At sunrise a wolf's tracks are plainly outlined on the muddy bank of the Gataga River in the Muskwa-Kechika Wilderness. All Canada Photos, John E. Marriot

The Current Status of the Parks System: Where Are We after One Hundred Years?

In 2006 Environment Canada published the *Canadian Protected Areas Status Report*. The purpose of the report was twofold: to evaluate the national and provincial park systems as a commitment to the International Union for Conservation of Nature (IUCN); and to demonstrate Canada's international commitment to establish a protected areas network.

The report noted that Alberta was the only province besides British Columbia to reach the IUCN protected areas target of 12 percent. (The bulk of those areas comprises three national parks: Jasper, Banff and Wood Buffalo, Canada's largest national park.) Manitoba had significantly increased its parks system, the government of Quebec had announced an 8 percent target for protected areas and many parks had been created in the Far North.

Internationally Canada's park system has much to be proud of and to present to the world. The United Nations Educational, Scientific and Cultural Organization (UNESCO), which advocates for the preservation of the world's most important natural and cultural sites, has designated thirteen World Heritage Sites in Canada, including Dinosaur Provincial Park, Gros Morne National Park and the Historic District of Old Québec. British Columbia is home to two sites: a portion of the huge Kluane/Wrangell–St. Elias/Glacier Bay/Tatshenshini–Alsek complex; and

Rocky Mountain Parks, which includes Mount Robson, Mount Assiniboine and Hamber provincial parks and the contiguous national parks of Kootenay, Banff, Yoho and Jasper. It is likely that Haida Gwaii will also be designated and Mount Edziza/Stikine/Spatsizi is being considered for nomination.

In 2010 BC boasted:

- 989 provincial parks and protected areas, totalling 13,142 million hectares (see map, page 23);

- 10,700 vehicle-accessible campsites and approximately 2,000 walk-in/backcountry sites;

- 6,000 kilometres of hiking trails;

- 20,257,000 recorded visits to parks. About 6 in 10 residents of British Columbia use a provincial park each year.

The auditor general of BC issued a 2010 report, *Conservation of Ecological Integrity in BC Parks and Protected Areas*, to address a number of questions regarding the planning and operation of the provincial parks system. Among the most telling issues were: 1) Does the Ministry of the Environment have the vision, plans and operational policies in place for the conservation of ecological integrity? 2) Is ecological integrity being conserved in each individual Class A park? And 3) Is the ministry reporting on the state of ecological integrity in protected areas?

The report highlighted the absence of a current master parks system plan. It suggested that numerous parks and ecological reserves lack adequate management plans and that the ministry falls short of meeting its commitment to ecological integrity. The response of the ministry to these perceived inadequacies was to plead fiscal restraint: millions of dollars would be required to fund the necessary inventory, planning and monitoring programs.

A clear need exists for an ongoing BC parks system plan, not as a traditional tool for identifying new parks, but rather as a means for the park system to evaluate how to best use, present and protect the province's hundreds of new parks. Simply designating them as "protected areas" does not preordain how they should be developed or managed.

A major dilemma for park administrators (apart from securing funding) is how to decide on the degree and type of public access for each new park in the system. Given the huge number of new parks, dozens of them will simply be "land banked" and remain relatively unknown, unvisited and unmanaged for decades.

But which new parks must be given priority for preservation of resource and cultural values? Can a case be made for one or several of the larger parks to be designated as high-profile destinations for easy access and multiple uses, like popular Wells Gray, Golden Ears and Manning parks, or others for high-density recreational use, like Sun Oka and Cultus Lake? These are the sorts of questions that must be asked in order to move toward rational growth and long-term preservation of the parks system.

Postscript

The results of the small steps that were originally taken to create a few BC parks have clearly exceeded the expectations of the park elders who undertook the early park reconnaissance in this large and magnificent province.

Despite its wounds the values of Strathcona have finally been protected, grown and diversified; its former geometric straight lines and boundaries now more clearly reflect watersheds and access to the ocean to create a more holistic park.

Who would have believed that the size of the early Devonian purchases would be eclipsed by those of Burgoyne Bay, Indian Arm, Fintry, Skaha Bluffs and others?

Or that Al Fairhurst's dreams would be largely realized by a system of over one hundred marine parks that now extends the entire length of the coast of British Columbia?

Or that a park the scale of Tweedsmuir would be matched by Muskwa–Kechika?

Or that Pacific Rim National Park would be joined by the Gwaii Haanas and Gulf Islands national park reserves? And that several large areas within the Great

Above: Ancient gnarled cedars, some estimated to be
well over 1,000 years old, are protected in Carmanah/
Walbran Provincial Park.

Bear Rainforest would be given conservancy status to protect the habitats of the grizzly and Kermode spirit bear?

Or that the international reputation of the West Coast Trail would be joined by hiking challenges along both the north and south coasts of Vancouver Island? Or that the Trans Canada Trail would be a near-reality, a continuous corridor across the province?

It would seem to pay to "dream no little dreams," but what dreams exist for the next century?

Are we satisfied that the vision of Premier Mike Harcourt to establish strategic land-use plans for all regions of the province has nearly been realized? What new large parks will be established when the Land and Resource Management Plans (LRMPs) for the Far North are completed? Do we need to ask what else is missing to complete the provincial park system? Parks staff recently identified a wish list of possible land acquisitions necessary to resolve issues with in-holdings, boundary conflicts and missing elements, a list that would likely require several hundred million dollars to implement.

However, a serious decline of government revenue has led to a fiscal retrenchment that includes parks budgets, fish and wildlife programs and staffing. A reduction in the number of park rangers and off-season closures of some parks has already generated considerable adverse publicity. Finding a balance between budgetary restraint and the need for parks planning will continue to be a challenge.

Two significant "ecological integrity" policy issues are emerging from the parks debate. First, how to manage the park biota—endangered species, large ungulates and forest cover—that will increasingly be subject to the uncertain effects of climate change and global warming. And second, whether to continue to allow big-game hunting in selected large wilderness parks in the face of increased public opposition.

Will the future growth of protected areas be based primarily on priorities identified by land trusts and characterized by near-urban parks with an emphasis on natural values? Will the new Gulf Islands National Park Reserve see future expansion and possibly the transfer in of more existing parks on Salt Spring and/or Galiano islands? Will the groups that support the dream of the Okanagan–Similkameen National Park proposal be successful? Will there be increased pressure on Canada to establish more Marine Protected Areas to protect the diversity of coastal marine resources?

New Challenges for the Second Century

It appears that the long-standing debate between "preserve and protect" versus "wise use" has grown more complex and will likely dominate the political agenda for the next decade. An overview of the topic might provide some perspective, and interested readers can turn to Muir, Nash, Pinchot, Ahrens, Haig-Brown and numerous other writers who make cases for both sides.

Over the past decade two topics have added a global perspective to the discussion of parks and their management. First, the Clayoquot and Great Bear

Rainforest areas raised the subject of how indigenous people and their traditional lifestyles interface with nature and what their role is in park management.

Second, and even more complex, is the link between the Protected Area Strategy and the issue of global warming. A 2010 report by Dr. Jim Pojar, *A New Climate for Conservation: Nature, Carbon and Climate Change in British Columbia*, suggests that the province has a moral responsibility to expand the total mass of protected areas by an additional 35 percent. The premise of the report, commissioned by the Working Group on Biodiversity, Forests and Climate, an alliance of environmental NGOs including the Canadian Parks and Wilderness Society (CPAWS), the Land Trust Alliance of British Columbia and others, is that the current system of protected areas is too small and fragmented to both protect habitat for migrant wildlife and biota and to serve as a carbon sink to deal with global warming.

Apart from this rather radical recommendation, the report comments on the future of the park system:

The park system is based in large part on physical enduring features that will not change much as climate changes, as species sort themselves out and as biological communities reassemble. The mountains, rivers and big lakes will remain, the interior plateaus will persist, morainal blankets and outwash terraces will stay as they are, even as the biota they support changes. The physical landscape is the template for ecosystems, the stage upon which the drama of climate change is playing out.

While the physical landscape of individual parks will remain relatively constant, climate change will almost certainly impact the distribution and even existence of numerous plants and animals found in these parks. The park may continue to look the same but new species will be found while others will be missing.

Dr. Pojar identifies a need to integrate nature conservation strategies with climate action strategies. The rationale for expanded protected areas is to provide more forest ecosystem to maximize carbon retention, biodiversity of habitats for ecological adaptation and corridors of refuge for migratory wildlife and endangered species.

CPAWS has also resurrected and greatly broadened the linear concept of the Great Divide Trails, not for recreational considerations, but for the protection of the diversity of wildlife and habitat. The ambitious Y2Y vision to protect and manage a corridor along the spine of the mountains that stretch from Yellowstone to the Yukon would have significance for several BC protected areas and might help abate current concerns for the future health of mountain caribou and of grizzly bears. CPAWS and others champion expansion of Akamina–Kishinena in the Flathead Valley to expand the cross-border complex of Waterton/Glacier National Parks. Perhaps by coincidence, BC Lieutenant-Governor Steven Point's February 2010 throne speech made reference to protecting the Flathead.

In November 2008 *National Geographic* magazine ran an article on the Muskwa–Kechika, a key component of the northern portion of the Y2Y corridor, extolling the area as a remarkable example of accommodating park protection and responsible environmental resource development. Only history will judge its success.

Recent action by the United Nations reinforces the concerns raised in both the Pojar and auditor general reports. The 2010 Nagoya Convention on Biological Diversity challenges the adequacy of our provincial park system to meet international expectations of our global responsibilities around global warming, climate change, biodiversity and species at risk. The 192 signatories of the Nagoya accord, including Canada, agreed to update the original 1992 Earth Summit protected areas figure of 12 percent to establish a new target of 17 percent for land areas and 10 percent for oceans.

Canada and British Columbia have done well to meet and exceed the original target and are well positioned to match the new expectations. Protected areas in BC now exceed 14 percent and both provincial and federal governments are committed to the new program to establish Marine Protected Areas along the BC coast. LRMPs are currently underway for northern regions of the province and proposals for new protected areas will also certainly be forthcoming, particularly for the Taku River Watershed.

The Elders and the Centennial

In 2005 CPAWS and former Lieutenant-Governor Iona Campagnolo sponsored an initiative to recognize the contributions of BC Parks elders. A history project was called for as part of the celebration of the parks centennial and in ceremonies in 2006 and 2007 twenty-two individuals were honoured for their contributions. They included notable scientists, citizen advocates and retired public servants.

BC Parks Branch honourees were: R.H. Ahrens, L. Brooks, C.J. Velay and G. Macnab, managers M. Goddard, J.C. Leman, D. Podmore and Jake Masselink, and naturalists Yorke Edwards, F. King, K. Joy and D. Stirling. Other honourees included officials from Parks Canada and regional park agencies, First Nations, the academic community and public spokespersons. In 2006 a bronze plaque to recognize their contributions was erected in Okanagan Lake Park, the site of a major park development project in the 1950s.

Acknowledgements

I would acknowledge and thank my wife Diane for her patience and support over four years of research, countless re-writes, and boxes of documents that clutter our family room.

And a thanks to everyone at Harbour Publishing who had faith in the public interest in the Centennial and provided able editors who I must admit turned my tedious narrative into more readable prose.

I would also like to recognize the vision and persistence of my colleagues with the Elders Council for BC Parks who still believe in the value and mission of parks and particularly to Derek and Phil for their quiet confidence in my resoluteness to complete the project. Thanks to both Tammy Liddicoat and Bill Merilees for generous assistance in fact checking and photo research. And to Ian and Russ for responding to my numerous requests for more information and updates.

1953—Pre- and Postwar "Elders" of the Parks Division of BC Forest Service (office, professional and field staff). Top row: R.H. Ahrens, J. Bailey, E.G. Oldham, Chess Lyons, L. Brooks. Row 2: G. Nicholson, R. Boyd, D.F. Macmurchie, C.J. Velay, D. Shaw, Les Cook. Row 3: Joe St Pierre, O. Johansen, E. Charlton, W. Rolls, Yorke Edwards, R. Lowry. Row 4: Len Shaw, Don Mckenzie, S.E. Park, E.A. McGowan, G.F. Macnab, M. Pope. Row 5: Sig Kristjanson, Robbie Robinson, F. McFarland, C. Fenner, G. Woods, B. Broadland. Row 6: F. Rainbow, S. Simard, D.K. Davidson, C. Lewis, D. Podmore, W. Hepper. Not pictured: C. Darkis, C. Heggie, D. Griffiths, N. Clarke, C.C. Hammond, J. Macintosh

Appendix A: The Park Act

March 1965 marked the passage of new landmark legislation: *The Park Act* (Chapter 20), compiled by Don Macmurchie working with R.H. Ahrens and other senior officials. This act, with numerous amendments over time, still serves as a core foundation for the park system of today.

Most importantly, this act defined the purposes for which parks were created, and now specifically identified conservation as *"the preservation of their natural environments for inspiration use and enjoyment of the public."* This officially broadened the mandate from previous recreation and tourism objectives and provided a set of principles and regulations by which parks would be managed.

The act increased protection from all forms of alienation, i.e., Class A parks, but also provided for Class B Parks and Recreation Areas, wherein parkland had less protection from resource development.

The act provided for both Nature Conservancy (NC) and Recreation Area (RA) designations, and the NC was given absolute protection to outstanding areas of scenic, flora and fauna environment. It could, for example, create "No Go" areas within Class B parks.

The new act was summarized in the following ministerial statements signed by the Hon. K. Kiernan, *Purposes and Procedures* (Parks Branch, 1965):

DEPARTMENT OF RECREATION AND CONSERVATION
PURPOSES AND PROCEDURES
PARKS BRANCH, 1965

Under the provisions of the *Department of Recreation and Conservation Act*, the *Park Act*, and other pertinent statutes, the Department is charged with the management and administration of parks.

The Parks Branch of the Department is established to execute the duties and responsibilities of the Department in all matters relating to the management and administration of parks.

For the purpose of administration, a park is any area designated a park under the provisions of the *Park Act* and includes dry land and water, the atmosphere above them, the flora and fauna upon and within them, and all their subsurface components.

The *Park Act* provides for the classification of parks to limit and guide subordinate exploitation of resources and for the establishment of nature conservancy areas to preserve natural ecologies. Parks of Classes A and C are reserved, absolutely, for recreational use, and no commercial or industrial exploitation is permissible except as may be necessary to planned recreational use or as may be authorized by the Lieutenant-Governor in Council. Parks of Class B are reserved for public pleasure and recreation, and no other exploitation is permissible except those which do not depreciate recreational values or which may be authorized by the Lieutenant-

Governer in Council. Nature conservancy areas are reserved, absolutely, for the preservation of outstanding scenic environments in their natural ecological cycles, and no exploitation or development, except that necessary to that preservation, is permissible.

In parks created for the pleasure and recreation of the public it is the purpose of the Branch to develop, maintain, and manage a comprehensive park system capable of accommodation those socially constructive activities which can be best enjoyed on such nonurban Crown lands as cannot be maintained as National, municipal, or local parks.

While the uses of parks are diversified, activities relating to nature and to an appreciation of man's cultural heritage and place in the universe are particularly appropriate to the Provincial system, and it is a purpose of the branch to provide adequate facilities for:

1. Sightseeing and viewing scenery.
2. Picnicking.
3. Strolling, hiking, and mountaineering.
4. Swimming and water sports.
5. Camping.
6. Boating and canoeing.
7. Fishing.
8. Nature study.
9. Skiing and winter sports.
11. Collecting and photography.
12. Outdoor sports and games.

It is recognized that the public, for whose pleasure and recreation parks are established, is the population of the future as well as that of the present, and it is a purpose of the Branch to so manage and preserve Provincial parks that their use may be equally enjoyed in perpetuity.

Among the responsibilities of the Branch, therefore, are those to

1. investigate and estimate present and future public needs for each of various appropriate activities;
2. examine and appraise the capacities of various lands to accommodate those activities;
3. recommend reservation or acquisition of suitable needed land and establishment of Provincial parks adequate to current and predictable public needs;
4. manage parks in manners enabling them to fulfil current recreational needs while insuring that their recreational values will be available, unimpaired to posterity.

To facilitate public enjoyment of appropriate activities and to preserve recreational values by minimizing inappropriate uses, it is a purpose of the Branch to designate and administer parks of the following types:

1. Nature conservancy areas, containing scenically outstanding examples of natural history uninfluenced by the activities of man, whose purpose is to preserve undisturbed natural environments.
2. Wilderness parks, containing expanses of unoccupied and undeveloped land, whose purpose is to preserve conditions similar to those which prevailed before the advent of European settlers and to provide opportunities to observe the regenerative processes of nature.
3. Cultural parks, containing geological, biological, historical, archaeological,

or other features representative of the public heritage, whose purpose is to perpetuate and display these features for their inspirational or educational effect.

4. Multi-use parks, offering space, cover, and topography in contrast with modern urban conditions, whose purpose is to provide opportunities for any two or more appropriate recreational activities.

5. Specialized recreation parks, containing a dominant feature facilitating intensive participation in a single activity, whose purpose is to provide maximum opportunity for enjoyment of a particular recreational activity.

6. Wayside parks, comprising more or less attractive nonurban lands adjacent to highways, whose purpose is to provide rest-places, camp-grounds, and similar amenities for the accommodation and convenience of motorists.

7. Marine parks, containing sheltered areas on waterways, whose purpose is to provide anchorages and moorages, camp-sites, and rest areas for boatmen.

8. Community parks, whose purpose is to make lands available to unorganized communities to accommodate local recreation needs which cannot be met on other lands.

It is a purpose of the Branch to conserve the recreational values of parks and, toward that end, it is a responsibility of the Branch to co-operate in all practical ways with land-managing agencies to promote and encourage maximum recreational use of nonpark lands.

December 2, 1965

MINISTER OF RECREATION AND
CONSERVATION

Appendix B:
The 5-Zone Zoning System for BC Parks

(Summary Table of Objectives, Criteria for Management, Use, Access),
from *Striking the Balance* (4th edition, September 1991)

	Intensive Recreation Zone	Natural Environment Zone
OBJECTIVE	To provide for a variety of readily accessible, facility-oriented outdoor recreation opportunities.	To protect scenic values and to provide for backcountry recreation opportunities in a largely undisturbed natural environment.
USE LEVEL	Relatively high density and long duration types of use.	Relatively low use but higher levels in association with nodes of activity or access.
MEANS OF ACCESS	All-weather public roads or other types of access where use levels are high (see "Impacts" below).	Mechanized (power-boats, snowmobiles, all-terrain vehicles), non-mechanized (foot, horse, canoe, bicycle). Aircraft and motorboat access to drop-off and pickup points will be permitted.
LOCATION	Contiguous with all-weather roads and covering immediate areas, modified landscapes or other high-use areas.	Removed from all-weather roads but easily accessible on a day-use basis. Accessible by mechanized means such as boat or plane.
SIZE OF ZONE	Small; usually less than 2,000 ha.	Can range from small to large.
BOUNDARY DEFINITION	Includes areas of high facility development in concentrated areas.	Boundaries should consider limits of activity/facility areas relative to ecosystem characteristics and features.
RECREATION OPPORTUNITIES	Vehicle camping, picnicking, beach activities, power-boating, canoeing, kayaking, strolling, historic and nature appreciation, fishing, snow play, downhill and cross-country skiing, snowshoeing, specialized activities.	Walk-in/boat-in camping, power-boating, hunting, canoeing, kayaking, backpacking, historic and nature appreciation, fishing, cross-country skiing, snowmobiling, river rafting, horseback riding, heli-skiing, heli-hiking, and specialized activities.
FACILITIES	May be intensely developed for user convenience. Campgrounds, landscaped picnic/play areas, trail, accommodation or interpretive buildings, boat launches; administrative buildings, service campgrounds, gravel pits, disposal sites, wood lots, parking lots, etc.	Moderately developed for user convenience. Trails, walk-in/boat-in campsites, shelters; accommodation buildings may be permitted; facilities for motorized access, e.g. docks, landing strips, fuel storage, etc.

	Intensive Recreation Zone	Natural Environment Zone
IMPACTS ON NATURAL ENVIRONMENT	Includes natural resource features and phenomena in a primarily natural state but where human presence may be readily visible both through the existence of recreation facilities and of people using the zone. Includes areas of high facility development with significant impact on concentrated areas.	Area where human presence on the land is not normally visible, facility development limited to relatively small areas. Facilities are visually compatible with natural setting.
MANAGEMENT GUIDELINES	Oriented toward maintaining a high quality recreation experience. Intensive management of resource and/or control of visitor activities. Operational facilities designed for efficient operation while remaining unobtrusive to the park visitor.	Oriented to maintaining a natural environment and to providing a high quality recreation experience. Visitor access may be restricted to preserve the recreation experience or to limit impacts. Separation of less compatible recreational activities and transportation modes. Designation of transportation may be necessary to avoid potential conflicts (e.g. horse trails, cycle paths, hiking trails).
EXAMPLES OF ZONING	Campground in Rathtrevor Beach Park; Gibson Pass ski areas in E.C. Manning Park.	Core area in Cathedral Park; North beach in Naikoon Park.

	Special Feature Zone	Wilderness Recreation Zone	Wilderness Conservation Zone
OBJECTIVE	To protect and present significant natural or cultural resources, features or processes because of their special character, fragility and heritage values.	To protect a remote, undisturbed natural landscape and to provide backcountry recreation opportunities dependent on a pristine environment where air access may be permitted to designated sites.	To protect a remote, undisturbed natural landscape and to provide unassisted backcountry recreation opportunities dependent on a pristine environment where no motorized activities will be allowed.
USE LEVEL	Generally Low.	Very low use, to provide solitary experiences and a wilderness atmosphere. Use may be controlled to protect the environment.	Very low use, to provide solitary experiences and a wilderness atmosphere. Use may be controlled to protect the environment.
MEANS OF ACCESS	Various; may require special access permit.	Non-mechanized; except may permit low frequency air access to designated sites; foot, canoe (horses may be permitted).	Non-mechanized (no air access); foot, canoe (horses may be permitted).
LOCATION	Determined by location of special resources; may be surrounded by or next to any of the other zones.	Remote; generally not visited on a day-use basis.	Remote; not easily visited on a day-use basis.
SIZE OF ZONE	Small; usually less than 2,000 hectares.	Large; greater than 5,000 ha.	Large; greater than 5,000 ha.
BOUNDARY DEFINITION	Area defined by biophysical characteristics or the nature and extent of cultural resources (adequate to afford protection).	Defined by ecosystem limits and geographic features. Boundaries will encompass areas of visitor interest for specific activities supported by air access. Will be designated under the Park Act.	Defined by ecosystem limits and geographic features. Will be designated under the Park Act.
RECREATION OPPORTUNITIES	Sight-seeing, historic and nature appreciation. May be subject to temporary closures or permanently restricted access.	Backpacking, canoeing, kayaking, river rafting, nature and historic appreciation, hunting, fishing, cross-country skiing, snowshoeing, horseback riding, specialized activities (e.g. caving, climbing).	Backpacking, canoeing, kayaking, river rafting, nature and historic appreciation, fishing, cross-country skiing, snowshoeing, horseback riding, specialized activities (e.g. caving, climbing).

	Special Feature Zone	**Wilderness Recreation Zone**	**Wilderness Conservation Zone**
FACILITIES	Interpretive facilities only, resources are to be protected.	Minimal facility development. Limited development for user convenience and safety, and protection of the environment, e.g. trails, primitive campsites, etc. Some basic facilities at access nodes, e.g. dock, primitive shelter, etc.	None.
IMPACTS ON NATURAL ENVIRONMENT	None; resources to be maintained unimpaired.	Natural area generally free of evidence of modern human beings. Evidence of human presence is confined to specific facility sites. Facilities are usually compatible with natural setting.	Natural area generally free of evidence of modern human beings.
MANAGEMENT GUIDELINES	High level of management protection with ongoing monitoring. Oriented to maintaining resources and, where appropriate, a high quality recreational and interpretive experience. Active or passive management depending on size, location, and nature of the resource. Visitor access may be restricted to preserve the recreation experience and to limit impacts.	Oriented to protecting a pristine environment. Management actions are minimal and not evident. Managed to ensure low visitor use levels. Visitor access may be restricted to protect the natural environment and visitor experience.	Oriented to protecting a pristine environment. Management actions are minimal and not evident. Managed to ensure low visitor use levels. Visitor access may be restricted to protect the natural environment and visitor experience.
EXAMPLES OF ZONING	Tidepools in Botanical Beach Park; Sunshine Meadows in Mount Assiniboine Park	Quanchus Mountains Wilderness in Tweedsmuir Park; Wilderness Zone in Spatsizi Park.	Central Valhallas Wilderness in Valhalla Park; Garibaldi Park Nature Conservancy Area.

Appendix C: Guiding Principles for Protected Areas

The following are from *A Protected Areas Strategy for British Columbia* (1993).

1. The first priority in the use and management of protected areas is to protect their ecological viability and integrity.

2. Protected areas are inalienable areas in which no industrial extraction or development is permitted. No mining, logging, hydroelectric development or oil and gas development will occur within protected areas.

3. The Protected Areas Strategy respects the treaty rights and interests that exist in British Columbia. Sustenance activities, subject to conservation objectives, and ceremonial and spiritual practices by Aboriginal peoples will be permitted in protected areas.

4. Recreational activities, facilities, services and cultural heritage policies in protected areas must be compatible with each area's objectives and the long-term protection of ecological viability and integrity, while enhancing the public's experience of the natural and cultural heritage of the province.

5. To ensure the long-term integrity of protected areas, their establishment will be coordinated with the integrated resource management of the surrounding lands and waters.

6. If land designated as a protected area is transferred to a First Nation as a result of treaty negotiations for purposes inconsistent with its continuation as a protected area, then other lands may be designated to maintain the provincial target of 12% in protected areas status.

7. Land and marine use guidelines will be developed that maintain and enhance biological diversity, cultural significance, scenic beauty, economic value and safety of coastal resources.

8. A management plan will be prepared for each designated protected area that is set in place through a process of open public consultation.

Endnotes

1   Elders Council, 10 Point Vision for Parks System. Following the Dunsmuir Conference in June 2006, the Elders Council reviewed the session results and arrived at the following ten key principles:

We envisage a parks system:
1.   with a bold new management model designed to engage all British Columbians in supporting their parks system. The government has gone it alone for too long.
2.   that is enjoyed by all British Columbians through the provision of more accessible recreation and educational opportunities and is located appropriately within a well planned system and in adjacent lands and gateway communities.
3.   where all governments continue to provide the legal and policy framework for parks, make ecological protection their priority, and resource it accordingly.
4.   that reaches out to other parks systems and the international community to gain support and to reduce inefficiencies and overlap between park systems.
5.   that establishes strong new relationships with First Nations.
6.   that builds on the "natural" in Supernatural BC to showcase BC's "green" entrepreneurial expertise and environmental best practices through investments in park infrastructure replacements and other improvements throughout BC.
7.   that is publicly accountable and performance focused through the development of a world class park-by-park monitoring and reporting regime that provides an annual public view of the state of our parks.
8.   that attracts visitors from around the world to enjoy a world class experience as a result of new trails, educational packages, senior adventures etc.
9.   that truly engages local communities and youth in park management support roles through the involvement of schools, local politicians, seniors outreach etc.
10. that is ready to welcome visitors to the 2010 Olympics and to attract visitors in 2011 to celebrate the hundredth anniversary of our provincial parks system.

2   Williston, Eileen, and Betty Keller. *Forests, Power and Policy: The Legacy of Ray Williston*. (Prince George: Caitlin Press, 1997), 229–33.
3   Ibid, 234
4   The biogeoclimatic zones concept, an ecologically based system of vegetation classification, was pioneered by Dr. Vladimir Josef Krajina at the University of British Columbia Botany Department and widely adapted and used as the basis for forest management in BC and Alberta as well as other parts of the world.

A Note on Sources

This document is not presented as a formal research monograph with each factoid or reference to a person, place, date and event documented with footnotes. Where there are events such as parks established or new legislation noted, they are usually on the public record. As such, the author is reasonably sure the basic core of his information is correct and factual. The primary source of information for this manuscript came from and can be verified from the following sources.

❧

The basic reference for the early days of national parks in Canada is *A Brief History of Canada's National Parks* by W.F. Lothian, published by Environment Canada.

In the fall of 2009, Public Broadcasting Service (PBS) ran a major multi-part TV series, "The National Parks: America's Best Idea," by noted filmographer, Ken Burns. The text of this series is available online from the U.S. National Parks website along with other numerous historical documents. This series provides a fascinating overview of the history of the National Park movement in America, much of which is similar to events in Canada. (By coincidence, 2011 will mark the 100th anniversary of the creation of the National Parks Service for Canada and it is expected several historical reference documents will soon be published or available online.) Information on both the U.S. National Parks and Parks Canada agencies can also be easily accessed directly from their home website including an alphabetical listing of parks each with their own website. A search by park name provides easy access to key data such as name, location, size, date of establishment and key park features.

The primary reference source for BC provincial parks is to review the annual ministry reports for both the BC Forest Service and Parks Branch, which usually provides information on the growth of the park system, construction projects, new policy, staffing, or program initiatives, and often gives both regional and provincial data sets concerning budgets, visitor use, opening of new facilities, etc., particularly for the period during the 1960s and 1970s; less so, in recent years.

The definitive source of data on the provincial park system, i.e., names of new parks, date of establishment, classification and size, can be found in the *Park Data Handbook* compiled in 1995. Also, the thesis by Ken Youds provides an analysis of changes to the parks list up to 1978; particularly, the confusing time in the 1950s and 1960s when major parks were being created, cancelled or reclassified and details to track massive changes to the park system resulting from the major hydro projects.

More detailed but much more difficult is to track specific legislative and executive orders as can be seen from new statutes and their amendments and Orders-in-Council (OICs) all of which can be found in the Legislative Library. There have been literally hundreds of OICs which can be generic documents implementing or amending policy effecting all parks, i.e., mineral claim staking, visitor control regulations, fees, or can be specific to individual parks such as name changes, reclassifications or boundary changes. To find, track and interpret documents from the legislature or those by executive orders can be rewarding but is also a time-consuming and tedious task.

An unpublished student paper by A. Rablen provides insight in to political dialogue of the 1960s and '70s and references two articles from *Saturday Night* magazine that provide a historical perspective on government economic policy of the day and how it affected the park system. (See articles by Roderick Haig-Brown and Donald Stainsby.)

The usual *Annual Reports* provide a wealth of details of several successive years of massive capital work programs and growth of visitor facilities; usually organized by region.

Three documents provide in-depth analysis of the park system and internal operations of the Parks Branch. First, the staff report prepared in 1976 by Glen Nuttall was the first major attempt to report on the state of the park system and analyze trends in visitor use including regional variances and an attempt to define costs of park management services. Also the *Annual Report for 1979* is possibly the most comprehensive compendium of information about the structure and operation of the Parks Branch and the parks they manage. It provides a summary of regional distribution of facilities that has since seen little expansion in the past four decades.

The Lee Report offered a candid review by the new branch director of administrative structure and organizational dynamics. It provides insight about the need for the agency to change to meet the demands of managing a greatly expanded park system, massive capital budgets and over ten million visits. Usually such documents are for internal use and are of interest only to employees personally affected by a new organizational structure. It identifies the main obligations of a decentralized public service agency, environmental management, planning, capital maintenance and visitor services, including a merged interpretation and information program.

Two other internal documents serve as benchmarks from which to evaluate the past and set the scene for what the park system might become. The first, *Natural Regions and Regional Landscapes for B.C. Parks*, provides an assessment of what park lands were protected and what remained to be added after the major expansion of the mid-1970s. This document presents a framework from which to define objectives for future growth and provides insights to the process of system planning.

The 1983 staff report *Recreation Area Policy—Implications for Legislative Change* was never published or released but if a copy can be accessed, it provides an excellent overview of the issues of the nomenclature used to classify parks, including the disingenuous nature for Class B and Recreation Areas as a means to offer less than full protection to parks. This largely unknown document provides historical perspective on the struggle to protect dedicated parkland and sets the scene for a major political impasse and ill-fated policy reforms.

The critical document of the late sixties and early seventies came from an outside source through the Wilderness Advisory Committee (WAC), whose report *Wilderness Mosaic* provides a summary of several contentious new park system proposals, boundary issues and recommendations for resolution, of which nearly all were accepted and implemented by Cabinet. It includes a discussion of the "wilderness" policy for British Columbia and also how to deal with questions of mineral claims in parks. It is clearly a landmark document that tries to resolve a series of policy issues affecting the park system that had been accumulating over seventy-five years. (Included is the Parks Branch submission to the WAC, which is a statement of their expectations to both protect and expand the park system.) In 1988 the Larkin report *Restoring the Balance* provided essential overview of resource exploitation in Strathcona and recommended new directions to restore integrity to the landmark park.

During this period, it is confusing to follow and use the summary statistics from the *Park Data Handbook* because dozens of parks were being established, cancelled, reclassified or undergoing major boundary changes, i.e., the number of *Recreation Areas* ballooned and then were re-classified. Today, most of them have now been established as Class A parks with boundaries protected by statute.

Two government documents mark the emergence of the modern park system. First *Striking the Balance*, a ministerial directive that went through four iterations and finally ended the threat of mineral claim staking in parks. It is the definitive policy statement on the goals and objectives and critical management policies for the provincial parks system. It also introduced a park zoning and classification system still in use. A copy can be downloaded from the Parks website.

Second is a series of documents collectively known as "Parks for the 90s," produced by the Parks Branch. They are best summarized in the large foldout map brochure used for householder and citizen public forum discussion on future growth of the park system. This map, which was the culmination of three decades of park system planning, became the shopping list for hundreds of new parks to be established during the 1990s. Chapter 8 and its information on property acquisitions were compiled by the author from his own experience in consultation with former and present staff members. Apart from some internal end-of-year summary listing, no overall tally and record of their purchases, donations and exchanges has been formally compiled and published.

Much data on individual transactions can be obtained by a detailed title search of the *Land Registry Office* but this would involve thousands of parcels of land because many properties consist of several legal parcels or the transaction included the transfer of numerous parcels located in different areas of the province. Estimating actual value of individual acquisitions is often complicated by the fact the transaction may also include donations, sale at less than market value, timber exchanges and/or service and access agreements. Also, this data is not comparable because the market value of property has increased tremendously over the past six decades.

In recent years, many acquisitions done in concert with several individual "land trust" groups have received more publicity and press releases were issued. While useful, those represent an incomplete data source. As part of their fundraising campaigns, individual trusts tend to publicize their own considerable accomplishments but, apart from a brief acknowledgment, seldom detail the contributions made by government, which in many cases provided the largest share of funding.

The book *Big Trees, Not Big Stumps* by Paul George, published by the Western

Canada Wilderness Committee (WCWC) in 2006 presents the twenty-five-year history of the campaigns of the WCWC. Of particular interest, the book concludes with a very useful thirty-page chronological listing of key events for the cause of conservation and parks in British Columbia. The two very readable and well-documented academic reviews by Wilson (for VILUP/Clayoquot) and Stanbury (for Great Bear Rainforest) present a comprehensive analysis of the public/political "logging versus parks" debate and how they influenced changes in government policy.

The major government policy document of historical importance was the Land Use Coordination Office (LUCO) manual providing guidelines for implementation of the Protected Area Strategy (PAS).

The document "A New Direction for Strategic Land Use Planning" (2005) provides a useful government summary overview of the Land and Resource Management Plan (LRMP) process. The 2002 paper by Frame, Gunton, Day provides an overview and analysis of the LRMPs and the role of their citizen representative regional planning tables as an exercise in "collaborative planning." The paper by Ronmark does a similar analysis of participants' views of the "management planning" process to prepare park master plans.

Unfortunately, the *Park Data Handbook* has not been updated since 1995 so the prime source of information about government decisions relating to the hundreds of new parks can best be found from dozens of press releases, which, in some cases, are several pages long and, unfortunately, many of them did not provide maps. During the 1990s, the government did occasionally produce a series of maps and progress reports regarding the PAS, which collectively do provide a means to identify the massive growth of the parks system. Because these maps and reports are intermittent and in different formats, it is difficult to get the full picture.

To the best of my knowledge, except for a series of Great Bear Rainforest (GBR) announcements and one map for Clayoquot and another for Muskwa–Kechika (M-K), there is no one document or series of maps that summarizes and celebrates the massive accomplishment that emerged from the LRMP planning process and the successful realization of PAS that reflects the scope and diversity of the present parks system. One way to understand the totality and growth of the park system is to view and compare a series of provincial highways and parks maps for 1991, 1999, and 2009, to realize the number of large parks added and now shown on the map. However, literally hundreds of new small parks do not show on the highway map. Unfortunately, many of the websites for individual parks do not provide adequate maps. It should be noted that over the past decade, governments changed the format and frequency of ministry annual reports and they are no longer a complete source of information. The Branch now only issues a brief consolidated summary of the park system. Fortunately, staff produced a brief year-end report for Parks 2007–08, which was separate from the ministry annual report. This other report includes a summary of expenditures, revenues, staffing, visitation, etc., and provides a status report and point of reference as we approach the Centennial.

In 2009, Parks Branch did publish a series of six regional guides showing provincial parks but they lack any narrative to explain how, when and where new parks were added. The *2005 Marine Park Guide* is dated and no comprehensive data set has been produced to highlight or map the current marine park system to reflect recent acquisitions and the massive expansion along the North Coast.

The Ministry of Environment–BC Parks website can be accessed for a variety of types of electronic and published information about both park system policy and visitor information. The definitive policy document *Striking the Balance* can be read online or downloaded.

The 1997 report, *More Than the Sum of Our Parks*, provides a detailed discussion of Aboriginal rights and the past and present interface of indigenous peoples with the growing number of new "protected areas" and proposed legislative and policy changes to recognize this reality. The paper by Dovetail Consulting (2001) then provides an excellent introduction to the subject of "co-management agreements with First Nations."

Both the federal and provincial governments have recently published a periodic *State of the Environment Report* that includes reviews on progress toward targets for biodiversity and protected areas. The *State of the Parks Report* (1997) by Parks Canada provides an introduction to the concept of "ecological integrity" as measured by species diversity, eco-system function and human stressors. These are factors that must be considered in conservation policies and draft master plans and tend to reflect a trend away from the recreational mandate of parks.

Two provincial reports, *Legacy Panel* (1999) and *Stewardship Panel* (2002), summarize recommendations from public consultation and offer a comprehensive review and range of policy options on complex questions of how to fund the growing commitments and obligations that resulted from doubling of the park system and providing outdoor recreation opportunities. The extensive brief submitted by CPAWS contributes a useful perspective on issues effecting management of such a large and diverse parks system. The adequacy of an operating funding for parks is a debate which is unfortunately an unresolved global budget issue for the present government. Hopefully, the occasion and opportunity for a forthcoming Centennial celebration may see a positive response.

Finally in early 2010, the Pojar Report, *A New Climate for Conservation*, re-examines the adequacy of "protected areas" in British Columbia in the context of global warming and sets the scene for a vigorous political dialogue to start the second century of the history of the parks system. The 2010 report of the Auditor General similarly reviews the issue of "ecological integrity" in the context of the *Parks Branch Program Plan* objectives and delivery.

Index